THE
HISTORY OF
CROATIA AND
SLOVENIA

THE HISTORY OF CROATIA AND SLOVENIA

Christopher Deliso

The Greenwood Histories of the Modern Nations
Frank W. Thackeray and John E. Findling, Series Editors

 GREENWOOD

An Imprint of ABC-CLIO, LLC
Santa Barbara, California • Denver, Colorado

Library of Congress Cataloging-in-Publication Data

Names: Deliso, Christopher, 1974- author.
Title: The History of Croatia and Slovenia / Christopher Deliso.
Description: Santa Barbara, California : Greenwood, An Imprint of ABC-CLIO,
    LLC, [2020] | Series: Greenwood histories of the modern nations |
    Includes bibliographical references and index.
Identifiers: LCCN 2020035103 (print) | LCCN 2020035104 (ebook) | ISBN
    9781440873225 (hardcover ; alk. paper) | ISBN 9781440873232 (ebook)
Subjects: LCSH: Croatia—History. | Slovenia—History.
Classification: LCC DR1535 .D45 2020 (print) | LCC DR1535 (ebook) | DDC
    949.72—dc23
LC record available at https://lccn.loc.gov/2020035103
LC ebook record available at https://lccn.loc.gov/2020035104

ISBN: 978-1-4408-7322-5 (print)
        978-1-4408-7323-2 (ebook)

24 23 22 21 20   1 2 3 4 5

This book is also available as an eBook.

Greenwood
An Imprint of ABC-CLIO, LLC

ABC-CLIO, LLC
147 Castilian Drive
Santa Barbara, California 93117
www.abc-clio.com

This book is printed on acid-free paper ∞

Manufactured in the United States of America

Contents

Series Foreword

The Greenwood Histories of the Modern Nations series is intended to provide students and interested laypeople with up-to-date, concise, and analytical histories of many of the nations of the contemporary world. Not since the 1960s has there been a systematic attempt to publish a series of national histories, and as series editors, we believe that this series will prove to be a valuable contribution to our understanding of other countries in our increasingly interdependent world.

At the end of the 1960s, the Cold War was an accepted reality of global politics. The process of decolonization was still in progress, the idea of a unified Europe with a single currency was unheard of, the United States was mired in a war in Vietnam, and the economic boom in Asia was still years in the future. Richard Nixon was president of the United States, Mao Tse-tung (not yet Mao Zedong) ruled China, Leonid Brezhnev guided the Soviet Union, and Harold Wilson was prime minister of the United Kingdom. Authoritarian dictators still controlled most of Latin America, the Middle East was reeling in the wake of the Six-Day War, and Shah Mohammad Reza Pahlavi was at the height of his power in Iran.

Since then, the Cold War has ended, the Soviet Union has vanished, leaving 15 independent republics in its wake, the advent of the computer age has radically transformed global communications, the rising demand for oil makes the Middle East still a dangerous flashpoint, and the rise of new economic powers like the People's Republic of China and India threatens to bring about a new world order. All of these developments have had a dramatic impact on the recent history of every nation of the world.

For this series, which was launched in 1998, we first selected nations whose political, economic, and socio-cultural affairs marked them as among the most important of our time. For each nation, we found an author who was recognized as a specialist in the history of that nation. These authors worked cooperatively with us and with Greenwood Press to produce volumes that reflected current research on their nations and that are interesting and informative to their readers. In the first decade of the series, close to 50 volumes were published, and some have now moved into second editions.

The success of the series has encouraged us to broaden our scope to include additional nations, whose histories have had significant effects on their regions, if not on the entire world. In addition, geopolitical changes have elevated other nations into positions of greater importance in world affairs and, so, we have chosen to include them in this series as well. The importance of a series such as this cannot be underestimated. As a superpower whose influence is felt all over the world, the United States can claim a "special" relationship with almost every other nation. Yet many Americans know very little about the histories of nations with which the United States relates. How did they get to be the way they are? What kind of political systems have evolved there? What kind of influence do they have on their own regions? What are the dominant political, religious, and cultural forces that move their leaders? These and many other questions are answered in the volumes of this series.

The authors who contribute to this series write comprehensive histories of their nations, dating back, in some instances, to prehistoric times. Each of them, however, has devoted a significant portion of their book to events of the past 40 years because the modern era has contributed the most to contemporary issues that have an impact on U.S. policy. Authors make every effort to be as up-to-date as possible so that readers can benefit from discussion and analysis of recent events.

In addition to the historical narrative, each volume contains an introductory chapter giving an overview of that country's geography, political institutions, economic structure, and cultural attributes.

This is meant to give readers a snapshot of the nation as it exists in the contemporary world. Each history also includes supplementary information following the narrative, which may include a timeline that represents a succinct chronology of the nation's historical evolution, biographical sketches of the nation's most important historical figures, and a glossary of important terms or concepts that are usually expressed in a foreign language. Finally, each author prepares a comprehensive bibliography for readers who wish to pursue the subject further.

Readers of these volumes will find them fascinating and well written. More importantly, they will come away with a better understanding of the contemporary world and the nations that comprise it. As series editors, we hope that this series will contribute to a heightened sense of global understanding as we move through the early years of the twenty-first century.

Frank W. Thackeray and John E. Findling
Indiana University Southeast

Preface

Almost a quarter-century after the end of the war in Croatia, sufficient time has passed to allow for both reflection and a certain measured expectation for the two most "different" former Yugoslav countries. Set apart from the others by shared geography and history, Croatia and its smaller northern neighbor, Slovenia, are at once Balkan and Western European in outlook and experience. As of 2020, they remained the only former Yugoslav republics to have joined the European Union (EU). That they would eventually do so was never a foregone conclusion; indeed, the fact that Croatia would be, at the dawn of this new decade, using its position as honorary EU president to try and revive the European enlargement drive to support other regional actors—including former adversaries like Serbia—indicates how remarkable the transformation has been.

A problem of imbalance arises with contemporary experience of Croatia and Slovenia. Academic research tends to be dominated, quite understandably, by the Yugoslav period and wars of the 20th century, to the detriment of earlier periods of history. Additionally, some of the globally most important natives have been "canceled out" of the historical narrative, a good example being Nikola Tesla—a Serb born in Croatia whose primary achievements were made in the United States.

Meanwhile, the two countries' increasing popularity as tourism destinations—Croatia for its islands and coastal towns, and Slovenia for its caves and mountain—is recasting their histories in entirely unexpected contexts for new generations of visitors who would hardly imagine any real conflict having occurred in these placid settings. Contexts change quickly too. Just a decade ago, the cruise-ship throngs debarking at the Croatian port of Dubrovnik, for example, were keen to visit the town's medieval Venetian sites in their own right; nowadays, an added attraction to these monuments is their association as filming locations for the epic fantasy series *Game of Thrones*. In an area of disputed histories, an added layer of total fictionality has become one of the most sought-after (if inevitably, for only a time).

Since writing about Balkan history is often considered a thankless task bound up with unending controversy, keeping this anecdote in mind may have a salutary effect. It is true that Croats, Slovenes, and their Balkan neighbors today continue to have disagreements and disputes over history and contemporary cooperation that often spills over into politics and society. However, almost two decades of research and travel in the former Yugoslav countries confirms for me that the various Balkan peoples also have many more commonalities than differences—linguistically, culturally, socially, and historically—and that these form the bedrock for a very unique European cultural view, one capable of understanding and working within the interstices of what is commonly presented as the West and East of Europe, but in reality is far more complicated than that.

To a great extent, much of the common culture found in this part of southeastern Europe owes to longer and deeper overlapping histories. Thus, this book also provides a panoptic view of larger civilizations and powers that affected the development of Slovenia and Croatia long before they were established polities, including the Illyrian, Roman, Byzantine, Venetian, Mongol, Ottoman, and modern Western European powers. In this light, readers will hopefully appreciate that the process of national formation was influenced by a plethora of events and trends that may be either well known (the 1683 Polish–Austrian victory over the Ottomans at the gates of Vienna) or obscure (the intrigues of the Narentine pirates of the medieval Dalmatian coast). In this review of history, there is nothing that can be excluded as everything is relevant to the ethnonational genesis and ground events that have made these two countries and peoples what they are today. Of course, this short volume can only suffice to be an introduction to the subject, but hopefully through the content and additional

sources cited the curious reader can find direction for future independent study.

Writing and researching this book has been a pleasure and has
allowed me to expand coverage of my core competencies as an Oxford-
trained Byzantine historian with practical analytic experience of contemporary Balkan politics, security, and society. In concluding this
foreword, I would like to acknowledge my editor, Kaitlin Ciarmiello,
and the rest of her team at ABC-CLIO, for bearing with me through
the long promise of bringing the book to fruition. Kaitlin's optimism
and helpful comments helped make the book better, while series editors Frank Thackeray and John Findling provided useful feedback on
the draft.

Timeline of Historical Events

32–27 BCE   Emerging victorious after centuries of war with
                the Adriatic Kingdom of Illyria, the Roman Empire
                establishes the Illyricum province on the Dalmatian
                coast.

10 CE   The Illyricum province is split into Dalmatia and
                Pannonia after local revolts, but remains under
                Roman rule.

305   The Dalmatia-born Roman emperor Diocletian
                retires, constructing a grand palace near Salona,
                which forms the basis for the later Croatian city of
                Split.

476   Collapse of the Western Roman Empire during
                barbarian invasion period leads to Ostrogoth rule.

535   Emperor Justinian the Great restores Eastern
                (Byzantine) Roman imperial rule in the Eastern
                Adriatic, establishing the province of Dalmatia.

568   Bayan, Khan of the Avars, plunders Dalmatia,
                cutting off Byzantine control of the land routes to
                northern Italy and Western Europe.

6th century	Slavic tribes settle parts of modern-day Slovenia and Croatia; they enter from both the north (via modern Austria and Czech Republic), settling in the Carinthia region, and south into today's Slavonia province.
623–658	Frankish merchant Samo unifies the Wends and other Slavic tribes of modern-day Slovenia, forging a short-lived but notable kingdom while battling Avars and Frankish troops.
6th–7th centuries	Avar and Slavic Croat invasions leave most of Roman Croatia in ruins, forcing survivors to flee to mountains or safer coastal sites, leading to the foundation of Ragusa (modern Dubrovnik).
7th–8th centuries	Slavic tribes from the former Roman Pannonian province settle in inland Croatia (Pannonian Croatia).
7th–10th centuries	The Duchy of Pannonian Croatia is established as a vassal state to the Avars and, for the longer part, Francia. The Franks consider it as a possession of their Carantanian region, further to the north.
745	The proto-Slovenian "Alpine Slavs" of Carantania (in present-day Austria and Slovenia) are incorporated into the Carolingian Empire and converted to Catholicism.
863–880	The monks Cyril and Methodius, two brothers sent to Great Moravia by the Byzantine emperor to proselytize, compete with the German-dominated clergy over the issue of Slavic-language liturgies, accelerating the spread of Christianity among the Slavs.
879	Branimir, Duke of the Croats in Dalmatia, is recognized by Pope John VIII as the ruler of the first autonomous Croat entity.
925	Pope John X recognizes Tomislav as King of Croatia, independent of Germanic Frankish rule. Under King Tomislav, Croatia gains prestige and fights off Hungarian and Bulgarian invasions.
976	Carantania-Carinthia becomes an autonomous administrative unit under Frankish Emperor Otto

	I. Carinthia is named the sixth duchy of the Holy Roman Empire, continuing to be influenced by a mixed Bavarian-Slavic nobility.
1000–1100	Parts of Carantania-Carinthia and neighboring German imperial regions become a military frontier zone (a "march") due to Hungarian military threats.
1058–1091	The medieval Croatian kingdom reaches its peak under the reigns of Petar Krešimir IV (1058–1074) and Dimitar Zvonimir (1075–1089). The death of King Stjepan II in 1091 marks the end of the Trpimirović dynasty.
1091–1102	Ladislaus I of Hungary claims the Croatian crown, sparking a war that ends with the "personal union" of Croatia and Hungary in 1102, ruled by Hungarian King Coloman.
1102–1527	The long-lasting "personal union" with Hungary leads to new innovations, such as the introduction of feudalism and the empowerment of Croatian noble families, including Frankopan and Šubić. Some measure of home-rule was given to the Kingdom of Croatia in the form of a *Sabor* (parliament) and a *Ban* (viceroy), appointed by the king.
1202–1254	Bernhard von Spanheim rules as Duke of Carinthia, continuing the Germanic dynasty in future Slovenian lands.
1286	Count Meinhard IV of Gorizia is given rule over the Duchy of Carinthia and the March of Carniola by Habsburg King Rudolph I of Germany in return for his support against the Bavarian kingdom.
1335	The Austrian House of Habsburg claims Carinthia and Carniola from the Gorizia-Tyrol branch, holding these core Slovene lands until 1918.
1300s	Habsburg helps the Dukes of Celje (in present-day central Slovenia) win effective control of Carinthia-Carniola through marriage alliances. Allying as well with Hungary, Celje extends its influence southward into Slavonia in the Croatian interior and supports Hungarian forces attacking coastal Dalmatia.

1342–1382	King Louis the Great reigns over the golden age of Croatian medieval history.
1409–1797	After Ladislaus of Naples sells Dalmatia to the powerful Venetian Republic in 1409, a new Italian influence—and decades of war for the coastal province—begins. While cities like Ragusa (Dubrovnik) become independent, the Venetians remain in control elsewhere on the Dalmatian coast until 1797 (and the Venetian Republic's collapse).
1500s	The first mentions of a common Slovene ethnic identity are noted.
1553	The Croatian Military Frontier (*Hrvatska Vojna Krajina*) is created to keep the Turks at bay, ruling directly from Vienna's military headquarters. The border region, which lasts officially until the late 19th century, is settled primarily by poor Serbs and Croats who enjoy freedom from serfdom in return for their military service against the Turks.
1583	Protestant scholar Jurij Dalmatin completes the first full translation of the Bible in Slovene.
1593	The Battle of Sisak marks the first major victory of Croatian forces (in coalition with Austrians and troops from modern-day Slovenia) over the Ottomans. However, it also sparks the so-called "Long War" between the Habsburgs and Ottomans, mainly fought in modern-day Romania.
1615	The "Uskok Wars" break out in Slovene territories between Venice and Habsburg Austria over the infamous Uskok pirates of Croatia, noted for decades of harassing Venetian and Ottoman commercial shipping.
1683	The Ottoman army is driven back at the gates of Vienna by a joint Christian army commanded by King John Sobieski of Poland, beginning their long period of retraction southward, no longer threatening Slovenes and Croats.
1741–1748	Croat nobles support the right of Empress Maria Theresa to take Habsburg throne in the War of the Austrian Succession; the empress, who would

rule until 1780, subsequently gives her support in Croatian affairs.

1797–1815	The Habsburgs finally gain control of coastal Dalmatia and Istria following the collapse of the Venetian Republic, while the inland Slavonia and Croatia proper remain under Hungarian control.
1830s	Intellectuals like Ljudevit Gaj of the Zagreb-based "Illyrian Movement" begin the process of national awakening by promoting the idea of a common literary language reflecting the common identity of the South Slavs, partly in reaction to creeping Austrian and Hungarian nationalist tendencies.
1847	A proposal that Croatian replaces Latin as the official working language in the Sabor is unanimously accepted, continuing the national awakening process.
1849	Emperor Franz Joseph imposes a new constitution that bans all political dissent, following Europe-wide populist revolts aimed at winning more national freedoms.
1850	Croat supporters of the "Illyrian Movement" agree on a joint linguistic standardization process with Serbian linguist Vuk Stefanović Karadžić's circle; they choose the southern Shtokavian dialect as the basis of the Serbo–Croatian language.
1867	The creation of the Austro–Hungarian Empire, or the "Dual Monarchy," leads to a lessening of tensions between Croatian and Hungarian nationalists who had taken rival sides. However, all outstanding issues were not resolved by a legal agreement the following year.
1914–1918	World War I causes large-scale loss of life and, coming out on the losing side, Croatia and Slovenia sever ties with the dying Austro–Hungarian Empire. A new country meant to unite the South Slavs of the Balkans is formed with its provisional headquarters in Zagreb: the "State of Slovenes, Croats and Serbs." It would soon be merged with the victorious Kingdom of Serbia and renamed

	"Kingdom of Serbs, Croats and Slovenes," with headquarters in Belgrade.
1920	The Treaty of Rapallo is signed, ending Italian claims to Slovene and Croatian territories secretly promised by the British five years earlier; Italy, however, takes considerable portions of ethnically Slovene populated border territories under Mussolini's rule, including the mixed city of Trieste.
1921–1929	The centralizing tendencies of the Belgrade government anger minority parties such as the Croatian Peasant Party of Stjepan Radić, who is assassinated by a Serb nationalist parliamentarian, angering Croats; Serbian King Aleksandar declares a dictatorship, renaming the country as the "Kingdom of Yugoslavia," stirring up nationalist feelings throughout the country.
1934	King Aleksandar is assassinated in Paris in a plot organized by the exiled Croat ultranationalist Ustaše and a Bulgarian-led Macedonian revolutionary organization.
1941–1945	The Nazi- and Vatican-supported "Independent State of Croatia" is created and run by Ustaše leader Ante Pavelić. The regime commits numerous war crimes against Serbs, Jews, Roma, and anti-fascist Croats. Prominent members are helped into exile in South America and elsewhere by the Catholic Church when the Communist forces of Josip Broz Tito finally defeat Germany and its Croatian and Albanian allies, paving the way for a second Yugoslavia.
1945–1991	The Socialist Federative Republic of Yugoslavia (SFRJ) comes into existence, led by Croat Partisan leader Josip Broz Tito, who serves as titular dictator until his death in 1980. While expressions of national identity are freer than that in the first Yugoslavia, the country is still run from Belgrade and highly centralized, with a one-party system. Croatia and Slovenia are two of the constituent Yugoslav republics, along with Serbia, Bosnia-Herzegovina, Montenegro, and Macedonia.

1960–1970	Industrialization and economic growth come to Croatia and Slovenia, trends that help them become Yugoslavia's wealthiest and most advanced republics despite the limits of worker-managed communism and nationalizations.
1970–1971	The "Croatian Spring" of student protests occurs, following similar demonstrations in Western Europe. Although unsuccessful in changing the system, such protests lead to a revised constitution in 1974 that devolves more powers and responsibilities from the central government to the national republics.
1980s	Ethnic nationalist sentiments in Yugoslavia, and particularly its diaspora communities, are stoked by a rapidly changing situation in Europe, the break-up of the Soviet Union, and a weakened economy. The emergence of Slobodan Milošević as Serbia's leader complicates the equation by increasing Serbia's power relative to other Yugoslav republics.
1989	While Yugoslavia remains a one-party Communist state, the *Hrvatska demokratska zajednica* (HDZ) is founded by nationalist dissidents led by former Partisan fighter and Yugoslav general Franjo Tuđman.
1990	At the Communist League of Yugoslavia summit, the Slovenian and Croatian delegations walk out in protest after Slobodan Milošević blocks their proposals, creating an existential crisis.
1990–1991	Franjo Tuđman's HDZ wins the first multiparty elections in Yugoslav Croatia, passing its own constitution. The party's ambitions for independence alarm the central government in Belgrade, and especially Croatia's 200,000-strong ethnic Serbian minority. Threatening to break away from any future independent Croatia, the Serb entity of Krajina declares autonomy and receives arms itself for defense from the Yugoslav People's Army (JNA).
1991	Croatia and Slovenia declare independence from Yugoslavia on the same day, while the Krajina

Serbs hold an unrecognized referendum, voting to remain in Yugoslavia. After a ten-day war, Slovenia is recognized as an independent state by Belgrade. Croatia similarly declares independence, but only achieves it in 1995, following a long and bloody war against the Serb-populated enclaves in Croatia, and in support of ethnic Croats in Bosnia.

1995   After four years of war, the Croatian Army launches "Operation Storm," forcing 90,000–150,000 Serb residents to flee. The Western-sponsored Dayton Agreements soon after cement the negotiated settlement to the Croatian–Serbian and Bosnian wars.

1998   Under United Nations (UN) negotiation, Croatia takes over the last areas that had been overseen by international peacekeepers.

2000   The nationalist HDZ government is defeated at elections, replaced by the Social Democratic Party of Croatia. New prime minister Ivica Račan begins reforms such as changing Croatia from a presidential to a parliamentary system while addressing the country's economic and social issues.

2001   Croatian war veteran General Ante Gotovina goes into hiding after being indicted for war crimes by an international tribunal.

2003–2009   A new HDZ government led by Ivo Sanader faces setbacks in negotiating EU membership due to issues like cooperation with the war crimes tribunal and territorial disputes with Slovenia. Sanader resigns unexpectedly in July 2009, leading to a long series of corruption trials.

2004   Slovenia joins the EU and North Atlantic Treaty Organization (NATO).

2005   General Ante Gotovina is arrested by Spanish police and extradited to an international war crimes court in the Netherlands, sparking anger in Croatia.

2009   Croatia joins NATO.

2011   Croatian–Slovene classical crossover duo 2CELLOS achieves breakout success after their rendition of

Michael Jackson's "Smooth Criminal" goes viral on YouTube. The duo goes on to release several bestselling and critically acclaimed albums of rock songs performed on classical instrumentation.

2012   Croatian nationalists celebrate when war veteran Ante Gotovina's guilty verdict is overturned on appeal at the international tribunal.

2013   Croatia joins the EU.

2015   Kolinda Grabar-Kitarović is elected as the first Croatian female president. In the same year, Croatia pulls out of UN-brokered arbitrations over border disputes with Slovenia, claiming that the latter had engaged in corrupt practices with arbiters.

2017   The UN arbitration body handling the bilateral border dispute concerning the Adriatic Bay of Piran and other areas releases its verdict. While Slovenia praises the ruling, Croatia refuses to accept it, citing its departure from the talks two years earlier.

2017   Slovenia wins the European Cup in basketball, upsetting heavily favored teams and showcasing talented players like the future NBA Rookie of the Year Luka Dončić.

2018   Croatia reaches the finals of soccer's World Cup, held in Russia. Despite losing to France, the historic run is considered one of the country's biggest sporting successes.

2020   Croatia hosts the rotating presidency of the EU from January through June.

CROATIA AND SLOVENIA

COASTAL ISLANDS

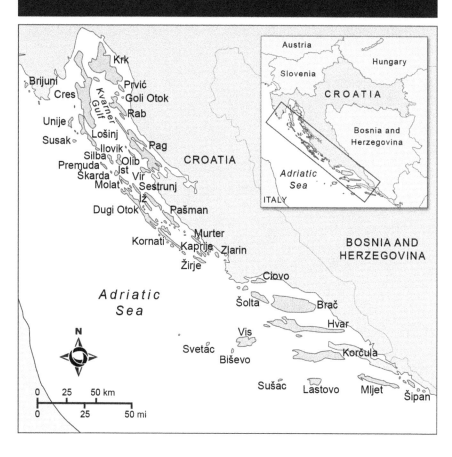

Austria
Slovenia
Hungary
CROATIA
Bosnia and
Herzegovina
Adriatic
Sea
ITALY

Brijuni
Krk
Cres
Prvić
Goli Otok
Kvarner Gulf
Rab
Unije
Lošinj
Susak
Ilovik
Pag
Silba
Olib
CROATIA
Premuda
Jst
Škarda
Vir
Molat
Sestrunj
Iž
Dugi Otok
Pašman
Murter
Kornati
Kaprije
Zlarin
Žirje
Ciovo
Adriatic
Sea
Šolta
Brač
Hvar
N
Vis
Svetac
Korčula
Biševo
Sušac
Lastovo
Mljet
Šipan

BOSNIA AND
HERZEGOVINA

0   25   50 km
0   25   50 mi

KINGDOM OF CROATIA (1868)

N

AUSTRIA

Lake Balaton

HUNGARY

DALMATIA

CROATIA

C.M.F.

Zagreb

C.M.F.

Rijeka

SLAVONIA

DALMATIA

CROATIAN MILITARY FRONTIER

SLAVONIAN MILITARY FRONTIER

Belgrade

BOSNIA

Zadar

Travnik

SERBIA

DALMATIA

Sarajevo

Split

Mostar

Adriatic Sea

HERZEGOVINA

Kingdom of Italy

Dubrovnik

MONTENEGRO

Cetinje

Skadar

Austro-Hungarian Empire

1

Croatia and Slovenia Today

The lands southeast of the Alps, bordered on the west by the Adriatic Sea and on the east by the Black Sea, with the great River Danube comprising much of a northerly informal border and the Aegean Sea comprising the ultimate border to the south, are generically considered as belonging to the Balkan Peninsula. This fascinating, geographically and culturally diverse and historic part of Europe has developed under the countervailing influences of neighboring powers over thousands of years. Today's Slovenia and Croatia, comprising the northwestern region of the Balkans, have always been somewhat different from the cultures and countries that emerged elsewhere on the peninsula; this difference was an oft-noted factor following their inclusion in Yugoslavia (an almost pan-Slavic larger state that existed in royalist and subsequently communist incarnations in the 20th century).

As of 2020, Croatia and Slovenia are the only two former Yugoslav republics to have become members of the European Union (EU), though several others continue to pursue membership. They are also North Atlantic Treaty Organization (NATO) members, whereas Serbia and Bosnia-Herzegovina are not. This speaks to the tectonic differences between the formerly Ottoman- and Byzantine-influenced central and eastern Balkans, and the Western-influenced Adriatic stretches of territory upon which today's Croatia and Slovenia were developed. With a foot in both worlds, these countries are not entirely one or the other, but something unique, sharing the post-communist transition legacy with the other former Yugoslav republics, as well as many deeply rooted customs, traditions, and social practices. Still, membership in Western clubs and economic growth based on new-found stability, especially, strong tourism industries, have improved the general outlook for these countries going into the future.

CROATIA

Geography

Croatia (*Hrvatska*), or the Republic of Croatia (*Republika Hrvatska*), is a mid-sized European country with a distinctly varied topography, defined by its elliptical coast; dotted with thousands of islands, this makes for one of Europe's most dramatic and varied maritime geographies in the Adriatic provinces of Istria and Dalmatia. Much of inland Croatia comprises forests, hills, or fertile agricultural plains, with a rugged set of mountains, the Dinaric Alps, running north-south down the coast. This mountainous region spills over into the neighboring Bosnia and Herzegovina; by contrast, Croatia's borders with Serbia and Hungary to the east and northeast comprise lowlands (the Pannonian Plain river basin).

Croatia's total area of 21,851 square miles makes it just smaller than West Virginia. The country's borders stretch for 290 miles between its easternmost and westernmost points and for 288 miles between its northernmost and southernmost points. Bosnia and Herzegovina, Hungary, Serbia, Montenegro, and Slovenia are bordering countries. Of these, Croatia shares the longest stretch of border with Bosnia and Herzegovina (627 miles). Croatia's capital city, Zagreb, is situated inland on the Sava River, while the country's next-largest cities (Split and Rijeka) are located on the coast.

When it won independence from Yugoslavia after a four-year war ending in 1995, Croatia reverted to historically defined regions based on prior iterations in the Austro-Hungarian and Ottoman Empires, as well as the medieval Venetian Republic and an autonomous entity on the Adriatic coast. There are twenty counties (*županije*) in Croatia within these regions, as well as one city with the special status of county—the capital, Zagreb. The inland agricultural region of Slavonia and Syrmia include the counties of Požega-Slavonia and important industrial cities, Vukovar and Srijem. The northern Zagorje region borders Slovenia and Austria. To the east, the province of Herzegovina overlaps with the larger historical region of the same name, comprising sections of Bosnia and Herzegovina. On the coast is the region of Istria and the expansive province of Dalmatia is to its south. In addition to Split and Rijeka, important coastal cities that are also popular tourist attractions include Dubrovnik, Zadar, and Šibenik.

Croatia is known for its jagged peninsulas and numerous islands that conceal idyllic beaches and natural areas. In total, Croatia has 1,244 islands, ranging in size from small outcroppings to large bodies, such as Krk, Cres, and Brac, each of which exceeds 150 square miles in area. Overall, Croatia boasts the third-longest coastline in the Mediterranean, after only Greece and Italy with 3,625 miles—twenty-first among all countries. European Union standards tests have consistently shown the Croatian coast to have some of the cleanest seawater in Europe, and 9 percent of the country's total land area is environmentally protected by law.

Rivers in Croatia are important to its population distribution, transit corridors, and historic division of regions. They flow generally in a west–east direction, down from the Alps and into the Central European river basin. The largest river in Croatia is the Sava, which originates in the Julian Alps in Slovenia and runs 615 miles before reaching the Danube in Belgrade in Serbia. The Drava is another tributary in this fundamental river system, the physical northern border of the Balkan Peninsula. Smaller rivers that flow into the Sava are the Kupa, Bosut, Lonja-Trebež, and Una. Like the Sava River, the Drava enters Croatia from Slovenia and forms much of the border with Hungary before flowing into the Danube. In Dalmatia, the Krka and Cetina rivers flow westward into the Adriatic Sea, providing electric power to large populations.

Croatia has many lakes, the largest being Lake Vransko (11.8 square miles), a natural lake near Biograd. The renowned Plitvice Lakes, in central Croatia's Plitvice Lakes National Park, comprise a chain of sixteen terraced lakes merged by waterfalls; the stunning sight is among Croatia's most-visited natural attractions popular with hikers and canyoners. The mountain peak of Dinara represents Croatia's highest point at 6,007 feet, rising out of the Dinaric Alps, with the low point being sea level. The country's mountains contain many caves, such as Kita Gaćešina, the longest cave in both Croatia and the Dinaric Alps (67,769 feet). One of the most visited, however, is the so-called blue grotto sea cave on Biševo island, which reaches depths of 36 feet and offers a constantly changing range of colors.

Croatia's varied terrain hosts a large number of animals, including 101 mammal species. This suffices to place Croatia within the European top ten for its mammalian diversity. Prominent species include the gray wolf, brown bear, Eurasian lynx, golden jackal, red fox, moose, chamois, deer, pine marten, and mouflon, a kind of wild sheep. The beloved domestic dog species, the Dalmatian, is a globally known breed originally from the region of Dalmatia. Tuna, swordfish, sea bass, sea bream, mackerel, and chum are among the 400 endemic fish species in Croatia's Adriatic Sea. The clean waters surrounding the islands also make the area a habitat for bottlenose dolphins.

Population, Demography, Languages, and Religion

Croatia had a population of 4,154,213 in 2016, ranking 126th in the world. The relatively unequal distribution of the population is a demographic characteristic of two centuries of emigration—either abroad or to the few urban centers. Almost two-thirds of Croatians today occupy just over 30 percent of the territory. Zagreb alone hosts 18 percent of the population. Ethnically, 90.4 percent of the population is Croat, a consequence of the expulsion of the former historic Serb minority during the 1990s war, only a small percentage of which has returned. Croatia is thus now one of the most ethnically homogeneous former Yugoslav countries. Serbs exist only in small numbers (4.4 percent); other minorities include Bosniaks, Italians, Germans, Czechs, Romani, and Hungarians. Life expectancy has risen to eighty for women and seventy-three for men. This has meant that Croatia, like many European countries, now suffers from an aging population, with 24 percent over the age of sixty.

Croatian is the mother tongue of 95 percent of the population, with the historic pockets of native Italian speakers on coast having all but disappeared since their expulsion after World War II (WWII). Interestingly, until the 19th century, Latin was the official language in parliament, though not spoken. Like Slovenia, since Croatia has a long joint history with Austria, German is a common second language. Modern Croatian is the result of an official post-1991 effort to disengage the common Serbo-Croatian language promoted during communist Yugoslav times. Linguists created this language adapting from three dialects of the South Slavic language family, using it in the Latin alphabet in Croatia. However, despite being written in Cyrillic, modern-day Serbian is almost identical to Croatian, and the populations in Serbia, Montenegro, Bosnia, and Croatia can understand one another easily.

The Catholic Church has deep roots in Croatia going back over 1,000 years, and the country remains one of the most devoted Catholic nations in Europe. However, Croatia has no official religion and the constitution enshrines secular freedoms. According to the 2011 census, 86.28 percent of Croatians were Catholics. Orthodox Christianity, primarily among the surviving Serb minority, comprises 4.4 percent of the population. Muslims, primarily ethnic Bosniaks, make up 1.4 percent of the population. Protestants make up 0.3 percent of the population. The country had a small but historic Jewish population that was all but destroyed during the Holocaust.

Economy

Historically, Croatia has looked to the sea for its livelihood, with everything from shipbuilding and fishing to trade and commerce making its inhabitants wealthy. The interior of the country has been more dependent on industrial and agricultural production, historically speaking. Today, tourism is a major industry for the service sector owing to Croatia's appeal as a summer holiday and cruise destination. About 20 percent of Croatian gross domestic product (GDP) depends on tourism; efforts continue to be made to diversify the national offering away from only summer- and coastal-type tourism and toward other areas and seasons.

Croatia is considered a developed European economy, on a secondary level after leading Western European ones, but generally stronger than other Balkan states. Along with Slovenia, it bases its credentials on memberships in leading international organizations. It joined the World Trade Organization in 2000, NATO in 2009, and EU in 2013. As of 2020, Slovenia and Croatia are the only former Yugoslav republics to be EU members, bolstering their stability and economic opportunities. Further, as of 2020, EU countries accounted for 68 percent of Croatia's exports; Italy was the leader with 14 percent, followed by Germany at 13 percent, and Slovenia at 11 percent. Regarding imports, 78 percent of goods come from EU countries. This is the outcome of the strategic redirection of the national economy following the dissolution of Yugoslavia.

Environmental Issues

Croatia relies on its biological and geographical diversity to attract foreign visitors and therefore has been keen to participate in conservation schemes since even before its EU membership in 2013. The country's first National Strategy and Action Plan for the Protection of Biological and Landscape Diversity was adopted in 1999 and extended in 2008. A significant threat to maritime environments noted by officials over the years has been the discharge of wastewater into the Adriatic Sea near cities popular with tourists. A 2009–2015 Coastal Cities Pollution Control Project 2 was launched to counteract this.

More recently, Croat environmentalists have been active on the fight against plastic waste, with a strong track record of participation at local levels in annual postsummer clean-ups of maritime waste. Croatia's long coastline tends to be afflicted by trash not only because of its popularity among cruise ships and general tourists but also because the strong currents and frequent storms in the Adriatic Sea draw in trash from countries further south in the Mediterranean. Nevertheless, Croats take great pride in their country's crystal-clear waters and thus remain proactive in their efforts to keep it clean.

National Regions, Symbols, and Governing Structures

The Republic of Croatia is organized into twenty counties, or *županije*. They exist within four traditional regions: Croatia proper, Dalmatia, Slavonia, and Istria. Within the *županije* are hundreds of *općine* (municipalities). These bodies administer local government. The municipal council (*općinsko vijeće*) is the seat of local self-government at that level, with local councils elected in direct elections every four years.

The national flag of Croatia or The Tricolor (*Trobojnica*) has been used since 1990, even before the country declared independence. It consists of three equally sized horizontal stripes in red, white, and blue. In the middle is the coat of arms, with a shield. Above the main shield is a crown with five smaller ones, attesting to historical Croatian crowns.

As in most European countries, Croatia is a parliamentary, representative democracy, in which a prime minister leads a cabinet of ministers in national government, with a national president also holding power but in a more ceremonial way, with certain exceptions such as leadership of the armed forces. These leaders come to power in elections held in a multiparty system, with elections held every five years for president and, theoretically, every four years for parliament. However, more often than not, internal developments within political life have forced parliamentary elections to be held earlier than expected, and new governments have been formed. This is also common in other European countries that follow this model.

The judiciary is independent of the executive and the legislature. All operate under the current constitution adopted on December 22, 1990. Independence from Yugoslavia was declared on May 25, 1991. The constitution has since been amended several times.

The Judiciary of Croatia

The judicial system in Croatia has a three-tiered, independent nature. The Supreme Court (*Vrhovni sud*) is the highest court of appeal. Judges are appointed by the National Judicial Council, with the lifetime office extending until age seventy. Parliament, following the proposal of the national president, elects the president of the Supreme Court for a four-year term. The lower two levels of the judiciary are county courts and municipal courts.

Special courts also exist in Croatia, including commercial courts and the Superior Commercial Court, misdemeanor courts, the Administrative Court, and the Croatian Constitutional Court. The State Attorney's Office, with its head appointed by the parliament, and a special State Attorney's Office known as USKOK investigate and prosecute serious organized crimes.

Security and International Institutions

The Croatian Army (*Hrvatska vojska*, HV) and the Croatian Ground Army (*Hrvatska kopnena vojska*, HKoV) comprise the major part of the Croatian Armed Forces. This professional army of 7,514 active duty personnel, as of August 2016, is supported by 6,000 reserve personnel. However, this number should drop as the unit is reorganized to fit future NATO requirements. The Croatian Army has been deployed for NATO peacekeeping in Afghanistan. Croatia already went through several restructurings of the military since beginning reforms, even before 2000, and after its membership in NATO in 2009.

The national president is the Armed Forces Commander-in-Chief, though daily administration goes through the government's Ministry of Defense. Croatia also possesses a significant navy (*Hrvatska ratna mornarica*, HRM), and the small Croatian Air Force (*Hrvatsko ratno zrakoplovstvo*, HRZ i PZO) has expanded in recent years.

The Croatian military budget has not exceeded the 2 percent of GDP figure that NATO expects its members to meet for several years. Unlike Slovenia, which won its independence in a fairly bloodless ten days of fighting, Croatia endured a devastating four-year war in the 1990s. For this reason, the country was long accustomed to spending billions on defense, which would lead to charges of war profiteering and corruption in the media and politics in the transition years following the war. Croatia's security has been stabilized, and it is unlikely to face another conventional war. Security threats arising from the 2015 migration crisis, owing to Croatia's location on the Balkan Route for migrant smugglers, could reoccur, requiring more effort from police forces rather than the army.

SLOVENIA

Geography

Slovenia (*Slovenija*), or the Republic of Slovenia (*Republika Slovenija*), is a small nation with a varied topography shaped by mountains and a curving seacoast that divide the country into mountainous and hilly regions interspersed with central plains. This richly forested country shares the Julian Alps mountain range in the western and northern parts overlapping Italy and Austria, respectively. In the southwest, the lesser Dinaric Alps runs from Slovenia through Croatia and further south, creating historical borders between various tribes, kingdoms, and states. The portion of the Dinaric Alps crossing Slovenia and Croatia is known as the Žumberak Mountains. The highest point of this subrange (called *Trdinov Grh* by Slovenes, and *Sveta Gera* by Croats) is also the highest border point between the two countries at 3,865 feet.

Comprising a total area of 7,827 square miles, Slovenia is almost as big as the U.S. state of New Jersey. The country stretches for 154 miles between its easternmost and westernmost points, and for 101 miles between its maximal north–south points. Slovenia shares boundaries with Austria, Hungary, Italy, and Croatia. Its border with Croatia (415 miles) is the country's longest common border. Slovenia's capital city, Ljubljana, is situated on the Ljubljanica River in the Ljubljana Basin in central Slovenia, between the Julian Alps and the karst formations (hence the provincial name, Karst) of the much smaller Dinaric Alps, and beyond that, the Adriatic Sea.

Since it only became an independent country for the first time in 1991, Slovenia has historically been divided into subregions based on its earlier existence in the Austro-Hungarian Empire. Thus the modern Slovenian regions are based on the four Habsburg crown lands of Carniola, Carinthia, Styria, and the Adriatic Littoral. The modern regions include Gorizia (*Goriška*), which stretches in a narrow north–south strip along most of the country's western border. Just to its east are the compact provinces of Upper Carniola (*Gorenjska*), and Inner

Carniola (*Notranjska*) just to its south. To the east of both is Lower Carniola (*Dolenjska*). Carinthia (*Koroška*) forms a small region on the northern border with Austria, where the bulk of the historic Carinthia now exists. Styria (*Štajerska*) is a large province taking up much of northeast Slovenia, with the small region of Prekmurje extending beyond it at the country's northeastern tip. Finally, Slovenia's small Adriatic coastline is called Slovenian Istria (*Slovenska Istra*, as distinct from the rest of the Istrian Peninsula, which continues southward into Croatia). However, the Slovenian coast can also generally be denoted simply as the Littoral Region (*Primorska*).

Slovenia is known for its extensive alpine forests, lakes, cave systems, and mixed geology. Despite its small size, it is proportionally one of the "greenest" countries in the world; with 36 percent of its total land area taken up by protected areas, Slovenia has the largest percentage of nature parks among EU states. Triglav, the country's highest point at 9,395 feet, is a peak in the Julian Alps. (It was also the highest point in the former Yugoslavia, when Slovenia belonged to that former federation.) The southwestern Karst Plateau (*Kras* in Slovene) is a limestone region of underground rivers, gorges, and caves. Indeed,

Spectacularly situated Predjama Castle stands in the mouth of Slovenia's Postojna Cave. Built in Renaissance style in 1570 on the ruins of earlier similar fortifications, the castle and its various noble rulers have been close to Slovene history and folk tradition for centuries. (Lachris77/Dreamstime.com)

Slovenia is well known for its caves. The longest, in Triglav National Park in the northwest, is the Migovec System, which runs 137,000 feet in length and reaches a depth of 3,190 feet. Slovenia's second-longest cave system, located in the country's southwest, is the Postojna Cave System (79,100 feet in length). Postojna Cave, in particular, has been accessible for visitors and has been a major outdoor tourist attraction since the 19th century. Approximately five miles from Postojna Cave is another much-visited site, the 13th-century Predjama Castle, an imposing structure built high in a rock face at the mouth of a cave, featuring numerous hidden tunnels.

Rivers (some of them underground) and lakes also play an important role in Slovenia's ecosystem. The alpine source of much of its waters gives Slovenia some of the purest water in the world. Rivers in Slovenia flow generally in a west–east direction. The major river passing through Slovenia is the Sava, which originates in the Julian Alps in the northwest corner of the country and flows for 615 miles before merging with the Danube in Belgrade, the capital of Serbia. The Sava has played a major role throughout history as it is the natural northern border of the Balkan Peninsula. It also flows along the southern edge of the Pannonian Plain, an area of great significance for the development of modern Slovenian and Croatian nations.

Two major tributaries flowing into the Sava include the Savinja, which flows for over sixty-three miles before reaching the Sava, and the Krka, which originates in southern Slovenian caves and runs for almost fifty-nine miles before flowing into the Sava. Other important rivers include the Drava, originating from the South Tyrol region of Italy, which passes through Austria and then Slovenia, before meeting up with the Mura, which itself originates in Austria and then passes through Slovenia and Croatia. Both are ultimately tributaries of the Danube.

Slovenia boasts of 321 lakes, mostly glacial in origin (with a few manmade ones).The deepest, at 520 feet, is the so-called Wild Lake (*Divje jezero*) in the west of the country. The most famous, however, is Lake Bled (*Bledsko jezero*) located in the Julian Alps in Upper Carniola in northwestern Slovenia. This glacial and tectonic lake is 6,960 feet long and 4,530 feet wide, with a maximum depth of ninety-seven feet. Set near the town with the same name and featuring a small island, Lake Bled is a popular tourist attraction.

The lowest point in Slovenia is sea level (the Adriatic Sea on the country's southwestern coast). This coastline stretches along the Gulf of Trieste (named after the nearby Italian city). While only twenty-nine miles in length, this provides vital access to the Adriatic. Slovenia's main towns on this coast are Koper (the country's main commercial shipping port), Izola (a historic fishing town), and Portorož, Slovenia's most popular seaside tourism destination. An ongoing problem has been the status of the Bay of Piran on the Croatian–Slovenian border; a 2017 international court ruling granted Slovenia access to international waters through a "corridor" in Croatian waters, but the latter did not respect the validity of the ruling, citing its abandonment of United Nations (UN)-sponsored negotiations in 2015 as a justification.

Population, Demography, Languages, and Religion

Slovenia's population of 2,102,126 ranks 147th in the world. Population distribution in Slovenia is fairly even, with the few and relatively small urban areas having the greatest population density. Over 65 percent of Slovenians inhabit urban and wider suburban areas. Even with its well-developed modern European economy, Slovenia has only one small city—the capital, Ljubljana (population 286,000). The few large towns in Slovenia's eleven urban municipalities include Maribor (95,586), Celje (37,628), Kranj (37,223), Koper (25,775), Velenje (25,329), Novo Mesto (23,275), Ptuj (17,870), Trbovlje (14,302), and Kamnik (13,685).

Owing to its low birth rate and high standard of living, Slovenia is among the European countries most affected by an aging population. In 2016, life expectancy was 78.2 years (74.6 years male, and 82 years female). The fertility rate being low, with 1.58 children born per woman, the population growth rate as of 2018 was only 0.03 percent.

In 2011, Slovenia changed its statistical collection methodology to exclude ethnic affiliation. The last census in which ethnic composition was identified was in 2002, which tabulated Slovenes as comprising 83.1 percent of the population, followed by Serbs (2 percent), Croats (1.8 percent), Bosniaks (1.1 percent), and the remaining 12 percent of the population including small communities of Italians and Hungarians, mostly living near their respective border areas and other unspecified ethnicities. This ethnic break-up has not changed significantly since 2002. Unlike other EU countries, Slovenia was relatively unaffected by the European migrant crisis of 2015 as it was not considered a destination country as ideal as Germany or Sweden by migrants.

The official language, Slovene, belongs to the South Slavic language group and has a number of regional dialects, reflecting its historic cultural overlap with Austria and Italy. Slovene is the native language of around 88 percent of the population, making Slovenia one of the most linguistically homogeneous countries in the EU. Despite (or perhaps because of) this situation, the government has given official-language status to the Hungarian and Italian languages spoken by the respective minorities. This bilingual status is maintained in the ethnically mixed border regions, with even passports being bilingual. However, this affects a very small percentage of the population (0.2 percent of the Slovenian population are Italian speakers, and 0.4 percent speak Hungarian as their native language). Slovenia also has the distinction of being home to a language considered "critically endangered" by UNESCO, the German dialect Gottscheerish. Before WWII, 4 percent of Slovenia's population was German-speaking. However, emigration and a state ban on the language under Communist Yugoslavia resulted in only a handful of elderly people in specific rural areas who still speak this 600-year-old Bavarian dialect.

Slovenia is a fairly secularized but nominally Roman Catholic country, with Slovenes and minorities like Croats, Hungarians, and Italians also including some Catholics. The historic decline in religious observance owes to general modern trends, but primarily to the persecution of religion during Communist Yugoslavia. Before WWII, 97 percent of the population was declared Catholic, whereas in 1991, after independence from Yugoslavia, that number fell to 71.6 percent. As of 2002, only 57.8 percent of Slovenians considered themselves Catholic.

While Protestantism has played a historically significant role in Slovenia, including the formation of the Slovene language and nation, less than 1 percent of the country is considered Protestant today. Mostly, this population comprises a significant Lutheran minority in the easternmost Prekumurje region. Slovenia's Jewish community today numbers only a few hundred people, who reside largely in the capital. Islam, considered the country's second-largest religious minority (2.4 percent), is associated primarily with the ethnic Bosniak community that came to Slovenia during and after the Yugoslav period on account of their common relationship between the federal republics. Similarly, 2.2 percent of Slovenia's population is Orthodox Christians, primarily comprising Serbs and Macedonians from former Yugoslav republics.

Economy

Although Slovenia, like the other former communist and socialist Eastern European countries, had to transform itself from a centrally planned economy to a market-oriented system, the transition was not nearly as painful as for many other countries in a similar situation. Historically, Slovenia was far ahead of the other Yugoslav republics in terms of development, and it was the site of the federation's most advanced technological development (e.g., hosting Yugoslavia's only nuclear power plant). Indeed, despite comprising only about one-tenth of the total federal population, Slovenia accounted for one-fifth of Yugoslavia's GDP and one-third of its exports. The country's relatively painless breakaway from the federation and lavish Western support meant that it had an advantage from the beginning. This was accentuated by its skilled workforce and advantageous location on a major European transport corridor with direct sea access.

Today, Slovenia is the wealthiest of the Slavic countries by nominal GDP. The country's per-capita GDP by purchase power parity in 2015 was equivalent to 83 percent of the EU average. The nominal GDP in 2018 was 42.5 million euros, a per-capita average of 21,267 euros. However, on a national level, this wealth is not equally distributed, with the central region around Ljubljana, the western Goriška region, and the Coastal-Karst region being the most prosperous. Alternately, the least wealthy parts of Slovenia are the Mura region, the Central Sava, and the Littoral-Inner Carniola.

After independence in 1991, Slovenia joined international economic organizations and wooed foreign investment on priority, even as civil war was waging to the southeast in Croatia and Bosnia. Slovenia thus joined the Central European Initiative in 1992, and became a founding member of the World Trade Organization in 1995. It then joined the Central European Free Trade Agreement the following year. The continuous pace of reforms brought Slovenia into the EU in 2004 when a total of ten countries joined at once. In 2007, Slovenia became the first new (2004 class) EU member to switch to the euro, replacing the Tolar, the currency it had adopted after leaving the Yugoslav Dinar behind. In 2010, Slovenia joined the Organisation for Economic Co-operation and Development (OECD), increasing its international economic network linkages further.

Slovenia's economy grew rapidly after joining the EU. However, setbacks occurred due to larger world events: the financial crisis of 2007–2010 and European sovereign-debt crisis. These events damaged Slovenian economic growth, severely affecting sectors like construction. In 2009, Slovenian per-capita GDP fell by 8 percent, a higher percentage than all but four other EU states. The economic crisis exposed a weakness in the Slovenian economy—its rapidly aging population—something which will have ramifications well into the future as it places a strain on the pension payments system. Nevertheless,

Slovenia continues to offer its workers one of the most generous retirement ages in Europe (fifty-seven for women, and fifty-eight for men), and rejected what would have been a modest increase in the retirement age at a 2011 referendum.

Today, while it still retains notable trade ties with other former Yugoslav states, two-thirds of Slovenia's foreign trade is with other EU countries, mainly, Germany, Austria, Italy, and France. Therefore, Slovenia's economy depends highly on foreign trade; the volume of this trade equals 120 percent of GDP (exports and imports combined). While traditional industries of agriculture (such as forestry, viticulture, and fishing) have fallen to just 2.5 percent of the GDP, with only 6 percent of the population engaged in these industries, Slovenia has been working hard to develop a name for itself in winemaking and organic foods. Tourism, and with it, the service industry in general, also comprises an increasing part of the national economy.

Environmental Issues

Slovenia's biological diversity is truly remarkable given its small size: around 1 percent of all the world's known organisms are found in a country that comprises only 0.004 percent of Earth's surface area. Successive governments have been accentuating this advantage ever since independence. Indeed, Slovenia signed the Rio Convention on Biological Diversity in June 1992, becoming a party to the convention on July 9, 1996. The government then came up with a National Biodiversity Strategy and Action Plan, which has been periodically updated ever since to protect endangered and unique species. These include the relatively rare Eurasian lynx, the endemic Carniolan Honeybee, and the Olm, an endemic aqueous salamander unique to Slovenia's underground caves.

Today, Slovenia has made a pristine environment one of its main selling points. While in some ways this restricts its economic growth, popular opinion tends to be proenvironment. For example, in early 2019, the environment minister canceled a tender that would have seen several hydroelectric plants come up along the Mura River following public concern—a move that was applauded by environmental groups. Nevertheless, areas of industrial production contribute to air pollution in parts of the country, as does a high volume of automobile traffic in Ljubljana.

Slovenia has added other accolades on the environmental front to showcase its attractions. Ljubljana was named Europe's Greenest Capital in 2016 by the EU, while in 2017, *National Geographic* called Slovenia "the world's most sustainable country," pointing to its management of tourism while protecting the environment. "Green certificates" for compliant tourism providers were among the concepts suggested in 2018 by internal green tourism organizers, who pointed to recent studies that indicated roughly 85 percent of foreign tourists chose Slovenia for its unspoiled nature. Such a trajectory indicates that in the coming years start-ups will focus more on bringing an environmental focus to their business offerings. This (and other larger EU environmental law developments) probably means that Slovenia has passed its peak in terms of heavy industry, and will now concentrate on other sectors like tourism and finance in the future.

National Regions, Symbols, and Governing Structures

Slovenia is divided into 212 municipalities, of which only eleven are classed as urban. Each municipality is led by a mayor (*župan*), popularly elected every four years, and a municipal council (*občinski svet*). Every municipality also has a head of the municipal administration (*načelnik občinske uprave*), appointed by the mayor to manage local administration functions. Population is distributed widely in this largely mountainous country, of which over half is covered by forests. Ljubljana, the capital and seat of government, is the country's only actual city (though a small one). The country's traditional regions are incorporated into two macroregions that have no administrative functions, but were organized for statistical purposes of EU policymaking. The first is Eastern Slovenia (*Vzhodna Slovenija*), which comprises the Mura, Drava, Carinthia, Savinja, Central Sava, Lower Sava, Southeast Slovenia, and Inner Carniola-Karst regions. The second is Western Slovenia (*Zahodna Slovenija*), comprising Central Slovenia, Upper Carniola, Gorizia, and the Coastal-Karst region.

The flag of Slovenia features equally sized horizontal stripes of white, blue, and red superimposed with the coat of arms of Slovenia slightly to the upper left side of the center. This coat of arms features a red-bordered blue shield on which stands a stylized mountain peak in white (a nod to Mount Triglav, the country's highest mountain) and running underneath it two wavy blue lines symbolizing Slovenia's sea and rivers. Above the mountain motif, three gold-colored stars represent the Counts of Celje, Slovenia's most notable medieval lords. The Slovenian national anthem, *Zdravljica* (A Toast), is based on a work by the 19th-century Romantic Slovene poet France Prešeren. Unlike many of the other "new" European countries that became independent after the Cold War, Slovenia did not create a new anthem, but merely continued using the one it had used as a federal republic during Yugoslav times.

Slovenia is a parliamentary democracy established following its declaration of independence from the Yugoslav Federation on June 25, 1991 (at the same time as Croatia). Although protests and political standoffs had been ongoing across Yugoslavia since at least 1988, Slovenia's declaration of independence was the first event to prompt a war. The immediate armed response from the Yugoslav Army (under the control of Belgrade, the Yugoslav capital in Serbia) occurred the following day. However, after what became known as the Ten-Day War (*Desetdnevna Vojna*), the Yugoslav Army withdrew and a truce was called. A total of sixty-three people were killed, making Slovenia's secession almost bloodless in comparison to the following wars in Croatia, Bosnia, and Kosovo. (Only the Republic of Macedonia, which declared independence on September 8, 1991, broke away from Yugoslavia completely peacefully.)

Slovenia was officially recognized by all European Community member states on January 15, 1992. It joined the UN on May 22 of that year. Comfortably insulated from the wars and accompanying problems affecting the rest of the former Yugoslavia, Slovenia spent the 1990s consolidating its ties with the West and implementing political and economic reforms.

The country's political system is similar to that found in most other European countries. The president, popularly elected every five years, is the nominal head of state, though actual power lies in the hands of the prime minister, the head of government. The government is formed by multiparty negotiations after parliamentary elections determine which parties have won enough seats to form a majority. The national president then ceremonially nominates a new prime minister, who nominates (after negotiations with coalition partners) a council of ministers to hold specific roles in the government. These new ministers are then elected by the parliament, also known as the National Assembly (*Državni zbor*). Parliamentary elections are typically held every four years, though special elections can be held earlier in special circumstances.

The Judiciary of Slovenia

The judicial system in Slovenia has largely thrown off Communist-era characteristics and generally resembles Western European judiciaries. It is among the three constitutional branches of government, but remains independent of the other two. Judges in Slovenia are given a permanent mandate. Further, they are appointed by the National Assembly, only after having been nominated by Slovenia's Judicial Council (*Sodni svet*). This council, however, is not part of the judicial branch.

The court system of Slovenia is multitiered, with three types of courts. The first, the basic or ordinary courts, are divided between civil and criminal and distinguished according to the importance of cases they hear. There are forty-four local courts for misdemeanors and minor civil cases (*Okrajna*) and eleven district courts for other cases (*Okrožna*). Third are the specialized labor, social security, and administrative courts. The second and higher tier of courts include four appellate courts (*Višja sodišča*), based in Celje, Koper, Ljubljana, and Maribor. An appellate court for labor and social security issues is also located in Ljubljana. The third tier, the highest court, is the Supreme Court of the Republic of Slovenia (*Vrhovno sodišče Republike Slovenije*), which generally only hears appeals involving the correct application of law. Lastly, Slovenia has a Constitutional Court, which is separate from the regular judiciary system.

Security and International Institutions

Slovenia is surrounded by peaceful, allied countries and as such has no military threats. The Slovenian Armed Forces is a small but efficient army that exists largely for joint peacekeeping missions abroad and to help in case of natural disasters at home. Since conscription was ended in 2003, Slovenia's military has become fully professional. Its commander-in-chief is the national president, though actual operational command is the responsibility of the general staff of the Slovenian Armed Forces. In 2016, military spending was only 0.91 percent of GDP—far below the 2 percent figure stipulated by NATO. International peacekeeping missions in which Slovenia has participated include Bosnia and Herzegovina, Kosovo, and Afghanistan.

Slovenia has membership in leading international organizations, including the EU, NATO, and the Organization for Co-operation and Security in Europe, as well as the OECD, International Monetary Fund, and other regional, European, and global organizations.

2

From Ancient Origins to the End of the Roman World (Prehistory–565)

PREHISTORY

The first recorded human settlement in today's Croatia dates to the Paleolithic Age. Neanderthals inhabited the Zagorje region in northern Croatia, and their bones and other remains have been found at several locations, most famously at the 130,000-year-old Hušnjakovo site near Krapina; this Paleolithic site is considered by archeologists as one of the world's most important and extensive. Early 20th-century excavations uncovered not only human remains but bones from prehistoric animals now extinct. Flint tools made by an even earlier civilization have been discovered at Šandalja Cave near Pula, on the north Adriatic coast, and in Punikve near Ivanec.

More permanent and settled Neolithic settlements appeared from c. 6000 BCE to c. 3000 BCE, with traces of notable settlements found on the Adriatic coast near modern Zadar and Šibenik, as well as at cave dwellings on islands like Hvar. Earthenware items reveal a more sophisticated day-to-day life of these populations, while some remarkable remains of defensive architecture from the Neolithic period have also been found, such as the defensive moat and stilted huts at the important Smilčić site near Zadar. Inland Neolithic settlements have also been found in the forested and arable lands between Croatia's great tributaries, the Rivers Sava, Drava, and Danube. Similar Neolithic settlements have been unearthed across the Balkans, for example, off the shore of Lake Ohrid in Macedonia far to the south.

It was in the tri-river region that the most important developments of the Croatian Bronze Age (c. 3000 BCE to c. 2200 BCE) occurred. On the banks of the Danube, an advanced civilization began using copper near today's Croatian city of Vukovar (lending this prehistoric culture the name Vučedol). The advanced new metalwork and ceramics attested by discoveries have led scholars to suggest a certain degree of cultural overlap with contemporaneous peoples from the nearby Carpathian Mountains, Dinaric Alps, and Eastern Alps. The ensuing Iron Age saw the settlement of the so-called Hallstatt (proto-Illyrian) culture and the Celtic La Tène culture in Croatia. In a period of significant migration and turbulence, these now-vanished peoples comprised the beginning of a more compact civilization in Croatia that merged into various tribes known collectively as Illyrians. The cultural orientation of these tribes was heavily influenced by their geographic dispersal; for example, those inland and further north were more oriented toward the Celts, whereas the coast-dwelling tribes were oriented toward ancient Greek and later Roman mores. In antiquity, a time of Greek colonization across the Mediterranean, this process extended to several islands in the Adriatic Sea off of today's Croatia.

Although much smaller territorially, the modern-day Slovenia has also delivered several truly remarkable finds from prehistoric times in its extensive cave systems and the now-protected marshlands near the capital, Ljubljana. Traces of human civilization here date back at least 250,000 years. In 1995, a prehistoric pierced cave bear bone was found in Divje Babe cave near Cerkno; possibly a flute of some kind, it may be the oldest musical instrument ever discovered. Seven years later, archeologists discovered Neolithic stilt pile settlements, and with them the "Ljubljana Marshes Wooden Wheel"—the oldest wooden wheel found in the world thus far.

ILLYRIAN TRIBES AND THE ROMAN CONQUEST (5TH C. BCE–10TH C. BCE)

The Illyrian civilization was, along with the ancient Greeks, Macedonians, and Thracians, one of the major inhabitants and influencers of the ancient Balkan region. While not nearly as culturally or artistically significant as the Greeks, the Illyrians played an important role in historic military affairs and commerce; faint traces of the Illyrian existence have been preserved in popular history. (One example is the ancient Illyrian King Pyrrhus, who was chronicled as having won a battle at too great a cost—hence the modern term, "a Pyrrhic victory.") In a less historical sense, the Greeks incorporated Illyrians into their mythological pantheon as they did with most other ancient tribes and cultures. The mythical "Illyrius" and his offspring were thus inventions of Greek imagination that sought to incorporate real peoples into their own cultural and religious worldview. In certain places in the Balkans, the names of the mythical "Illyrius" offspring have survived as place-names.

In the case of the Illyrians, the remaining evidence is so scant that their language—if there even was a single one—is unclear, with scholars having run through numerous theories that often have had more to do with national ethnopolitical preferences and ideologies than with actual facts. Similarly, little is known of their religion, except that it (like other ancient belief systems) was pantheistic. Human and animal sacrifice among the Illyrians has been attested, and their funerary beliefs involved placing household items, jewelry, and weapons alongside the dead to assist in their journey to the afterlife. Such items have been recovered from burial mounds (tumuli) scattered across the Balkans.

The presence of the Illyrians in Croatia and Slovenia dates back to well before the Common Era. However, there are very few linguistic or archeologically unique remains. Indeed, most of what we know about the Illyrians comes from ancient Greek and Roman authors. Tracing the Illyrian point of origin is also difficult because, as with many other now-disappeared ancient cultures, their tribal affiliations were loose and heterogeneous. Lacking any simple and compact ethnic identity, the Illyrians were and are hard to pin down. The most probable theory about the origins of this Indo-European people is that they migrated westward into today's Balkan region from the plains north of the Black Sea. It is also possible that the Illyrians were simply descendents of local Bronze Age cultures already present.

It is likely that, as with other descriptors for peoples that the Greeks considered "barbarians" (notably, the later Slavs), the name "Illyrian" was used as a blanket term for a number of disparate tribes scattered across the central Balkans, such as the Liburnians and Pannonians—basically, all those people who lived north of ancient Macedonia and Thrace, and beyond the limits of what was considered "civilization" by the ancient Greeks. (This possibility is reaffirmed by Roman author Pliny the Elder's reference to "Illyrians proper" when describing the inhabitants of the south Dalmatian coast of today's Croatia, in his 1st-century CE work *Natural History*.) What is most striking about the Greek and Roman portrayal is of the Illyrians as a naturally warlike people, constantly a threat on both land and sea as pirates.

Therefore, we should take with a grain of salt the depiction (created by Greek and Roman authors) of "Illyrians" as occupying vast lands from Albania to Slovenia along the Adriatic Sea and inland across the Balkans up to the Morava River. There was no strong Illyrian sense of ethnic self-awareness—much less a territorial empire. As a strict political–geographical entity, Illyria would be known as the Roman province of Illyricum after the Croatian coast was annexed by the empire following a series of wars in the 2nd-century BCE.

These wars were preceded when one of the main Illyrian tribes of the coast, the Dalmatae, revolted. These ancient Dalmatians, of course, are responsible for giving the south and central Croatian coastal region the name it still bears. Declaring independence in 180 BCE from Illyrian King Gentius, these coastal Illyrians managed to create a capital at Delminium (modern-day Tomislavgrad). Rather uniquely, the Dalmatians chose to form a republic along the lines of the ancient Roman Republic. This decision, of course, challenges ancient Greek and Roman views of the Illyrians as bloodthirsty and uncultured barbarians.

The dominion of the Dalmatae spread northward from the Neretva to the Cetina Rivers, and as far east as the River Krka. However, this Dalmatian Illyrian expansion would prove to be short-lived as the Romans began their trans-Adriatic conquest only twelve years later. The prolonged and violent wars that ensued (known to ancient Greek and Roman authors as "the Illyrian Wars") went on for approximately 150 years. The Dalmatae fought hard but were unable to match the superior and better-equipped Roman forces, and were forced to pay tribute after their defeat in 156 BCE.

To a large extent, the mighty Roman Empire had a hard time suppressing the Dalmatae owing to their unique nomadic lifestyle and the rugged, mountainous geography in which they lived. The mountainous interior (that extended into today's Bosnia-Herzegovina) were all but impenetrable for heavily armed troops with long supply trains, though perfect for guerrilla warfare waged by Dalmatae chieftains who erected a series of small stone fortresses in this remote hinterland. On the coast, pirates could easily outfox the Roman military, especially commercial fleets, given the innumerable hidden coves and other hiding places found throughout the Adriatic coast. While the elite of Dalmatian society not living in coastal cities enjoyed stone houses, the shepherds and cattle-breeders that performed the vital duties of feeding the populace inhabited humble dwellings, as simple as mountain caves. All these factors contributed to creating a highly mobile and dangerous military threat that continually vexed Roman efforts to crush local rebellions.

With the eventual overall victory of Rome and incorporation of the Western Balkans into the empire, the Illyrian Wars ended after 27 BCE. Then, in 10 CE Emperor Augustus chose to divide the Illyricum province to administer his expanded empire. The northern and more inland reaches of old Illyria became the Pannonian province (after a related ancient tribe living there). In the south, Dalmatia came into being, though its territory was not consigned merely to the littoral but also swept inland. Latin civilization and customs thereafter took hold generally throughout Illyricum, replacing the semi-independent tribal structures of the various tribes and augmenting the vestiges of Hellenistic culture that had taken hold previously during the Greek colonization of a few Adriatic islands. North of Dalmatia, some cities on the Istrian coast and on the northern Adriatic coast of present-day Slovenia and Italy were incorporated into the Roman province of Italia. Much of Istria had already long been annexed by the Romans well before the end of the Illyrian Wars in 27 BCE.

Following the turn of the millennium into the Common Era, the Illyrian tribes were slowly assimilated into the Greco-Roman cultural sphere, with preexisting local cultural and belief systems acquiring further similarities. The geographic proximity and trade ties of Illyria and the Greco-Roman world had already created cultural synergies. In terms of religion, the Dalmatae's religious beliefs (which had been attested for at least 400 years by that point) bore close similarities to the Greco-Roman pantheon. For example, the major pastoral deity, Vidasus and his wife Thana, were equated with the Roman Sylvanus and Diana. Likewise, the war god Armatus equated with the Roman god Mars. Today, archeologists have discovered testaments to Dalmatian deities in the form of stone reliefs (often decorated with nymphs) on Croatian cliff faces. The valley Imotski Dolina is also remarkable for containing remains of an actual Dalmatae temple used from the 4th to 1st centuries BCE. Such findings have given historians and archeologists a more complete understanding of the life and beliefs of this major Illyrian tribe.

ROMAN CROATIA AND SLOVENIA

Following centuries of war against and within the Illyrian tribes of the Balkans, Roman rule brought their culture, gods, language, and an extended and much-needed period of peace and development. Roman mores were adopted mostly in the coastal cities, as well as in some well-situated inland Balkan metropolises, such as Singidunum (modern-day Belgrade), Serbia, Serdica (modern-day Bulgarian capital of Sofia), and Stobi (now an archeological site on the Macedonian plain). In the often mountainous countryside of Croatia, Slovenia, and other Balkan lands, however, indigenous beliefs and practices were more likely to survive among nomads and local chieftains.

However, the events leading to this peace in future Croatian lands were precipitated by some of the most dramatic events in general Roman history, which occurred at roughly the same time as the annexation: the victory of Caesar's adopted son, Octavian, over Mark Antony and his lover Cleopatra, Queen of Egypt, at the naval Battle of Actium in 31 BCE. Occurring south of Croatia in the Ionian Sea off of Greece, the battle brought the Final War of the Roman Republic to an end, ushering in the age of imperial Rome. Four years later, Octavian was given the honorary title of Augustus—as he is also known—and thereafter carried out constitutional reforms over the next three decades that would govern the Roman Empire. The rule of Caesar Augustus marked the beginning of the famous *Pax Romana,* a long and largely peaceful period (from 27 BCE until the death of Marcus Aurelius in 180 CE). The Mediterranean became a "Roman Lake," and the end of chronic civil wars allowed for renewed cultural and architectural development across the burgeoning empire.

Dalmatia made a particularly fateful contribution to the Roman Empire as the birthplace of Emperor Diocletian (244–311 CE). Although born into a poor family, he distinguished himself as a military officer, serving under the emperor Carus. When the latter died during a military campaign, Diocletian defeated his son, Carinus, and became emperor in 284. Diocletian's rule was particularly important for several reasons. First, he brought much-needed stability to the empire, ending the so-called Crisis of the Third Century, a fifty-year period marked by barbarian invasions, civil war, and social unrest. Diocletian created political balance by appointing fellow military officer Maximian as coemperor over the Western Empire, while he himself ruled in the East, and later appointed Galerius and Constantius as coemperors in specific areas. This "Tetrarchy," proved more capable of joint military action to drive out barbarians and stop the major threat of the

Persians in the east. Without Diocletian's creative administration and military acumen, it is likely the Roman Empire would have imploded.

However, the Dalmatian-born emperor is also known for an equally fateful but darker policy—his persecution of Christianity (303–312), the longest and bloodiest such persecution in imperial history. By the 3rd century, the new religion had spread across the empire, becoming an irritant to rulers who upheld the traditional pagan worship. Under the official persecution of Diocletian (and coemperor Galerius in Greece), believers were forced to be "crypto-Christians" and worship in secret, lest they be executed or left to be killed by wild animals in arenas as a form of spectator sport.

In a very real way, however, the proliferation of new martyrs to the faith strengthened not only Christian resolve but also imperial sympathies. Indeed, Diocletian's eventual successor (Constantius's son Constantine) negotiated the 313 Edict of Milan, by which the persecutions were ended and Christianity came to be tolerated. Constantine, who would be eventually known as Constantine the Great and the founder of the Byzantine (Eastern Roman) Empire, converted to Christianity on his deathbed in 337, in the new capital he had built, Constantinople (today's Istanbul, Turkey). The Byzantine Empire would later adopt Christianity as its official state religion under Emperor Theodosius in 380. Among much else, Theodosius's decision gave the Bishop of Rome (a position that would become the Papacy in time) clerical authority in the Western Roman Empire. This would create an intra-Christian rivalry between the Bishop of Rome and the Patriarch of Constantinople that persists to this day. The Balkans, and Croatia and Slovenia in particular, would become the line of division, as the easternmost region of former imperial lands over which the Latin-speaking, Catholic Roman Church had influence. This religious fault line between Catholic and Orthodox persists to this day, and has long affected politics, war, and society.

Overall, Roman rule brought great benefits to the future Croatian and Slovenian lands. The Dalmatian and Istrian coast just north of it benefited particularly. In addition to the cultural, social, and educational benefits, the empire built new roads to connect cities and commercial ports with land routes accessing Rome and other imperial destinations. The major coastal route (the Via Flavia) connected the Dalmatian and Istrian settlements with those of the southern Adriatic and, to the north, Aquileia. (A flourishing Roman city, the latter is today a small Italian town west of the Slovenian border.) The road from Aquileia westward passed through two modern Slovenian cities, Emona (modern Ljubljana) and Cellia (modern Celje), both wealthy trading cities protected by towers and replete with marble palaces and wide squares.

Following the contours of the Adriatic, the Roman roads carried on both eastward into Pannonia and southward along the Istrian and then the Dalmatian coast. Settlements on this route included Tarsatica (near modern Rijeka), Salona (near modern Split), and Narona, a town in the Neretva River valley. At Narona, a second Roman road (the Via Aurelia) ran northeast and inland through Sirmium to Mursa (modern Osijek).

The coastal region just north of Dalmatia, known as Istria, was incorporated into the Roman Republic by 177 BCE. Its major coastal city (today's Pula) grew in prominence after 45 BCE when Julius Caesar declared it Rome's tenth province. While the city suffered heavy damage during the civil war that followed Caesar's assassination three years later, it was rebuilt in grand fashion and given a rather verbose name, following its main patron, Iulia, the daughter of Caesar Augustus (Colonia Pietas Iulia Pola Pollentia Herculanea). Surrounded on ten sides by city gates (remains of which still survive) and boasting advanced water systems and a massive arena, Pula became a symbol of the Romanization of the Eastern Adriatic.

Under the Romans, the Istrian, Dalmatian, and Pannonian provinces indeed underwent a remarkable transformation in architecture. The remnants of Roman structures are not only archeologically valuable but have also become some of Croatia's best-loved and most-visited tourist attractions, revealing a remarkable sense of aesthetics between urban functionality, military genius, and the stunning natural landscape of Balkan highlands and the Adriatic Sea.

One of the most impressive Roman constructions is the Arena at Pula. Today, it is the only surviving Roman amphitheater with four side towers and is one of the best-preserved arenas anywhere in former Roman lands. Originally a wooden structure when work began on it in 27 BCE, the structure eventually morphed into a massive limestone amphitheater with multiple gates, aqueducts, and tunnel entrances by the time of its completion in 68 CE. Under Emperor Vespasian in 79 AD, the arena was enlarged again to make room for the brutal but riveting Roman spectator sport, gladiator fighting. Pula was also notable for its Temple of Augustus, built in honor of the first Roman emperor between 27 BCE and 14 CE. Decorated with intricate friezes, this temple set on a porch of Corinthian columns is now considered one of the finest preserved Roman temples outside of Italy.

A different but equally magnificent Roman structure in Dalmatia, the Diocletian Palace, today makes up half of the "old town" of modern-day Split. It was completed in 305 CE when the Dalmatia-born Emperor Diocletian was preparing for retirement. He commissioned the grand structure near Salona, the Roman predecessor to Split. However, far from a simple aristocratic retirement home, the Diocletian Palace (built strategically on a peninsula jutting into the Adriatic) included a large fortress for the Roman military. This garrison section comprised about half of the palace's area. The other half was devoted to Diocletian's residence and spacious gardens. Although Diocletian was only able to enjoy the palace for a few years until his death in 312, the structure was maintained and used for centuries by subsequent Roman leaders in what was the Dalmatian province's main administrative center. Today, the Diocletian Palace has become a UNESCO World Heritage Site and, despite partial destruction and renovation over the centuries, remains the best-preserved example of a Roman palace in the empire's former territory. One of its most important and impressive features is its Temple of Jupiter, the chief Roman god, which was set in the palace's western quarter and decorated with sculpted reliefs of gods and heroes.

Large-scale, sophisticated Roman settlements were not only built on the Adriatic coast, however. Inland (near the country's modern capital

Diocletian's Palace, the most striking ancient site in the Croatian city of Split, was built at the turn of the fourth century as a retirement villa for the eponymous Roman emperor. The heavily fortified structure, which played an important defensive role for ancient Salona in Dalmatia, today comprises much of Split's historic old town. (Carolannefreeling/Dreamstime.com)

of Zagreb) extensive remains have been found of Roman Andautonia, a major commercial and administrative center on the Sava River for roughly 400 years. The extensive remains of Andautonia today reveal a city of some wealth, with remains of houses with heating systems, public baths, and artwork, such as wall paintings and mosaics, as well as fine glassware and silver jewelry.

Overall, the Romans built or renovated over thirty cities and towns in today's Croatia and Slovenia. The former Illyrian capital of Delminium (near today's Tomislavgrad in neighboring Bosnia and Herzegovina) was rebuilt and expanded by the Romans, who also built military highways, the remains of which are still visible, to keep watch over the marauding mountain Dalmatae who avoided Roman rule. In modern times, votive tablets, sculptures, inscriptions, and other material have been found by archeologists, indicating that this remained an important and relatively peaceful city for 400 years of Roman rule. For defensive purposes, the Romans also built their own network of hillside fortifications, including Tilurium between today's small inland towns of Gardun and Trilj.

BARBARIAN INVASIONS AND THE END OF THE ROMAN WORLD (380–565)

Defense indeed became a greater and greater priority with the swift decline of the Western Roman Empire in the 5th century. The creation of Constantinople by Constantine the Great two centuries earlier had influenced a gradual power shift away from Rome and toward the Eastern Mediterranean, where the Eastern Roman (Byzantine) Empire became prominent in political and military leadership. While the Byzantines still referred to themselves (and would for over 1,000 years) as "Romans" (*Romaioi*), Greek gradually became the lingua franca of daily life by the 7th century. However, this influence was less pronounced in Dalmatia and Istria, where Latin and Western Roman influence was more prominent.

A second implication of the imperial shift eastward, one which coincided with increased barbarian invasions of the 5th century, was that the Balkan region, far from the capital of Constantinople, became more difficult to defend. However, this unfavorable situation had been apparent for centuries already by the time of the Western Roman Empire's fall to the Ostrogoths in 476. Most significant in this regard was the Gothic War (376–382). Before the war, the Romans had allowed the Goths to settle as refugees south of the Danube as they sought to escape from the Huns in the north. However, the arrangement quickly failed and the Goths revolted. In the ensuing anarchy, numerous Roman settlements and towns were ravaged, and the emperor, Valens, was killed by the Germanic barbarians. In 380, a Western Roman army had to drive marauding Goths back from Illyricum in the west.

Emperor Theodosius, who inherited this dismal situation, was unable to achieve total victory in the Gothic War. The empire was forced to adopt a policy of accommodation toward the Goths to end their rampage in Thrace (in the eastern Balkan region of present-day Turkey, Greece, and Bulgaria). Unlike the usual Roman preference for total victory over barbarians, the treaty gave the Goths the status of *foederati*—that is, an autonomous, recognized group that could be called upon for Roman military service but which was allowed to keep its customs and lands. Some of these Goths (who later divided further into the Ostrogoths and Visigoths) were settled in Thrace, others in Illyricum and Pannonia, and others throughout the empire.

While Theodosius's advisors had hoped the Goths would become "good Romans" as previous subdued barbarians before them, this did not turn out to be the case. Instead they became occasional allies and enemies, and sought their own terms in diplomatic relations. The 382 policy of accommodation was fateful in that it established a certain way of dealing with invaders and local populations that would be inherited by later Byzantine rulers, and indeed even by the Ottoman Turkish Empire that succeeded it after 1453.

In 395, the death of Emperor Theodosius prompted the Goths, under new King Alaric, to declare the peace treaty of 382 void. Amidst a power struggle between the presumptive leaders in the empire's east and west, Roman armies could not defeat Alaric, whose Goths pillaged westward across Thrace and Macedonia into Greece. Finally, Alaric was awarded what he sought—a senior Roman military appointment. In 398, he was made senior commander (*Magister Militum*) over the Illyricum province of modern-day Croatia. However, over a decade of failed treaties, wars, sieges, assassinations, and other barbarian invasions left Rome vulnerable. In 410, Alaric finally succeeded in sacking the city.

Although it was no longer a major center of power (it had been replaced by the Italian Adriatic city of Ravenna as capital of the Western Roman Empire), Rome still represented rich pickings. Its population of 800,000 still made it the world's largest city, and it had symbolic, historical, and emotional importance in Europe and beyond. Thus, its fall, for the first time in 800 years, was met with great shock everywhere. The Germanic barbarian invaders looted widely before continuing their assault southward throughout Italy. After Alaric's death later that year, they returned north and, expanding into Gaul, declared a kingdom.

A much-weakened Western Roman Empire lingered on at Ravenna for a few decades. But in 455, another barbarian group (the Vandals) sacked Rome again, causing yet more devastation. In 476, the Western Roman Empire finally collapsed as the last Western Emperor, Romulus Augustus, was overthrown by the Germanic barbarian Odovacer, who pronounced himself King of Italy. In 453, the death of famed warlord Attila the Hun led to the swift defeat and disappearance of that civilization. Like the Goths, Alans, and others, the Huns had been raiding Byzantine lands in the Balkans for decades by that time. Power was taken over by Pannonian-born Ostrogoth Theoderic (454–526), who had received a Byzantine education and sought to restore a form of Roman civilization, overseeing a subempire from the Croatian coast across Italy and into Visigoth-controlled Spain. However, with his death, the Ostrogothic kingdom began to decline.

The end of the Hunnic Empire in the 450s had meant semi-independence for numerous groups, some of which, like the Ostrogoths, took local power across the Balkans, including in Pannonia and Dalmatia. In the second half of the 5th century, barbarian groups formerly subjugated to the Huns such as the Gepids, Rugii, Heruli, Suebi, and Ostrogoths became *foederates* of the Eastern Roman Empire, under the style of treaty accommodation introduced by the Theodosian system for the Goths in 382. Theoderic's death in 526 and the ensuing crisis of dynastic succession left the Ostrogoths significantly weakened until 535 when Byzantine Emperor Justinian I declared war on the Ostrogoths, attempting to restore imperial control over Italy and other former imperial lands lost in the west since the barbarian invasions began. For his military achievements, building works like the Church of St. Sophia and a legal code which is today considered one of the most important examples of early European law, Justinian (482–565) is often considered one of the greatest Byzantine emperors.

The war, which lasted twenty-one years, resulted in widespread devastation in Italy and the general Adriatic area. In the early years, the war was a great success, with the emperor's top general, Belisarius, continuously defeating the Ostrogoths in battle, marching into southern Italy from Africa, and working his way northward. However, his sudden recall to Constantinople allowed the barbarians to recover some territory. However, Justinian did for a time return Dalmatia to imperial control during the wars with the Ostrogoths. It also became the Theme (a Byzantine Greek term for a military province) of Dalmatia, and would remain so well into the Middle Ages.

The future Croatian province actually played a key role in preparations for the final, and successful, Byzantine campaign. In 550–551, Justinian assembled a large army of 20,000 soldiers at Salona on the Dalmatian coast under the command of Narses, the imperial chamberlain. Moving his troops to the Italian port city of Ancona the following year, Narses and the Byzantine army defeated the Ostrogoths at the Battle of Taginae. The defeat marked the end of Ostrogothic rule there, and the remaining Ostrogoths were gradually absorbed into another Germanic barbarian tribe that had previously invaded, and which would have a longer influence—the Lombards. The Ostrogoth defeat, in the long term, would prove quite advantageous for their own enemies to the north—the Frankish tribes that would eventually play the greatest role in shaping north and central Europe.

However, other events in the 6th century aside from war were also occurring that decisively marked the end of Roman antiquity and the beginning of the early Middle Ages. Chief among them was a massive outbreak of Bubonic Plague in 541–542. According to historians of the time, the plague was initially brought to Constantinople by rats aboard grain ships. The suddenness and extremity of the plague depopulated and impoverished the empire at a crucial moment in European history. Over the course of two centuries of outbreaks, the plague killed an estimated twenty-five to fifty million people. In the context of the late Roman world, this catastrophe (which had the largest impact on Constantinople, Egypt, and the Eastern Mediterranean coastal cities) killed an estimated 13–25 percent of the entire world population at the time. There is no question that the Justinianic Plague hastened the decline of ancient civilization and benefited the rise of barbarian populations on the empire's edges. The depopulation along the empire's southern frontiers also helped, indirectly, the rise of Arab tribes gravitating toward the competing new religion of Islam from the mid-7th century.

The death of Justinian in 565 and extinguishment of the Western Roman Empire mark a symbolic end to ancient Rome, its worldview, and some of its populations. It is at this point that the ancestors of today's Croats and Slovenians step into the picture.

3

From the Avar Khanate and Slavic Migrations to the Kingdom of Croatia and Union with Hungary (565–1102)

THE AVAR KHANATE IN THE BALKANS AND WARS WITH BYZANTIUM (568–626)

After 565, new waves of migrating populations and barbarian invaders very quickly reversed the gains the late Justinian had made during the long campaign in Italy, where the rising Lombard power replaced the Ostrogoths. The Byzantines had also neglected the Balkans because of the great war in the east against the Persian Empire, also waged under the late emperor. Due to these events, a sort of anarchy prevailed elsewhere in the empire, particularly around the northern edges of the Black Sea and north of the rivers Sava and Danube, where a range of rival nomadic tribes fought one another.

From 567, one nomadic group, the Avars, had made inroads due partly to Byzantine partronage; a decade earlier, Justinian had paid off these Asiatic warriors to fight another tribe, the Gepids. However, the Avars simply replaced the Gepids in the region, and soon represented the biggest threat to the empire in the Balkans since the Goths. The origins of the Avars have been disputed as they left no written records and largely vanished from the historical record by the 9th century. (A 2018 genetic study concluded that the Avars were a mixed Mongol-Turkic people, similar to the inhabitants of today's Central Asian republics.) They began to arrive from north of the Caucasus, across the Black Sea steppes of modern Ukraine and Romania, in the early 6th century. The Avars were never homogenous, instead forming a loose confederation of tribes and negotiating with other groups—most significantly, the Lombards to the west—as they sought to increase their lands and power.

During their forays across the northern Balkans, the Avars created settlements across the vast Pannonian Basin, an area including parts of modern-day Croatia's province of Slavonia, and stretching across the Hungarian Plain and northern Serbia as far as western Ukraine. (This included parts of the former Roman province of Pannonia.) The Avars' shamanistic, non-European society brought a new element to the emerging post-Roman Balkans. Like other tribal societies from the east, their sense of identity was expressed by a tribal name that often reflected a legendary sense of prestige, rather than an ethnic identity. Power was held ultimately by a powerful khan, with a limited wealthy aristocracy and subject tribes of various ethnicities. The Avars were respected by the Byzantines for their skilled horsemanship and prowess in archery. While considered barbarians, they did exhibit some artistic skills, as attested by the ornate, Byzantine-styled jewelry and ornaments found in the graves of Avar warriors in Hungary.

Despite Justinian's patronage, Avar ambitions quickly increased following the Byzantine emperor's death. In 568, Avar Khan Bayan besieged Sirmium (today's Sremska Mitrovica, on the Sava River, near the border between Serbia and Croatia), a city that had been established by ancient Illyrians and thereafter had served as the Roman capital of Pannonia. Bayan could not capture the city, but dispatched 10,000 skilled horsemen from a subject Turkic tribe, the Kutrigurs, to raid Dalmatia, launching a war between the two powers that would last for almost forty years. Seizing Dalmatia's all-important Roman coastal road, Khan Bayan cut off Byzantine military access and left the residents of Roman Croatia's coastal cities vulnerable as well. Sirmium was finally taken in 581, and other Roman-origin cities and towns across the territory of modern Croatia were largely destroyed and depopulated. With the Byzantine army preoccupied by war on the eastern front with the Sassanid Persian War (572–591), Avar raids became more frequent and intense, especially in the central and eastern Balkans, as far south as Macedonia and Thrace. But after the cessation of hostilities in 591, a Byzantine counteroffensive pushed the Avars away from their newly conquered lands; instead, the Avars turned their forces on Dalmatia. However, the impoverished province was not an enticing target, and harassment from the Byzantines led the Avars to head further north to attack the more vulnerable Franks in today's Slovenia and Austria.

Fighting continued intermittently over the following two decades, with the Avars first raiding successfully almost up to Constantinople, but eventually being driven back deep into their own territory on the Pannonian Plain, as Byzantine armies sought to keep the Danube—vital to their own inland naval route—safe and operational. However, another war with the Persians (from 602 to 628) forced the empire to withdraw some troops from the Balkans. The Avars took advantage of this by relaunching their raids southward from 612. Numerous Byzantine Balkan cities were captured by the Avars, including Salona on the Dalmatian coast. The Avars continued to be a thorn in the empire's side until 626 when they attempted a joint siege (with the Persian army and Slavic tribes) of the capital, Constantinople. According to popular legend, the city's Orthodox Christian patriarch, Sergius, achieved divine intercession by waving an icon of the Virgin Mary atop the city walls. (The actual icon is today housed in Dionysiou Monastery in Greece's isolated monastic community of Mt. Athos.)

New Populations: The Bulgars and the Slavs

After the failed siege of 626, the Avars withdrew to their lands in the northern Balkans and did not pose a serious threat to the Byzantine capital again. In fact, their empire began to fall apart amidst fighting between their Turkic Bulgar clients, the Kutrigurs, and Onogurs. Their decline and eventual disintegration was hastened by the conflicts and expansions in the Balkans of other peoples, such as the Turkic Bulgars. Like the Avars, this new population was pagan and warlike, and under the rule of a khan. Entering the Balkans like the Avars had, across the steppes north of the Black Sea, the Bulgars both settled the Pannonian Plain (under Avar control) and later established their power base in modern-day Bulgaria (partially, that is, some of the Roman provinces of Thrace and Macedonia). This tribe achieved superiority over the Avars by about 680 and would subsequently from time to time be an ally or threat to the Byzantine Empire for control of the Balkans.

However, unlike the Avars and some of the Slavs, the Bulgarian conversion to Orthodox Christianity in the 9th century (a subject to which we will return later) brought them into a Byzantine cultural orbit distinct from that of the Croats and Hungarians of the Pannonian Plain.

Strictly in terms of population, most contemporary sources agree that another migrating group from the east—the Slavs—became the most numerous and the most settled. They began to arrive in distinct waves from the 5th to 7th centuries, and at different times were either allies or enemies of the Avars. In the 6th century and up to the failed siege of Constantinople in 626, some Slavic tribes were pressed into military service by the Avars, though as a society they were not nomadic and less geared up to waging war than their nomadic neighbors.

The Slavs are particularly important for the present study because they largely comprised the ancestors of modern Slovenes and Croats. Attested in Byzantine sources from the 6th century as *Slavi* or *Schlaveni*, the Slavs (known to themselves as *Sloveñi*) were a loose confederation of tribes that emerged from the Black Sea steppes and Eastern Europe, coming westward in various waves. Like the Goths, Avars, Gepids, and others before them, the Slavs headed for the fertile grasslands and rich forests of central and southeastern Europe. Etymologically, their name derives from the early Slavic term *Slovo* (meaning "the word"). It is widely believed by scholars that the Slavs used this term as a reference to people who could speak a mutually understandable language—something they contrasted with the Germanic tribes, which they called the *Nemci* (from the term *nem*, meaning "mute," or "incapable of speaking"—this name is still used informally to refer to Germans in Slavic languages like Serbian).

Although scholars have proposed numerous theories about the origins and relative homogeneity of the Slavs, there is general agreement that they—along with all the other tribes of what is referred to by scholars as the Great Migration Period—came to Europe seeking arable, fertile land and the wealth of established communities. Unlike the Avars, who were largely pushed out of the trans-Caucasus by Turkic tribes, some of the Slavs at least came to the Balkans and Central Europe to take land deserted by the Goths and other Germanic tribes, following the latter's defeat by Attila the Hun and the gradual move westward to Italy.

Some Slavic tribes migrating to Europe came from beyond the River Dnieper, and quickly expanded to settle a remarkably large swath of territory from the Carpathian region and the Danube and Pannonian basins to the Western Balkans and as far south as the Peloponnese in Greece. Unlike the Turkic tribes and the Avars, the Slavs were not nomadic horsemen looking primarily for pasturage; rather, they sought to make extensive settlements in forested areas, as well as near lakes, rivers, and marshes. From the 6th century, they began to create their own simple villages, while also resettling towns abandoned by the previous Gothic inhabitants. Relying primarily on farming rather than plunder, the Slavic tribes also engaged in woodwork and trade.

Over the following centuries, the Slavic migrations created three general groups by which they are categorized today: the East Slavs (Russians, Ukrainian, Rusyns, and Belarusians); the West Slavs (Czechs, including Bohemians and Moravians, Slovaks, and Poles); and the South Slavs (Serbs, Croats, Slovenes, and Macedonians). Although originally Turkic, the Bulgars would become Slavicized by the 9th century due to their earlier cultural contacts in Pannonia, and later due to their geographical and cultural proximity to the Macedonians to the west. Before the development of wealth through agricultural and slave labor resulted, in the 7th century, in a clan-based system of rule, most Slavic settlements were communal in nature. Farmland, pasturage, and cattle were the shared property of the individual tribes. Tribal leaders exerted their authority only locally as villages tended to be scattered and geographically dispersed. While this autonomous lifestyle and general abundance of natural resources were broadly beneficial, the lack of any large or cohesive political structure also made the Slavs attractive prey to more warlike and nomadic populations like the Avars.

THE FIRST SLAVIC POLITIES: SAMO'S KINGDOM AND THE WHITE CROATS (623–850)

By the mid-6th century, various Slavic tribes had either been forced into alliances by the Avars or subjugated by them completely. In truth, the Turkic nomads needed them for their own semiempire to be able to compete with the might of Byzantium. The Avars relied not only on Slavic food production and labor but also on their skill and craftsmanship when it came to designing siege weaponry, bridges, and boats. Along with other subject peoples (like the Kutrigurs, Huns, Sabirs, and Gepids), Slavs were recruited into the Avar armies that were active in the Balkans and Central Europe until the mid-7th century.

Inevitably, this dominant relationship incurred resentment, and various Slavic tribes were inclined (sometimes with the blessings of Byzantine or Frankish leaders) to revolt against their Avar overlords. According to the 7th-century Frankish Chronicle of Fredegar, resistance to the Avars accounted for the remarkable, if short-lived, Kingdom of Samo (ruled 623–658). Named after a Frankish merchant-warrior respected by the Slavs for his bravery in battle, this polity came into existence following Slavic anger at being pressed into Avar service, while having their wives and daughters taken by the Turkic nomads. Samo succeeded in uniting the Wends, a Slavic tribe in present-day Slovenia, with other Slavic tribes spreading over to today's Czech and Slovak Republics. The unprecedented Slavic freedom movement also benefited the Onogurs, a local Turkish tribe and longtime enemy of the Avar-allied Kutrigurs. In 632, nomad leader Kubrat defeated the Avar-Kutrigur forces on the Pannonian Plain, creating something the Byzantines would call *Patria Onoguria* (homeland of the Onogurs).

Amidst this infighting among the Turkic powers, other Slavic tribes joined Samo's tribal union. From 632, he was supported by Valuk, the first Duke of Carantania. This area in the eastern Alps and extending through modern Slovenian, Austrian, Czech, and Slovak lands was the home of the proto-Slovene Slavic tribes. Under Valuk and his successors, Carantania had its capital at present-day Karnburg (near Klagenfurt in Austria). The principality maintained its independence until 745 when it was incorporated into Bavaria and then the emerging Frankish Empire. These so-called Alpine Slavs had little sense of national identity, but they did enjoy a greater degree of peace and tranquility than their Slavic cousins—no doubt a result of their protected mountainous location. Indeed, in the 7th century, at the time of Samo's uprising, it seems that none of the various powers—neither the Lombards in the west, Franks in the north, nor Avars and Bulgaria in the east—could control this territory in the southeastern Alps. In this somewhat protected environment, the Slavs of Carantania and the neighboring Carinthia (*Koroška* in Slovene, now situated mainly in Austria) were able to form communal entities (*župe*), with limited nobility. The same was the case for the Slavs of what would later be called Carniola (now mostly in Slovenia).

As the emerging Frankish power to the north and Lombards in Italy had supported the Slavic uprisings of Samo and Valuk against the Avars, the Byzantines encouraged another Slavic population, the Croats, to fight the common enemy. The origins of the Croats as a people remains a very controversial subject, with numerous theories suggested and various medieval texts cited. Although it was written only later, in 950, Byzantine Emperor Constantine VII Porphyrogenitos's work *De Administrando Imperio* (On the Governance of the Empire) is probably correct in its claim that Byzantine Emperor Heraclius (610–641) invited a new group the so-called White Croatsto come to Pannonia and help fight the Avars. Although there is evidence that Avar

Slovenia's Mt. Triglav rises up to 9,400 feet in the Julian Alps and has long been a source of national pride. The mountains that today comprise Triglav National Park were the original home for the migratory proto-Slovene "Alpine Slavs" who colonized the region in the early medieval period. (Corel)

society continued at least for some time in Pannonia and Dalmatia, it eventually died out or was incorporated by the newcomers, who established a Croatian duchy in Dalmatia (which, like Illyricum before it, included inland parts of today's Bosnia, not only the coast).

The White Croats had been neighbors of a similar migratory Slavic people, the "White Serbs," who also migrated at about the same time to the territory of today's Serbia and Macedonia. It is important to note that the name "white" had nothing to do with the color of these people's skin (nor anything else), but rather to the fact that in medieval times, a specific color was ascribed to each cardinal direction on the compass. In other words, the naming of a color referred to a vague point on the map from where they had come.

The location of the original White Croatia is still debated by scholars, but it is thought to have been generally somewhere between modern Slovakia, Czech Republic, Poland, and Ukraine. An even greater mystery about the Croats is the origin of their name (in Croatian, the country is called *Hrvatska* and the people, *Hrvati*). Since similar names are found in ancient Greek (among other) texts from centuries before the Slavic migrations, one school of thought among scholars claims that the origins of the Croats is actually in a trans-Caucasus people of Iranian-European descent. In their ancestral Eastern European home-land, those White Croats (*Bijeli Hrvati* in Croatian and *Biali Chorwaci* in Polish) who did not migrate to modern-day Croatia actually preserved their sense of ethnic identity and their name until the early 20th cen-tury, particularly in Lesser Poland (historical Galicia). Still other White Croats who did not migrate to the Balkans in the 7th century were eventually assimilated by the emerging Slavic nations of the Czechs, Poles, and Ukrainians.

BAVARIAN INFLUENCE IN CARANTANIA AND CAROLINGIAN FRANCIA'S EXPANSION IN PANNONIA (660–822)

Even as the Slavic migrations saw the Croats and Alpine Slavs begin to establish themselves in modern-day Croatia and Slovenia, a new power was rising quickly to the north: the Franks and, to the south of them, the Bavarians (of the eponymous German province that still exists today). Frankish culture was Catholic and looked to the Latin-speaking culture of Rome rather than the Greek-speaking Byzantine Empire for its cultural influence, while also retaining aspects of its own indigenous culture (such as sagas and heroes).

The Franks were long-attested Germanic tribes that had fought for and against the Roman Empire. First mentioned in the 3rd century CE by Roman sources, these tribes were settled along the River Rhine, in the Roman hinterland, and were known for their frequent raids into imperial lands. Over time, the Franks increased their influence across a vast area spanning the rivers Loire and Rhine. As the Roman Empire fell apart in the 5th century, Frankish kings consolidated their rule, adding large portions of Roman Gaul—modern-day France—the country with which the Franks are still associated. As it developed into what became known as the Merovingian Empire, the Frankish kingdom was characterized by a cultural synthesis of native Germanic and Roman customs and laws.

By 800, when Pope Leo III crowned Charles (better known as Char-lemagne) "Holy Roman Emperor" in a Christmas ceremony, this implied a claim not only to a legitimate heir to the Roman Empire but also as a defender of the Holy See. By that time, the Vatican had been weakened to the point that Pope Leo's life was being threatened by Roman mobs, while the Vatican held temporal power over only a few territories, the Papal States in Italy. For the pope to be awarding imperial titles to Western kings was fairly ludicrous, in Byzantine eyes at least, but tolerated. Although at times ceremonially used and held by leaders at odds with the Church, the title continued to be held by German and Austrian kings into the 1800s.

Under Charlemagne, the Franks conquered the Lombards, and then, in 788, the Duchy of Bavaria, which bordered the Slavic lands of Central Europe. Charlemagne continued the Bavarian policy of establishing on the southern Bavarian borders tributary, militarized Marches (military borders protected in return for tribute). This March was created precisely to stave off the Carantanians, Serbs, and Czechs. Other lands inhabited by Slavic peoples that would be taken by Charlemagne included Bohemia, Moravia, Austria, and Croatia (Pannonia and part of Dalmatia).

The Carolingians and the Croats found a common enemy in the Avars, who were at the time making their last stand in a much-diminished Khanate. Charlemagne called on Dalmatian Croatian Duke Višeslav and Croatian Prince Vojnomir of Pannonian Croatia for support. Their joint offensive destroyed the Avars once and for all. For his part, Vojnomir was himself obliged to convert from paganism to Christianity and recognize Frankish sovereignty over Pannonian Croatia and Slavonia, all of it rich farmland and pasturage in the interior. The Franks placed Pannonian Croats under Eric, the margrave, or military commander of Friuli (modern-day Rijeka) on the northern Croatian coast after Charlemagne's conquest of Istria. From there, Eric wanted to carry on the campaign south along the coast, but his forces were defeated by those of Duke Višeslav in the Battle of Trsat. The margrave's death in the lopsided battle was a blow to the Carolingian Empire and helped convince Charlemagne to turn his attention to a weaker Slavic enemy who proved easier to subdue: the above-cited Carantanians and Carniolans, the "Alpine Slavs" of the future Slovenian state.

These developments brought the Frankish Empire into direct conflict with the Byzantine Empire, which still retained several city-states and islands in Dalmatia. Treaty negotiations began in 799 but were not helped by the pope's elevation of Charlemagne to the status of Holy Roman Emperor the following Christmas, a gesture seen as a provocation by Constantinople. Talks were followed by a brief war, but finally ended in a tentative peace in 812 (known as the *Pax Nicephori* treaty, after its initiator, Emperor Nicephorus). The deal allowed the Byzantines to retain control over the coastal cities and islands they possessed in Croatia, while in return they supported Frankish rule over Istria and the Dalmatian interior. While a major division of territory and acknowledgment by Constantinople that the Frankish Empire was practically an equal party, the treaty did not stop local Croats from occasionally rebelling. However, more often than not the Croats (particularly in Dalmatia) found that their interests aligned with those of Byzantium in light of common enemies such as the expending Bulgarian state.

The Byzantine *Thema* and City-States of Dalmatia

Since the Byzantine reconquest of the Adriatic in 535, the empire had for the most part been able to hold on to key cities like the administrative and ecclesiastical capital of Jadera (Zadar), the new city of Ragusium (Dubrovnik), Cattarum (Kotor in today's Montenegro), Spalatum (Split), Vecla (now Krk), Crespa (Cres), Arba (Rab), and Tragurium (Trogir). These well-fortified settlements, some of them on islands, provided a safe haven for the autochthonous Latinate Dalmatian population. Being more civilized and wealthier imperial subjects, they had historically been victims of raids by the Avars and Slavs; this situation continued into the 7th century, and, even when a semiautonomous Duchy of Croatian Dalmatia was established, its duke did not have control over these coastal cities but was mostly relegated to the inland, Slavic-populated settlements in today's Croatia and Bosnia.

Nevertheless, the barbarian raids that ravaged the coast from time to time contributed in some way toward forming some of the city-states that continue to exist in modern Croatia. For example, when in 639 the Avars destroyed Salona (modern Solin), residents occupied and added to the remnants of the nearby Palace of Diocletian, naming the new city Spalatum (today's Split). Similarly, another Avar attack (together with the Slavs) around 615 destroyed the Roman city of Epidaurum (modern Cavtat). Its inhabitants went on to build the important city of Ragusium (Ragusa in Italian, Dubrovnik in Croatian), which survived as an independent city-state for centuries and which will be discussed in more detail in the following chapter.

The native coastal Dalmatians would, over the years, pass under the nominal control of various powers—most prominently, the Venetians—but retained their own Roman law, independent customs, and even a Latin-based language (Dalmatico) similar to Italian and with several regional dialects. Although spoken by fewer and fewer people over time, Dalmatico did not go extinct until the turn of the 20th century. As such, the native Dalmatians remain the closest descendants of ancient Romans in Croatia today.

For the Byzantines, a Theme (*Thema*, in Greek) was a sort of military-civilian province not simply equitable to a Frankish frontier March. Imperial divisions of territory into Themes helped rationalize administrative and military command over lands that were often geographically complex and ethnically diverse. Dalmatia, however, was no ordinary Theme as it was far from the imperial capital, on a coast dotted with islands, and near to both barbarian populations and established rival powers. Linguistically and religiously, the Dalmatian city-states would over time become more aligned with Roman Catholicism than Byzantine Orthodoxy.

What is most remarkable about the Dalmatian city-states, however, is how they were able to remain largely independent of both the land-based powers that formed intermittently over time to the east (the Avars, Franks, Croats, and Serbs), as well as the maritime powers to the west, such as the Venetians and, for a time, the Normans. This speaks to the strategic advantage that all sides perceived in keeping these well-set and fortified cities prosperous. Although they never posed a military threat to the inland duchies and kingdoms, they did provide a degree of naval defense and access to a Mediterranean-wide maritime trading network.

REVOLT AND REINCORPORATION: FRANKISH RULE, THE CARANTANIANS, AND THE REBELLION OF LJUDEVIT POSAVSKI (745–822)

The annexation by the Carolingian Empire of much of Central and Western Europe helped solidify the cultural orientation toward Germanic, Catholic society that would have a lasting impact, particularly in the future Slovenia. After the disintegration of Samo's realm in 658, Alpine Slavs established the Principality of Carantania in the Eastern Alps, which was independent from 660 to 745. After then, it fell under the Bavarian sphere of influence and was later generally incorporated into the Frankish Empire. Until around 820, it was ruled as a semi-independent tribal polity. Borut, a ruler in the mid-8th century, was the first documented Slavic prince (*knjaz*) of Carantania. He was notable among local Slavic pagan rulers in that he converted to Christianity. In fact, the Carantanians as a people were the first Slavic nation to convert to Christianity. Looking for unity in the face of yet another Avar invasion, Borut's successor, Prince Hotimir, asked Bishop Vergilius of Salzburg to send evangelists to Christianize his people into the Roman Catholic faith. In 755, an Irish monk named Modestus was sent to Carantania along with several clerical colleagues and achieved this task.

However, not all Carantanians were happy about giving up their ancestral ways, and rebellions against Frankish Christianity did break out. In response to revolts, the Carantanian principality was turned into a Frankish March. Over time, this tactic would increasingly become the preferred way of dealing with unruly Slavic populations on the hinterlands, right up through the time of the Austro-Hungarian Empire many centuries later. The new March later emerged as the feudal Duchy of Carinthia.

In the early 9th century, Alpine Slavs of Carantania were moved en masse from modern Slovenia and Austria and settled in the Lower Pannonian Basin region—officially, the Balaton Principality, a place in today's Hungary. (Latin sources dubbed this *Carantanorum regio* or "The Land of the Carantanians," indicating a clear ethnic continuity perception on the part of the Carolingian leadership.) In fact, the name Carantanians or Quarantani is attested in Latin sources until the 13th century.

As noted, the Carantanians generally supported the best-known rebellion of the early 9th century, that of Pannonian Croat Duke Ljudevit Posavski (ruled 810–823). Posavski ruled from the fortified town of Sisak (a Croatian town in today's eastern district of Slavonia) on the confluence of the Kupa, Sava, and Odra rivers. This rich agricultural land, only thirty-six miles from the modern Croatian capital of Zagreb, was one of the main settlement points of Croats who had not continued further southwest to the Dalmatian coast. The rebellion started in 818, after Frankish Emperor Louis ignored Posavski's diplomatic entreaties, concerning the perceived ill-treatment of Pannonian Croats by Margrave (Frankish military commander) Cadolah of Friuli (today's coastal city of Rijeka) in northern Dalmatia. Although Cadolah (ruled 800–819) enjoyed initial successes in Pannonia, his penchant for torturing even children did not endear him to local Slavs, and Ljudevit had no trouble in mustering reinforcements from the Carantanians and Serbs to the east. They were thus easily able to repel a second assault by Margrave Cadolah, who died of disease in Friuli in 819.

This setback forced the Frankish emperor and his advisors, deliberating from the northern capital of Aachen, to devise a plan for a massive invasion of Croatian Pannonia from three sides. Ljudevit's men partially repulsed the first one and defeated Borna, a Croat lord of the northern Dalmatian coast, but were forced to retreat to a heavily fortified enclave, while ordinary Croats hid from the Frankish troops in swamps and forests. Although the Franks lost many soldiers to disease in the marshy conditions, they ultimately won the war when Ljudevit was forced to escape to Serbian protection around 822.

From Duchy to Kingdom: The Croats of Dalmatia (845–928)

Beyond Pannonia, the first Croatian political dynasty to be formed by the descendants of the 7th-century White Croats was created in the Dalmatian hinterland (not the coastal city-states). Writing in 950, Byzantine Emperor Constantine VII stated that the Croats divided their territory into eleven counties or administrative regions (*županije*). The major ruling dynasty of the first Croatian Duchy was the House of Trpimirović, who ruled from the 9th to the 11th centuries, overseeing Croatia's transformation into a kingdom that united, for a time, Pannonia and Dalmatia. Due to occasional instability, leaders of this clan were temporarily replaced by the House of Domagojević from 864 to 878 and again from 879 to 892. The Croat dukes were originally considered vassals of the Carolingian Empire and took part in complex three- and even four-sided wars for the coast with Byzantium and Venice, as well as with the expansive Bulgarian Empire to the east. Indeed, the degree of rulership was never geographically simple, and considerable overlap constantly occurred due to changing facts on the ground and flexible peace treaties.

The Duchy of Croatia (*Kneževina Hrvatska*), also known as *Dalmatinska Hrvatska* and Littoral Croatia, was the second political entity to include a part of the modern Croatian state after the Pannonian Duchy. While the Byzantines (and later Venice) continued to hold more influence over the Dalmatian city-states, the Croats' Slavic culture would over time begin to make inroads with the Latinate coast-dwellers—particularly after the Croats began to convert in large numbers to Roman Catholicism in the 8th and 9th centuries.

The Duchy did not have a single capital; rather, over its centuries of existence, it developed several seats. Dukes often ruled from the hilltop Fortress of Klis near Split, which commanded a strategic view of passages to the Adriatic Sea from the Balkan interior, and was thus strategically significant through the Ottoman-European Wars centuries later. Solin (the ancient Salona, sacked by Avar-Slav raids) was another ducal possession as were Knin, Bijaći, and Nin. Just south of the Croatian Duchy was a different competing maritime power: the Narentine Slavs known mostly for their paganism and piracy, most frequently preying on Venetian shipping. At their peak in the 10th century, the Narentines controlled territory from the rivers Cetina to Neretva, as well as the important islands of Brač, Hvar, Korčula, Mljet, Vis, and Lastovo. These geographical facts at first held Croatia back considerably in its goal of establishing a naval presence. However, Croat maritime expansion and development of a commercial fleet and navy picked up after the 11th century when the Venetians decided to end the Narentine threat once and for all, annexing some of their territories at the same time.

In an earlier antipiracy raid, in 839, the Venetians under Doge Pietro Tradonico attacked both Narentine- and Croat-held coastal territory. This resulted in an important peace treaty between Venice and Duke Mislav of Croatia. Mislav was succeeded by Trpimir I (ruled 845–864)—who is considered the actual founder of the Trpimirović dynasty. Under his rule, the Croatian Duchy managed a complex series of threats while expanding its territory and cultural–religious development.

Ruling from an expanded Klis Castle, Trpimir chose first to fight the Byzantine army forces guarding the empire's coastal cities, like Jadera (Zadar), in 846. Then, just nine years later, a threat emerged from the eastern mountains in the form of an invading army led by the powerful Bulgarian Khan, Boris I. However, after limited fighting, Trpimir turned to diplomacy and reached a peace treaty with the Bulgars. This would prove most auspicious as the Bulgars were becoming a major power in the Balkans, and limiting hostilities with them was a wise idea for Croatian stability.

Trpimir also displayed his diplomatic acumen in his negotiations with the Vatican, issuing in 852 a Latin charter in Biaći which confirmed his predecessor Mislav's gifts to the Archbishopric in Split. The document also restates Trpimir's plan for church construction, as well as the first Benedictine monastery in the Croatian Duchy; it was to be located in Rižinice, an area between Klis and Solin. Both of these religious constructions quite understandably made the pope and the Catholic Church quite pleased as they continued to expand their influence in non-Catholic lands.

After the death of Trpimir, a Vatican-backed noble, Branimir Domagojević, led a coup in 879. Taking advantage of this situation and the decline of the Carolingian Empire, Duke Branimir sought to make himself—and Croatia—indispensable to the Vatican. In a letter, Branimir wrote to Pope John VIII to inform him of Croatia's split from Byzantium and of its allegiance to the Holy See. The pope lost no time in holding a special service in St. Peter's Basilica, in which he gave his blessing to Branimir and his people—a symbolic but important gesture in the Croatian nation-building process. Branimir attempted to prove his value to Rome, for example, in the following year when he answered the pope's call for a Croatian-armed escort against Narentine pirates for a Vatican delegation traveling off the southern Dalmatian coastline. Even though the mission was not entirely successful, it did indicate goodwill on the part of the Croatian duke. In fact, after the cessation of hostilities with Bulgaria in 853, the Croats became known for their ability to provide reliable security escorts for Papal delegations traveling to Bulgarian-held territory across the often dangerous mountains of inland Dalmatae and Bosnia.

When Duke Branimir died in 892, control reverted to the House of Trpimirović: specifically, to Trpimir's third and only surviving son, Muncimir (ruled 892–910). Under Muncimir's reign, Croatia took a more moderate and independent course between the Byzantine Empire and Papacy, while the duke sought to resolve some internal problems Branimir had sparked between Catholic leaders in Croatia. At the same time, instability in neighboring Serbia saw Muncimir take into his protection rivals to the throne there, while keeping a wary eye on the approaching Hungarians (Magyars) who crossed the Carpathians from the Eurasian steppes during his reign and invaded Pannonia to the northeast, defeating Croat Duke Braslav there and endangering Dalmatia. However, Muncimir is probably best known for being the predecessor (and, probably, the father) of Tomislav, Croatia's last duke (around 910) and its first king (925–928).

Aside from his involvement in important ecclesiastical matters, King Tomislav had to deal with potential invaders from the east. In 926, after having captured most of the Balkans, threatened Byzantium, and successfully demanded to be crowned as emperor by the pope, Bulgaria's Simeon I took his armies through Serbia and Bosnia to fight King Tomislav's forces. It turned out to be a terrible mistake as the Croats won a decisive victory over the invaders. Despite Croatia's estrangement from Byzantium at various times, King Tomislav was a more moderate leader than some of his predecessors and saw the common threat that the Bulgarians posed to both Croatia and the empire.

Simeon's ambitions to seize Constantinople were well known. The Croats had tolerated the Byzantine Theme of Dalmatia; it was not hostile to Croatian interests, and indeed the empire had struck a deal by which the Croatian leaders shared in the revenues generated by these few port cities. Although well defended from the sea, where the Byzantines still maintained a naval presence, they were less well defended from any land attacks coming from the east. If Simeon could seize the Byzantine Adriatic cities, it would make a major statement regarding Bulgaria's claims in the Balkans. The only thing that stood in their way was the Dalmatian Croatian army, which met them in a historic face-off. Known as the Battle of the Bosnian Highlands, the showdown between the two sides occurred in the mountains of Bosnia near the rivers Bosna and Drina—at the time, the border area between Dalmatian Croatia and the Bulgarian Empire. In the fighting, the Croats used superior positioning and surprise to achieve a crushing victory over the forces of Bulgarian commander Alogobotur.

After Simeon died in 927, an emissary of Pope John X mediated a peace treaty between the Croats and Bulgarians. The former had affirmed its regional strength in the decisive battle, while the latter would no longer prove a serious threat to the Croats. Meanwhile, the Croatian victory allowed the Byzantine to Empire to hold on to its Dalmatian coastal Theme (in gradually diminished form) through the 12th century.

FRANKISH PATRONAGE, THE MISSIONS OF SS CYRIL AND METHODIUS, AND EARLY CHRISTIANITY IN CARANTANIA AND CROATIA

As has been seen, a major recurring theme in the history of the Croats and Slovenes (and indeed, all the peoples of the Balkans) is the battle for spiritual allegiances between the two former capitals of the Roman Empire. On the one side was the pope, ruling from Rome over only a small collection of Italian states but wielding influence in the royal courts of a rapidly developing Western Europe. On the other side was the Orthodox patriarch, whose authority rested on that of the Byzantine emperor in Constantinople. In this battle for hearts and minds, the migratory Slavs along with the Turkic Bulgars (who would gradually be assimilated by Slavic culture) were the main focus of Byzantine and papal interest and competition. Several key events would create an ideological and physical dividing line between the different Slavic peoples of the Balkans that persist to this day.

A major event that has been noted, the pope's crowning of Charlemagne as Holy Roman Emperor on Christmas Day 800, was one that really put the Byzantines on notice. At the time, both Eastern and Western Churches were in full communion, but the prospect of a Latin pope granting titles—much less the title of "Emperor of the Romans"—was unthinkable. In the Orthodox view, the pope was simply the bishop of Rome, one of several original bishops of the Christian Mediterranean. The patriarch of Constantinople, while also simply another bishop, was traditionally considered "first among equals" due to his imperial patronage. His role would become continuously more important over time as Arab expansion put large areas of North Africa and the Middle East, where other Orthodox Christian patriarchates had been established originally, under Muslim rule.

Adding to the shock over the coronation of Charlemagne was the relative abruptness with which this break in practice occurred. In 800, popes had only been nominated by Western cardinals for the previous forty-eight years. Back in the 6th century when Justinian had recovered Italy, a new policy was adopted by which the Byzantine emperor could nominate and approve new popes, leading to a number of Greek-speaking Greeks, Syriacs, and Sicilians serving as pontiff between the years 537–752, a period generally known as the "Byzantine Papacy."

Nevertheless, a major ideological dispute that would contribute to a crisis of Orthodox legitimacy in the West overlapping with this era was the periodic outlawing of religious icons (a policy known as iconoclasm). It was started by Byzantine Emperor Leo III and has been interpreted partly as a reaction (primarily by the poorer and non-Greek Eastern elements of society in the Byzantine Middle East) to the rapid advance, from the mid-7th century, of the new religion of Islam. Sweeping north and west out of Arabia, the new religion took a radically austere view against the depictions in artistic form of any holy personages. Worse than the unknown destruction of priceless icons during the iconoclast period was the ideological alienation created between and within Christian communities. The first period of iconoclasm as Byzantine state policy lasted from 730 to 787; a second occurred between 814 and 842. This period roughly overlapped with the consolidation of Frankish power and the Bulgarian Khanate's replacement of the Avar one.

It was in this context that the growing division and competition between pope and patriarch continued and played out among the new populations of the Balkans. Even four years before his coronation, Charlemagne had subdued the remnants of the Avars and converted them to Catholicism. He then created a general March across the former Pannonian Basin that had constituted the Khanate's heartland for centuries. The eastern half of this March was granted to the various Slavs—first in 840 to Prince Pribina (800–861).

Originally expelled from his homeland by a rival prince, Pribina was notable for building the first documented Christian shrine among the Slavs in 827 in his hometown of Nitra, an important medieval Slavic city located in today's Slovakia. Prince Pribina's place of exile in 846, the lakeside Balaton principality, existed until 871 when it was divided between the Frankish Carinthian and Eastern Marches. He remained loyal to the Frankish King Louis the German and was rewarded for this with numerous properties, vineyards, and churches in the area around his principality.

A concern for the Franks at this time was the powerful Great Moravia, the first significant West Slav kingdom. With its heartland along the River Morava in today's Czech Republic, it would expand to include parts of modern Hungary, Slovakia, Serbia, Poland, and Ukraine, becoming a major player in the geopolitics of the time. However, what Great Moravia lacked was a reliable legal and linguistic system. Thus, a year after early Slavic church supporter Pribina died in 861, Moravian leader Prince Rastislav (ruled 846–870) made an official request to Byzantine Emperor Michael III and the learned Patriarch Photius to send teachers to Moravia. This request, which was fulfilled in 863, would have momentous repercussions for European history and Slavic people in general. Rastislav turned to the East rather than the West because he wanted to reduce the existing influence of Frankish Catholic priests in his territory. In the 850s, he had supported the deposed Ratpot of Pannonia against the Franks, and fought off a Frankish attack against Moravia, while also supporting the rebellion of Carloman, a Frankish prince, against his own father, King Louis the German (ruled 843–876).

The missionaries who were sent, brothers and clerical scholars Cyril and Methodius, were both erudite men and aware of the local Slavic dialect (probably, a forerunner of today's Bulgarian and Macedonian languages) spoken in the vicinity of Thessaloniki, their hometown. This Byzantine city on Greece's north Aegean coast was well-defended by walls from the expanding Bulgarian Empire in the 9th century, though the indigenous people of the historic province of Macedonia to the north had become increasingly Slavicized with the migration waves that reached as far as the Peloponnese in southwestern Greece at various points. Cyril and Methodius would use the colloquial Slavic language of their home region as the basis for the liturgical language they created, Old Church Slavonic, using an innovative new alphabet (referred to as Glagolitic). Later this was simplified to an alphabet named in honor of the missionaries, known as Cyrillic, at the Preslav Literary School in Bulgaria and the monasteries surrounding Lake Ohrid in Macedonia, then a center of the expanded Bulgarian Empire.

The first task that Cyril and Methodius set for themselves was translating the Bible into the Slavic tongue. This made it considerably easier for the Slavs of Great Moravia to understand Christianity— to which they had already been converted by the Franks—than it had been in Latin, the common language of Western Christendom, but far removed from the common parishioner's daily life. Naturally, the Byzantine missionaries' success alarmed and irritated the Frankish political leaders and priests under papal control. Any deepening of Byzantine influence so far north into Europe was a direct challenge to the pretensions of the so-called Holy Roman Empire of the Franks. The success of Cyril and Methodius incurred the jealousy of pro-Latin German missionaries, and the whole issue subsequently became a matter of Vatican intrigue. Pope Adrian II, impressed with Methodius' arguments in favor of a Slavonic liturgy and the importance of Christian unity, even made the evangelist Archbishop of Sirmium (modern-day Sremska Mitrovica in Serbia).

In 869, Pope Adrian sent Methodius back from Rome with this title and jurisdiction over all of Moravia and Pannonia, including the Croats living there. Soon after, however, Ratislav died; his successor sided with Frankish King Louis and his German bishops, deposing and imprisoning Methodius. Even though Pope John VIII later secured the release of the Byzantine missionary, he was ordered to stop using the Slavonic liturgy and was declared a heretic for doing so in 878. Despite being exonerated by the pope, Methodius was soon forced out of Moravia by the jealous German bishops determined to uphold a Latin-only policy. This policy would be upheld for centuries, and Methodius and his followers were exiled; many found refuge in the court of Boris I of Bulgaria, where they developed Slavonic literacy further. There is no telling how different European history would have been without the interference of the Carolingian German bishops against the Slavic peoples and their missionaries; quite possibly, the West Slavs might have adopted the Cyrillic alphabet rather than the Latin one.

In addition to the literary and cultural developments that Cyril and Methodius brought to the Slavic peoples, the enduring legacy of their missions was a sharp division in Christian orientation. Despite being almost constantly at war with Byzantium, the Bulgarian Empire accepted and supported the work of the Byzantine prelates, and the lands under imperial possession (large parts of today's Serbia, Bosnia, Montenegro, Macedonia, and of course, Bulgaria) would accept Byzantine Orthodoxy, whereas Slavic populations either directly under the German boot or simply under Vatican influence (from Great Moravia to Carantania, Carniola, Pannonia, and Dalmatia) would orient themselves toward Roman Catholicism.

Despite its future Catholic orientation, it is worth noting that Croatia—even in its most distant coastal parts—did not go unaffected by the literary work of Cyril and Methodius. Indeed, a church graveyard on the island of Cres preserves a stone tablet recording three generations of the Valun family. Known as the Valun tablet (*Valunska ploča*), this 11th-century artifact is written in both Glagolitic and Latin. Another, more impressive limestone tablet of almost six feet in height (the Baška tablet or *Bašćanska ploča* in Croatian) was found near the Church of St. Lucia on the island of Krk. It contains a lengthy Old Church Slavonic inscription written in Glagolitic, and dates from around 1100—almost 150 years after Cyril and Methodius's mission to the Slavs of the neighboring Moravia.

The historical personage most associated with advancing the use of Slavonic as a liturgical language was Bishop Gregory of Nin. For his efforts, this early 10th-century prelate often found himself at odds with the Archbishop of Split and the papacy. However, Gregory's efforts helped deepen Christian worship among the local population. Croatia's increasing significance in ecclesiastical matters was attested in the Vatican's decision to hold two Church Councils in Split (in 925 and 928), events attended by King Tomislav himself.

Among the major outcomes of these events was the accentuation of Latin-rite over Slavonic-rite masses supported by Gregory and the final decision to make Split the unquestioned archbishopric of Croatia. Interestingly, the pro-Split contingent justified this seniority by claiming that Split was the original home of Christianity in Croatia; they claimed that a certain Domnius, a disciple of the Apostle Peter, had been martyred there after having tried to convert the local Roman population. However, it is more likely that the "Domnius" involved was actually Salona's first bishop, who was indeed a victim of Roman martyrdom, but in the early 4th century under Emperor Diocletian. Today, Domnius remains the patron saint of Split, with a large church named in his honor.

CIVIL CONFLICT, A BRIEF APOGEE, AND THE "PERSONAL UNION" WITH HUNGARY (928–1102)

Following the death of King Tomislav in 928, Croatia entered a period of gradual change that led to an internal crisis. While Tomislav had united Pannonian and Dalmatian Croatia together under the same banner for the first time, the royal model turned the country into a feudal society in which peasants were robbed of their land and became serfs. This had a deleterious impact on the kingdom's ability to field a strong army.

Tomislav's successors, Trpimir II (928–935) and Krešimir I (935–945), served generally as custodians of the first king's achievements, preserving relations with both the Byzantines and the Vatican, while avoiding conflict with rival powers. However, Croatia was notably weakened under the reign of Krešimir's son, Miroslav, as some outlying regions of the new kingdom sought to break away. Miroslav was in fact killed, after only four years in power, by his own *ban* (provincial viceroy) Pribina, acting on behalf of a usurper, Michael Krešimir II (949–969). However, both Michael and his wife, Helen, were generally respected throughout the country and made lavish donations to the church, particularly in the Dalmatian coastal cities. Good relations with the Byzantine Empire were preserved under Michael's son Stjepan Držislav (969–997). According to contemporary chronicles, he was granted royal insignia and titles, and the Croats held more control over the cities in the Byzantine Theme of Dalmatia.

Around the same time, on Croatia's northern periphery, events occurred that increased the Germanic consolidation of influence over future Slovenian lands. In 976, Carantania-Carinthia was named as an autonomous administrative unit by Frankish Emperor Otto I. This drew the land of the "Alpine Slavs" further under Germanic influence, with Carinthia (named the sixth Duchy of the Holy Roman Empire) ruled by a mixed Bavarian-Slavic nobility. This development also consolidated the power of the papacy and the Latin rite over any further spread of the Old Church Slavonic movement.

Meanwhile in Croatia, Stjepan's death in 997 led to a messy civil war in which each of his three sons wielded authority at various times over the following three decades. Amidst the infighting of the brothers (Svetoslav, Krešimir III, and Gojslav) Croatia was weakened, allowing rivals to slowly encroach on their territory. Most egregious were the Venetians, who under Doge Pietro II Orseolo took the Dalmatian coastal cities of Zadar, Trogir, and Split, and subsequently defeated the Narentines at sea, seizing the pirates' islands of Korčula and Lastovo. The Venetian leader even claimed the title of Duke of Dalmatia (*dux Dalmatiæ*) for himself. Despite some efforts to reverse these losses, Krešimir III was defeated by a Venetian-Lombard alliance and forced to become a Byzantine vassal until Emperor Basil II's death in 1025. One of the most successful Byzantine emperors, Basil had indirectly preserved Croatia on another front when his army crushed the Bulgarian army in Macedonia in 1018, forestalling another attempted expansion northward in 1018.

In Croatia, a gradual period of consolidation followed Krešimir III's death. His son, King Stjepan I (1030–1058), put the Narentines under Croatian authority in 1050. He was succeeded by King Krešimir IV (1058–1074), known as "the Great." Croatia reached its medieval apogee. Krešimir negotiated with the Byzantines, who were distracted on other fronts at the time, to declare him supreme ruler of the cities in the Theme of Dalmatia; while the Theme did not disappear, it had become a de facto part of the Croatian kingdom. This territorial transfer included the strategic city of Ragusa (the future Dubrovnik) and the Duchy of Durazzo (Durrës in modern-day Albania). This gave Croatia a restored and much-expanded naval and trade presence up and down the Eastern Adriatic coast.

The fortunes of Croatia and Krešimir IV expanded further due to a major historical event that had occurred just before his rule: the Great Schism of 1054. Although the significance of this East–West divide were not truly appreciated at the time, the mutual excommunication of Roman and Byzantine religious leaders would mark the point of no return in a centuries-long deterioration of relations between the Catholic and Orthodox Churches. In 988, Basil II had succeeded in converting the Kievan Rus' (the forerunners of today's Russian, Ukrainian, and Belarusian nations) to Orthodoxy, which was a major blow to the papacy that would have an impact felt until the present day. In 1054, the pope's demand that the Byzantine Orthodox recognize him as the supreme Christian leader was a step too far, with relations reaching an all-time low. Croatia, set as it was on the Eastern Adriatic line of separation between Byzantine and papal influence, was able to use this position to its advantage during the fallout of the Schism. Even as he extracted concessions politically and territorially from his Byzantine allies, Krešimir IV won papal patronage, and allowed the Catholics to expand their influence and the use of Latin-rite liturgy (something not popular with regular people and priests, especially in Istria, who preferred the Church Slavonic devised by Cyril and Methodius two centuries earlier).

Under Krešimir IV, Croatia reached its medieval territorial peak, stretching from Pannonia down into today's Bosnia and Serbia, and southward along the Adriatic coast, through Montenegro and into today's Albania. The kingdom's twelve counties each had their own militias, and the royal court's functions, titles, and structure became more elaborate.

The king's only major strategic mistake occurred late in his rule, in 1072, when Krešimir supported a Bulgarian-Serbian uprising against the Byzantines, who promptly encouraged a new population from the west, the Normans, to besiege the Croatian island of Rab. Although unsuccessful, the Normans somehow captured the Croatian king himself; the humiliating negotiations that followed saw Croatians give up Split, Trogir, Zadar, Biograd, and Nin. Very quickly, however, Venice took advantage of the instability and seized these territories from the Normans.

The decline of the Trpimirović dynasty marked the gradual decline of an independent Croatia. Krešimir's successor, Demetrius Zvonimir Svetoslavić (1075–1089), had been a *ban* in Slavonia, and later the Duke of Croatia, but only became king due to the patronage of Pope Gregory VII, reasserting Roman Catholic influence over the country. Demetrius Zvonimir also adopted an anti-Byzantine policy by helping the rising power of the Normans, who had expanded from France to Britain and Southern Italy. Various Norman princes had fought the Byzantine for control of the peninsula's southern tip and the island of Sicily from the 1040s, managing to drive them out of this historic Byzantine territory by 1071. Although of humble birth, one Norman prince, Robert Guiscard (1015–1085) distinguished himself in battle several times and took a leading role among the rival Norman princes, even saving the pope at one point. The result was a formidable Papal-Norman alliance that would be vital to the Crusades.

Between 1081 and 1085, Croatia's Demetrius Zvonimir assisted Guiscard in his war against the Byzantine Empire and Venice for the East Adriatic and Ionian coast, as far south as Greece. Guiscard even defeated the great Byzantine emperor, Alexios I Komnenos, and captured a couple of Ionian islands before being recalled by the pope. Although he soon returned to Greece, Robert contracted fever and died, leaving Norman southern Italy in a disorderly state of internal conflict. However, in driving the Byzantines out of Italy, the Normans did end the centuries-old Orthodox traditions of the south, strengthening the position of the papacy across the Italian peninsula.

Another alliance of convenience for the Croatians, and one that would be much more important for their long-term future, was King Demetrius Zvonimir's decision to marry Helen of Hungary two decades earlier in 1063. The Hungarians (or Magyars, as they were called and still call themselves) were the final major population to follow the time-honored migration path from Asia and into Central Europe. Like the Slavs and Bulgars, they put down roots and established themselves as a native population over time. Their original territory of occupation was the Pannonian Basin, the general area populated by Franks, Moravian Slavs, Serbs, and Croats. The royal marriage began a process of intermingling between the nobilities of both kingdoms that would soon lead to a historic union.

Daughter of King Béla I of the Árpád dynasty, Helen was also the sister of the future Hungarian King Ladislaus I. Although Helen and Demetrius Znonimir had a son, he died at an early age, meaning the Croatian throne passed (after the king's death in 1089) to the elderly Stjepan II (ruled 1089–1091). With his death, the Trpimirović dynasty became extinct, leading to a power struggle and outbreak of civil war.

During this crisis, Demetrius Zvonimir's widow, Queen Helen, sought to retain power and successfully rallied some of the leading Croatian noble families to her cause. Presenting herself as the legitimate successor to the royal line, she proposed that the Croatian kingdom be given over to her nephew, Ladislaus of Hungary. The prospect of annexing more territory was obviously enticing to the Hungarians, but historians still disagree over the extent to which Ladislaus was considered as a rightful successor or invader by the Croatian people at the time. In places like Slavonia, his arrival in 1091 met no resistance, while deeper into the countryside some Croat nobles put up armed resistance.

Although he was soon forced to return to Hungary to fend off an attack from Cuman nomads, Ladislaus appointed his own nephew, Prince Álmos, to run the newly Hungarian parts of Croatia, which included the future capital of Zagreb. Nevertheless, rival Croatian nobles elected their own king, Petar Snačić, who had his power base in Knin. His resistance forced Álmos to escape to Hungary in 1095.

When Ladislaus died in the same year, his nephew Coloman became king. He returned his focus to Croatia. Returning with a large army, he defeated the Croatian forces and killed King Petar in the 1097 Battle of Gvozd Mountain. After five years of negotiations with Croatia's ruling families and representatives of the fortified Dalmatian coastal cities, the Croatian nobility officially recognized Coloman as king. He was crowned in the town of Biograd in 1102, assuming the title "King of Hungary, Dalmatia, and Croatia." Seeking to make the circumstances of his elevation seem more cordial than colonial, the arrangement became referred to as a "personal union" between the two countries. The event marked the end of an independent Croatia and the beginning of eight centuries of division between different European powers.

4

Between Empires: Hungary, Venice, Habsburg Austria, and the Ottoman Invasions (1102–1557)

THE RISE OF VENICE, NARENTINE PIRACY, AND THE FOURTH CRUSADE (697–1204)

Early medieval Croatia developed under the influence of another rising power that would emerge seemingly from nowhere to dominate the entire Mediterranean in only a few short centuries—Venice. Although not connected territorially, Croatia's Dalmatian cities fell under the cultural, commercial, and eventually political influence of this Italian city-state.

The maritime empire that would eventually become known as *La Serenissima* (Most Serene Republic of Venice) on account of its beauty and grandeur began its existence rather inauspiciously. This territory of swampy lagoons in a foggy bay between small rivers on Italy's eastern Adriatic, directly opposite the Croatian coast, had been inhabited since ancient times by the Veneti, the tribe that eventually gave Venice its name. With the chaotic downfall of the Western Roman Empire, the islands in Venice's bay attracted other native peoples seeking safety from invading Goths, Huns, and Lombards in the 6th century. Along with the nearby Ravenna, the transplanted imperial capital down the coast, Venice formed part of a Byzantine-ruled Exarchate, connected only by sea. Thus from its earliest days as an organized political entity, Venice had to look to the Adriatic, across it to Croatia, and further into the Mediterranean, to ensure its prosperity.

Historical tradition attributes Venice's emergence as a republic to the year 697 when the first *doge* (duke), Paolo Lucio Anafesto, was elected by the city's leading aristocratic families. Venice would keep its republican status until the year 1808 after the French Emperor Napoleon conquered much of Italy. But during the Middle Ages, the city flourished as a commercial empire, with the Doge of Venice being one of the most powerful men in all Europe. In the 9th century, Venetian merchants notoriously stole the relics of St. Mark from Alexandria in Egypt, causing the doge of the time to announce the building of a church to the apostle. As homage to Venice's patron saint, the grand Cathedral of St. Marco was built to house the relics. Development also increased and connected the city's 118 little islands by over 400 bridges and interspersed by an intricate network of navigable canals, creating a unique and spectacular city that still attracts millions of tourists every year due to its beauty and historic character.

The Venetian Republic's political and social systems differed from those of other contemporaneous kingdoms and empires in several ways. One was the manner by which Venice elected leaders, administered government, and oriented its interests. Being built on a relatively small location and strategically fixed toward the sea and maritime commerce, Venice developed wealthy familial dynasties who lived peaceably enough due to geographical proximity and common interests. The large majority of residents were wealthy and engaged in commerce, giving the republic a distinctly aristocratic air and educated bearing. Politically, the republic evolved over time away from a simple autocracy (with power held largely by the doge) into a more sophisticated polity known for its separation of powers. This consisted of the *Maggior Consiglio* (Great Council), comprising 480 representatives from Venice's most prominent families. Further subcouncils and specialized administrators were added in the 12th and 13th centuries, including a Senate. Under this system, responsibility for decision-making was mutually conferred. The Great Council was also sufficiently powerful and united by common interests that it could check the power of the doge, a more stable and advantageous system than was the case in European aristocracies of the time. The latter thus suffered frequent instability and civil strife due to arguments over dynastic succession.

To protect the burgeoning prosperity that came with everything from trade in salt to silk, Venice created a formidable navy that assisted the Byzantines from the 8th century into the early 11th century. The coast and islands of the future Montenegrin and Croatian states were key areas of common contact. But as Venice established itself as a trade empire across the Mediterranean, creating linkages to Africa, the Middle East, and Asia, its wealth made it more independent-minded and attracted the attention of enemies. In the early 9th century, steady attacks from Arab navies resulted in the Byzantine Empire's temporary loss of small parts of Dalmatia and southern Italy. The large Aegean island of Crete was taken. The Venetians, allied at the time with Byzantium, were obliged to defend the internally conflicted empire at sea. However, the frequent deployments of Venetian navies to the distant south of Italy left their commercial fleets susceptible to attacks from the feared Narentine pirates of Dalmatia.

Taking their name from a stronghold near the outflow of the Neretva River, these pagan Slavs were descendants of the tribes Emperor Heraclius had sent in the 640s as a buffer against the Avars in Dalmatia. However, unlike the Croats, the Narentines remained pagan and concentrated on raiding commercial ships for their income. Settling in primarily islands and some coastal towns, the Narentines were considered by contemporaneous Byzantine sources as the people of "Pagania" (because they were pagans, not Christians). The places to which they would retreat after raids included islands like the modern-day Korčula, Hvar, Brač, Sušac, and Mljet, as well as Dalmatian coastal towns like Makarska, Brela, Zaostrog, and Gradac. For pirates, Croatia's hilly, clustered, and isolated islands offered a perfect geographical setting for hiding from the larger ships of the Byzantine or Venetian navies.

Bordering the Narentines were other Slavic tribes whose territories and power were fluid. The most significant of such political entities, south of Narentine Pagania and Croatia, was Zahumlje. Also set along the Neretva, Zahumlje extended inland into the mountainous terrain near modern-day Mostar in Bosnia. Zahumlje also reached up the Dalmatian coast from Kotor (in modern Montenegro), and north past Dubrovnik, to the Narentine town of Makarska. The Dubrovnik area town of Ston was Zahumlje's major Dalmatian settlement. The nearby Pelješac Peninsula (today, Croatia's longest, extending forty miles into the sea) provided Zahumlje access to the Adriatic. In his

De Administrando Imperio of 950, Byzantine Emperor Constantine Porphyrogenitos refers to the people of Zahumlje as "Serbs," and indeed their territorial and cultural reach extended inland into the Serbian principalities. Never fully independent, Zahumlje at different times received tribute in gold from Byzantium, was annexed by Croatia, and raided by Bulgarians. But in providing a buffer against Narentine expansion and occasional troop support to Byzantine expeditions against the Arabs in southern Italy, Zahumlje played an important role in the development of medieval Croatia.

Throughout the 9th century, the princes of Zahumlje would be of less concern to Venice than the Narentines. After a failed peace treaty in 830, Doge Pietro Tradonico sought to deal with the pesky pirates of Dalmatia more strongly, dispatching a fleet eastward in 839. Narentine leader Ljudislav, predictably enough, broke a hastily established treaty the following year, inflicting heavy casualties on the Venetians—who were then forced to deal with an Arab raid, giving the Narentines the opportunity to raid north along the Istrian coast and even onto Italian shores by 846.

To counter the Arabs and Narentines, the Byzantine Empire began sending larger fleets to Dalmatia in the 860s in alliance with the Venetians. To further protect Venetian commerce from piracy in the Adriatic, Doge Orso I Participazio and his son Giovanni II Participazio also allied with Croatia. Venice also restored an older treaty with the Franks, and the next doge, Pietro I Candiano, landed Venetian troops in Dalmatia in 887. However, despite initial victories, the Venetians were soon defeated when the Narentines brought in neighboring Slavic troops; the doge himself was killed in the battle. By the end of the 9th century, Narentine Pagania and several of its islands had been partially annexed by Serbia. These developments made life more unpredictable for Venetian leaders in other ways, as in 912, when the Prince of Zahumlje, Michael, kidnapped the doge's own son and sent him as a sort of trophy to the powerful Bulgarian Tsar Simeon.

Through the first half of the 10th century, instability in Zahumlje and Croatia allowed the Narentines to increase their power once again; the islands of Brač and Hvar seceded from Croatia, rejoining the Narentines, who also seized Vis and Lastovo. These developments alarmed the Venetians, sparking another war in 948 that ended in humiliation for Venice, which was forced to pay tribute to the pagan pirates to guarantee safe maritime passage.

Finally, however, Venice prevailed over the Narentines and other Slavic tribes with a decisive naval intervention in 1000, organized by Doge Pietro II Orseolo. This key event, which ended the Narentine threat and thus eliminated the last obstacle to Venetian dominance in the Adriatic, was greatly assisted by coincidental events on the mainland. In 998, the expanding Bulgarian Empire had overrun Serbia, Dalmatia, Pagania, and Zahumlje, laying waste to inland villages and almost seizing the well-fortified city of Ragusa (Dubrovnik) before returning to Bulgaria. Faced with this existential threat from the east, Slavic tribes like the Narentines could not simultaneously fend off the Bulgarians coming from the west and the Venetian offensive from the east. Doge Orseolo's victory over the Narentines gave Venice a new opportunity to begin colonizing parts of Dalmatia, Istria, and the islands. The Venetian influence here, which began with commercial and security interests, would subsequently acquire lasting cultural, political, and linguistic dimensions as well.

For the next two centuries, Venice's relationship with Croatia remained a complex one, influenced by the Republic's ever-changing relationship with the Byzantine Empire, as well as the rise of the Croatian kingdom and its subsequent Union with Hungary in 1102. But most significant, in the bigger picture, was Venice's own growing wealth and prestige. Its economic status, foreign connections, and naval power gave it increasing leverage with the kings of Europe and successive popes, while clever trade deals saw the Venetian Republic gain a coveted tax-free status with the Byzantines. In return, Venice continued to provide naval support to Byzantine operations; this arrangement would prove disastrous for the Byzantines in the long term. As its once-formidable naval capacities were outsourced to Venice, the empire became less capable of defending its vast territories of Aegean islands and the coastline of Greece and Anatolia—not to mention the capital of Constantinople itself.

This weakness was exploited in one of the darkest chapters in Western history—the Fourth Crusade of 1204. During the crusade, Western armies that had been exhorted by the pope to fight once more in the Holy Land were rerouted to seize Constantinople by Venetian Doge Enrico Dandolo. A shrewd businessman, the doge knew from past Crusades how profitable these expeditions could be. He thus offered to provide ships to the crusaders in return for material compensation. When individual crusaders could not pay their way, the military adventure was rerouted under the pretext of aiding a pretender to the Byzantine throne. The looting of the great capital by fellow Christians that followed the invasion exceeded the far better known Sack of Constantinople by the Ottoman Turks in 1453. This disgraceful enterprise greatly enriched Venice, which received vast territories, gold, and priceless artifacts (including the four bronze horses that now front

St. Marco's Basilica) from Byzantium. The Byzantine Empire was dismantled into three successor states, and would not rule Constantinople again until 1261. The Fourth Crusade (for which Pope John Paul II formally apologized in 2004) played a crucial role in allowing the Turks to establish an empire that would reach the gates of Vienna in 1529 before slowly retracting to its heartland in modern-day Turkey.

While the Fourth Crusade is fairly well known, the role of Croatia in the lead-up to it is not. Even if the Orthodox and Catholic populations had their differences, the concept of a religiously inspired invasion of another Christian country in the name of religion was anathema to many in Europe. What would make the ideologically questionable adventure of 1204 somewhat acceptable was the precedent that Doge Dandolo had set in 1202 when the crusaders were arriving from all over Western Europe. Unable to pay for their transport, some of these fighters accepted Doge Dandolo's proposition to invade the Dalmatian city of Zadar, which had broken away from Venetian control and gone over to the Kingdom of Hungary-Croatia. The business-minded Venetians saw the massed crusader armies as a perfect tool for recovering the Adriatic city and seizing its wealth. The idea of a holy war by Catholics against Catholics was so unthinkable that the pope, Innocent III, threatened to excommunicate anyone who took part. Nevertheless, it happened.

The Siege of Zadar began on November 10, 1202, and lasted two weeks before the Venetians and crusaders entered and plundered the city. Zadar's residents, who had displayed flags decorated with crosses to try and appeal to the crusaders' moral values, largely fled to local towns like Nin and Biograd, as well as the islands. With the wealth returned to Venice as partial payment, the precedent of a Christian crusade against another Christian country had been set, making the Venetian-led armada's continued voyage to Constantinople the following spring somewhat more palatable in the West. The fact that by 1202 the Venetian Republic was able to ignore Vatican condemnation, field a fleet sufficient to transport a massive military force, and dictate terms to the Holy Roman Empire and other leading European powers indicates just how strong Venice had become since its inauspicious origins as a fetid lagoon.

CROATIA UNDER THE HUNGARIAN ÁRPÁD DYNASTY AND THE MONGOL INVASION (1102–1301)

The long-lasting "personal union" with Hungary paralleled and influenced Croatia's relations with Venice, Byzantium, and fellow

Slavic neighbors, such as Zahumlje, Serbia, and Narentine Pagania. Union with the larger and stronger Hungarian state unquestionably helped Croatia preserve its independence and identity during turbulent periods of invasions and dynamic political trends. It also led to new sociopolitical innovations in Croatia, such as the introduction of feudalism and the entrenchment of Croat noble families. Some measure of home-rule was given to the Kingdom of Croatia in the form of its *Sabor* (parliament) and a *Ban* (viceroy or duke) appointed by the Hungarian king.

Like the Goths, Avars, Bulgars, and other pagan tribes before them, the Hungarians (Magyars, in the Hungarian language) swept into Central Europe from Asia. With ancient roots in south Siberia and Central Asia, the Magyars inhabited parts of modern-day Russia before forming a tribal federation (with minor participation of some Turkic peoples) and moved west in the 9th century. Occupying the Carpathian Basin, they established the Principality of Hungary and became an instant new factor in the ongoing power struggles of the northern Balkans between the Byzantine Empire, Slavs, Franks, and dying Avar civilization. However, the Hungarians' occasional involvement as mercenaries for different sides eventually made them targets of retribution, and they were forced to resettle west of the Pontic steppes in the later 9th century. This first Hungarian dynasty was named after Grand Prince Árpád, son of Álmos, who had led the tribal federation into the Carpathian Basin around 895. The dynasty of the Árpáds (Hungarian: *Árpádok*, Croatian: *Arpadovići*) would rule the Principality (and, after 1000, Kingdom) of Hungary until 1301.

While frequently divided by internal rivalries, succession crises, and royally ordained blindings of potential competitors to the throne, the Hungarian dynasty gradually succeeded in consolidating territory from the Carpathians and westward across the Pannonian Plain—the western half of modern Romania and Hungary itself. The Magyars also became diplomatically important when some, but not at all, ruling families began to convert to Christianity. The diplomatic clout of Hungary was attested by intermarriages with Venetian nobles and Byzantine royalty. Croatia's incorporation into the Hungarian Kingdom also brought it more firmly into the orbit of the Vatican and Catholicism (indeed, several rulers of this initial Hungarian dynasty would be canonized, some in medieval times and some even in the 20th century).

Hungary achieved this status because under King (and later Saint) Stephen I it aligned itself completely with the West and especially the Vatican. A direct descendent of Árpád, Stephen was crowned on New Year's Day 1000 in his capital of Esztergom. Significantly, Pope Sylvester II gave King Stephen complete administrative authority over

Hungary's bishoprics and churches. Stephen soon forced the remaining pagan Hungarians to convert to Christianity and eliminated rivals friendly to the Orthodox Byzantine Empire—at that time, still a major Balkan power at war with the Bulgarians. Further, King Stephen replaced the Hungarian language's runic-like script with the Latin alphabet; he even went so far as to declare Latin Hungary's national language and established monasteries, churches, and cathedrals. In the context of Saint Cyril and Saint Methodius' Slavic-Orthodox missions to Great Moravia less than 150 years earlier, this consolidation of Catholic influence in the heart of Central Europe met the papacy's strategic objectives of keeping Orthodoxy from expanding further (indeed, just twelve years before King Stephen's coronation, Byzantine Emperor Basil II had converted the rising Kievan Rus population to the Orthodox faith).

King Stephen also imposed Western feudalism in Hungary, a system which spread to the Croatian kingdom. In governance, he also copied the Frankish administrative model, further bringing Hungary into the Western fold and further from the people's roots as Asiatic nomads. Hungarian-controlled territory was split into counties (*megyék* in Hungarian), each under a royally appointed count (an *ispán*, Latin *comes*). This delegation of powers resulted in a larger army and robust tax collection system that would make Hungary one of the wealthiest countries in medieval Europe for a time. Following Croatia's 1102 incorporation into the kingdom, similar structural changes also came to areas under Hungarian control, with a royally appointed *Ban* overseeing administration locally. In 1225, this position was divided so that two *Banovi* oversaw the country (one for "Croatia and Dalmatia," and the other for Slavonia). As with Hungary, Croatia was divided into counties (*županije*), each under a count (*župan*). As had been the case before 1102, these Croatian counts came from about twelve local noble families with concentrated power bases in local regions of the kingdom. Their overall political and economic power included influence in religious matters. The Croatian Catholic Church was administered by two (often bickering) archbishoprics, one in Split on the coast, and the Slavonian one in Kaloča (today's Kalocsa in Hungary).

Following the Árpád dynasty's 1102 unification with Croatia, the kingdom spent much of the 12th century in constant conflict with Venice over the Dalmatian and Istrian coastal cities. For example, while King Coloman controlled most Dalmatian coast cities by 1107, his death in 1116 emboldened the Venetians to attack and defeat Croatian *Ban* Cledin, capturing Biograd, Split, Trogir, Šibenik, Zadar, and important islands. Although King Stephen II, Coloman's successor, failed to recover these cities, Venetian Doge Ordelafo Faliero died in the fighting, making the Venetian adventure in Dalmatia a costly one indeed. While a truce was signed, several similar wars between Hungary-Croatia and Venice broke out, with most of the contested territories going back-and-forth. Zadar, however, remained for the most part under Venetian control. However (as previously discussed), its revolts and desire to rejoin Croatia through the latter half of the 12th century gave Venice the pretext it needed to have the knights of the Fourth Crusade recover the city for it in 1202.

The antagonisms between the two powers would not be permanent, however, partially because of the enormous wealth Hungary had amassed under King Béla III (ruled 1172–1192), as well as the military ambitions of King Andrew II (ruled 1205–1235). Determined to make amends for the Fourth Crusade, King Andrew resolved to organize a Fifth Crusade, with the blessings of the pope and commitments from other Western powers. In 1217, the Hungarian king gathered a massive army (32,000 soldiers from the Hungarian side alone) and was named leader of the Fifth Crusade. Designed to recover territories in the Holy Land that the Ayyubid Muslim dynasty had seized from previous crusader statelets, the Fifth Crusade was, like its predecessor, made possible by Venetian naval transport. Croatia played a role in this as King Andrew and his army left from Zagreb and then traveled by sea from Split on their journey to the Middle East.

While the crusade did not result in any grand victory, it did reassert Hungary's position as a leading power in Western Christendom. That status would, however, be damaged considerably two decades later, with the Mongol invasions of 1241–1242. Under legendary conqueror Genghis Khan (1162–1227) and his generals, this "Golden Horde"—known for their lightning-quick mounted raids, civilian massacres, and total devastation of anything in their path—successfully invaded an incredibly vast swath of territory ranging from China and Central Asia to Russia, the Caucasus, and Eastern Europe.

Having received several threatening letters since 1237 demanding an unconditional surrender, Hungarian King Béla IV was well aware of the Mongol threat. However, his refusal to turn over thousands of Cuman nomads who had previously been defeated by the Mongols gave the latter a pretext for war. The Hungarian king was also disliked by local nobles due to his recentralization program of lands and privileges, meaning that few lords were eager to come to his aid. In general, Western European leaders underestimated the existential threat posed by the Mongols. Ironically, though the Hungarians' ancestors had been (like the Mongols) steppe nomads skilled in light cavalry fighting, two centuries of settled life in cities and agrarian towns on a largely unfortified plain had reduced their military size and changed its way of fighting. By the time of the invasion, the king had about 10,000 armored knights (Hungarian, Croatian, and some allied European knights).

Unfortunately for Béla IV, this army was up against Genghis' grandson, Batu Khan (1205–1255), and his top general, Subutai (1175–1248), one of the greatest military strategists of all time. Unbeknownst to the Hungarians, Poles, and others in Eastern Europe, Subutai had built up an elaborate intelligence-gathering network within Europe itself. This Mongol spy network fed information back to the general's headquarters, allowing him to plan his invasion meticulously a year in advance. Coordinating three large armies (one invading north through Poland, another south through Wallachia, and his own, with Batu, in the center through Hungary), Subutai obtained victories on all fronts. The invasion of Hungary began with the Battle of Mohi (April 11, 1241), in which the Hungarian army was totally destroyed.

The battle showcased Subutai's tactical ingenuity. The Mongols needed to cross the Sajó River to reach the Hungarian army's camp. After defending crossbow soldiers inflicted casualties on a Mongol raiding party as it tried to cross the river's one bridge, Subutai used catapults to launch giant stones across the river onto the Hungarian defense, while secretly building a pontoon bridge of his own further downstream at night—all the while concealing the presence of the much larger main Mongol army. By the time the Hungarians were aware of the threat, it was too late. Soldiers attempting to flee were cut down, and the king himself barely escaped. The Mongols decimated the Great Hungarian Plain, avoiding most of the fortified areas, leaving their residents to starve as agricultural areas were destroyed. Well over 20 percent of Hungary's population was killed (over one million people) in the Mongol invasion.

After the battle, another Mongol general, Khatun, was sent with 20,000 soldiers to capture the Hungarian king as he fled with survivors to Croatia. Although the Mongols destroyed Zagreb, King Béla IV escaped to Dalmatia, moving through towns and islands to avoid the Mongols. Unaware of the king's location, the Mongols attacked several Dalmatian cities in vain and were instead harried by Croatian guerrilla fighters. Indeed, an enduring legend (which would resurface in the 19th-century Croatian national revival period) claimed that valiant Croats defeated a larger Mongol force at the Battle of Grobnik Field (*Bitka na Grobničkom polju*). This battle at the "field of graves" was allegedly fought at Čavle, near the coastal city of Rijeka. While such legends are (at very least) exaggerations, it is certain that the Mongol cavalry was at a disadvantage fighting between the stark and mountainous Dalmatian terrain and the strongly fortified coastal cities. Whether or not due to a great Croatian victory, the Mongols did indeed leave Croatia in 1242, plundering as they went through the Balkans back to Mongolia, following the news that Genghis Khan's son, the Great Khan Ögedei, had died. Contemporary European leaders and churchmen regarded the event as a divine miracle.

The Mongol invasion left Croatia and especially Hungary in ruins. Returning from his Croatian hideout to Hungary, King Béla IV began to rebuild the country, with an emphasis on fortresses—not only on key border points but also in the interior of the vast Hungarian Plain. While this program was expensive and led to the empowerment of regional dukes, it also turned out to be critical for the future; indeed, when the Mongols invaded Hungary again in 1286, the country was much better prepared, with a network of stone fortresses. The heavily armed knights of King Ladislaus IV defeated the Mongols near Pest (one-half of the future Budapest on the River Danube). This defensive system would also prove important in subsequent centuries when the Ottoman Turks emerged as the major threat from the south.

Venetian Influence in Croatia and the Republic of Ragusa

In the wake of the Mongol invasions, Venetian influence grew, as the Hungarian monarchy was preoccupied with rebuilding cities and towns devastated by the invaders. However, places that had been largely spared by the Mongols—the islands and fortified coastal cities of Istria and Dalmatia—were also places that already had the strongest cultural, economic, and political connections with the Venetians and the Byzantine and Roman Empires before them. The coastal cities, which had already been centers of culture and architectural magnificence for well over a millennium by the 13th century, provided the best conditions for developing a distinct Croatian culture, one with strong Italian influence. In cities like Dubrovnik (Ragusa) on the southern Dalmatian coast, the phenomenon of cultural intermingling was already completed by the 13th century; there, the original Roman-Italian populations merged with Slavic settlements to form a unified city. In all such places, both Venetian-Italian and Croatian languages were used. In some cities, competition occurred not only between Venice and Hungary but between the former and its commercial rival on the other side of the Italian peninsula, Genoa.

Such was the case with Pula (known as Pola to the Italians) on Croatia's Istrian coast. The city famed for its ancient Roman Arena and maritime importance had been annexed in 1148 by the Venetians, who would battle Pisa for the city decades later, and eventually lose it to Genoa following a naval defeat in 1397. However, there were also moments of cooperation during this time, such as when Pope Gregory IX forged a Venetian-Genoese alliance in 1238 to stave off the Pisans and the Germanic Holy Roman Empire. Thus, while the rival Italian city-states in turn built up and sacked the port city several times, Pula's development was primarily led by and oriented toward Italy rather than Hungary. The city (which would finally become Venetian-administered from 1331 until the Republic's fall in 1797) became part of the Italian cultural imagination. Indeed, no less a personality than the great medieval poet Dante Alighieri immortalized Pula in his *Divine Comedy*.

From the 1260s onward, Venice took over an increasing number of other Istrian towns in today's Croatia and Slovenia, such as Poreč, Umag, Novigrad, Sveti Lovreč, Motovun, Kopar, and Piran. The most important possessions in Istria, like Rovinj (held by the Venetians

Pula's Roman Arena (built from 27-67 BCE) has been a focal point of public life since ancient times. Even in the Middle Ages, when Roman traditions were long out of use, the arena had a role in hosting medieval fairs and knightly jousting tournaments. Today it is a popular spot for concerts and other performances. (Conceptw/Dreamstime.com)

from 1283 to 1797) were developed lavishly in the prevailing Italian style of the late Medieval and Renaissance periods. Much of this heritage remains to the present day in architecture like the coastal town's defensive walls, Venetian-style mansions, and, adjoining the Church of St. Euphemia, a pointed *campanile* (bell tower) like that of St. Marco's Basilica in Venice. Indeed, the Republic's distinctive lion symbol is engraved in several places in Rovinj, where famous Venetian families (such as the Balbi clan, whose name adorns a central city, Arch) left their marks.

The Venetians built their littoral possessions similarly further south down the coast into Dalmatia. One of the best surviving examples of a Venetian urban space (though naturally renovated and retrofitted over the years) is the town of Hvar on the eponymous island. This strategic large island with a protected inner harbor was given further security with Hvar Town's land-side walls, guarded by two hillside fortresses from 1278. The walls guarded a flourishing public area centered on the typical *piazza* (square, or *pijaca* in Croatian) lined by palatial structures and the town's cathedral. These and other structures such as the *loggia* (governor's palace), arsenal, and clock tower combined Venetian and local Croatian architectural stylings and methods, creating a distinctive look that fused Venetian preferences with the result of local materials and craftsmanship. Hvar remains today, as does Rovinj and indeed much else of the Croatian coast, a very popular tourist destination due largely to this distinctive Italianate architecture, one ideally suited to the coast's natural beauty and contrast of a glittering sea and hilly greenery.

The most singular example of Venetian influence in Croatia, however, was a unique city-state: the Republic of Ragusa (in Croatian, *Dubrovačka Republika*). This self-governing and forward-thinking polity managed to preserve its independence, for the most part, from 1358 until 1808. Since antiquity and the arrival of Greek colonists in the Croatian littoral, a tendency toward independence and self-reliance had manifested in a region where geographic and climatic factors also influenced native ingenuity and self-sufficiency. Based on the antiautocratic ideals of the Venetian Republic, and indeed competing with it in the world of maritime commerce, the Ragusan Republic demonstrated just how much, given the ideal cultural, geographic, and political conditions, Croats could achieve at a time when much of the Balkans remained primitive and underdeveloped.

The territorial expansion of Dubrovnik occurred over time, well before it became known as a leading city. In 1050, Croatian King Stjepan I extended the city's borders to Zaton, ten miles to the north.

This gave Dubrovnik access to a vital freshwater supply. The king also gave the city an adjoining harbor, Gruž—modern Dubrovnik's main commercial port. Dubrovnik later passed into Serbian hands when the surrounding area was part of the Kingdom of Zahumlje (also referred to simply as Hum). As in previous centuries, the small kingdom's capital was at Ston. In the 13th century, Zahumlje was part of the Serbian Miroslavljević family dynasty. These holdings were inherited and passed down until, in 1325, King Stefan Uroš III sold Ston and the strategic Pelješac Peninsula to the Ragusans. By 1426, the republic's borders also incorporated mainland areas from Neum to the Prevlaka peninsula, as well as the islands of Lastovo, Mljet, Koločep, Lopud, and Šipan. The territorial expansion of a new republic in an area that had once consisted of just two separate and mistrustful Latinate and Slavic settlements was a major factor in giving Ragusa the capacity to sustain and defend itself from potential attacks or sieges from land and sea.

While Ragusa and its territories had been mostly Venetian dependencies following the Fourth Crusade of 1204 and the Mongol Invasion of Hungary and Croatia in 1242, Hungary eventually recovered and its kings returned their attention to the Croatian coast. Thus, a century later, Hungarian King Louis I exploited internal discord within the Croatian nobility and gathered allies from Austria and the Holy Roman Empire to take on the Venetians in battle; this resulted in the 1358 Treaty of Zadar. The agreement forced Venice to give its Dalmatian cities and islands to Hungary-Croatia (however, Venice was allowed to keep its Istrian holdings). While Venice would later recover some of its lost Dalmatian territories, the 1358 treaty was a boon for Ragusa, which thereafter achieved real independence from both Venice and Hungary. The city-state was able to preserve good relations and remain on favorable terms with both powers because it occupied a key maritime position that connected the mineral-rich Balkan interior with the Italian mainland across the Adriatic. Furthermore, since the 1358 treaty prevented Hungary from becoming a naval power, there was no potential for the empire to invade Ragusa—in any case, the king was well aware of coastal Croatia's historic penchant for independence. Five years after the Ottoman Turks' capture of Byzantine Constantinople in 1453, the Turks would become a Balkan power for the next four centuries. Ragusa was thus forced to pay the sultans an annual tribute to preserve its independence after 1457.

Unlike other parts of the Balkans held firmly by the "Ottoman yoke," the Republic of Ragusa extracted great economic advantages from its vassal status. It was exempted from Ottoman taxation and, unlike other states, was allowed to sail into the Ottoman-controlled Black Sea for commercial purposes. The port was extremely strategic to the Turks as from Ragusa began the Balkan land route for commercial items; it passed through Bosnia's Sarajevo and Novi Pazar in Serbia, southward through Skopje in Macedonia, and eastward through the Bulgarian city of Plovdiv and through Adrianople (Edirne) before reaching Istanbul (the Turkish name for Constantinople). Through the 15th and 16th centuries, Ragusa thus became a major economic and political competitor for Venice.

While the 1358 Treaty of Zadar codified the Ragusan Republic's independence from Venice, in fact the former was administered in a way following that of the latter. A Grand Council, drawing its members from the city's wealthy aristocratic families, presided over urban affairs. There was also a Minor Council and a Senate similar to Venice. In place of the Venetian doge, the Ragusan head of state (with limited powers) was known as the *rector* in Italian (*knez*, or duke in Croatian). Rather uniquely, a new rector was elected each month by the Grand Council, who was thereafter not eligible for re-election for two years; this clever scheme was designed to prevent any one noble family from taking too much power over the republic. Aside from urban affairs, the Grand Council oversaw local magistrates and authorities in the republic's counties (both on the Dalmatian coast and on the islands). This granted a larger degree of autonomy and decentralized rule (including unique statutes in each island) than was the case in much of contemporaneous autocratic Europe.

At its peak, the republic had a total population of about 90,000 people, of which only a small percentage inhabited the walled city itself. Resembling imperial Rome, Ragusan society was divided into three classes: the aristocratic nobility, the citizens (artisans and shopkeepers), and plebeians (peasants). Slavery was forbidden (after 1416), a very enlightened policy at the time. But so too was intermarriage between classes, and only Roman Catholics were allowed to become Ragusan citizens. Nevertheless, despite the social stratification of the republic, local leaders did show a general preference for good governance and justice, and even freedom. Indeed, the word *Libertas* was emblazoned on the Ragusan flag, and the entrance to the city's Lovrijenac Fortress was inscribed with the Latin motto *Non bene pro toto libertas venditur auro* (Freedom cannot be sold for all the gold in the world).

Ragusa was marked by the same Venetian architectural influences as elsewhere on the Dalmatian and Istrian coastal cities and islands. Unfortunately, a 1667 earthquake that killed over 5,000 citizens destroyed most of the city's important original structures, including many of the Gothic and Renaissance villas, palaces, churches, and other public buildings. Aside from Ragusa's outer walls, the only important surviving original architecture were the Sponza Palace and the front facade of the Rector's Palace. Thus, the modern Dubrovnik that greets visitors today—while still visually stunning—is far different than the city that existed before 1667. The postearthquake construction works tended to follow a Baroque style that was less grand than the earlier Renaissance architecture of the city.

Another unique, enduring mark of Venetian influence in Croatia was the development of Latin- and Italian-based local dialects in the coastal cities and islands, dialects collectively known as Dalmatian and Istrian; while the former died out in the late 19th century, the latter is still used in a few towns in Istria. The Dalmatian dialects were spoken in towns like Zadar, Trogir, Split, and of course Dubrovnik, as well as on islands like Krk, Cres, and Rab. Vegliot, a northern dialect of Dalmatian, was spoken on the island of Krk (Veglia, in Italian). In the south, Ragusan was the primary Dalmatian dialect and was considered an official language in the Ragusan Republic. Today, numerous documents in the Dalmatian language have survived from the medieval period, including official documents, inventories, and even literary works from the Ragusan Republic.

Dalmatian evolved originally from the local Latin that was spoken during the Roman occupation of Croatia from Rijeka on the Dalmatian coast down to Kotor (in today's Montenegro). The Dalmatian or *Dalmatico* language was first mentioned in the 10th century and developed further by contact with Venetian and Croatian languages. The former is a Romance language, very similar to Italian, whereas the latter comes from the Slavic linguistic group. Dalmatian was seen in some places as a mark of superior culture, as in the Republic of Ragusa, where Croatian was prohibited from oratory in the senate for some time. Nevertheless, over the centuries, Croatian would predominate (in Ragusa and elsewhere) from the 16th century as the ethnic balance and political culture continued to shift. However, the Dalmatian language has left lingering influences in the Croatian dialects of the coast even today—one of many singular elements that have set littoral Croatia apart from the inland areas over the centuries.

THE SECOND HUNGARIAN DYNASTY AND THE OTTOMAN INVASIONS (1301–1541)

In the 14th century, the royal union between Hungary and Croatia entered a new dynastic period, colored by the influences of changes, both internal and across Europe. The Mongol invasions of a few decades earlier had devastated the country, limiting the power of the king. The newly fortified countryside fell under the rule of about a dozen noble families—as was the case in Croatia too. The diversification of European royal powers post-1204 continued with the intermarriage and resulting land claims of different aristocratic families. Crusading continued, and with it the claims of European aristocrats to large areas from Italy to Greece to the Middle East—essentially, fragments of the former Byzantine Empire.

This trend of the High Middle Ages is exemplified by the first post-Árpád king of Hungary, Charles I. He was a representative of the Capetian House of Anjou, which itself descended from French royalty and had won extensive holdings in the Mediterranean due to the Crusades. Charles I was the grandson of Charles II of Naples and Mary of Hungary. Indeed, the only reason he became king was because of Queen Mary's determination to keep the Hungarian bloodline of the legendary Stephen the Great intact—even if it meant having to go through her maternal bloodline as male heirs had died out by 1301.

Charles I (ruled 1308–1342) became king following a brief civil war, and had the difficult task of uniting Hungary and restoring royal control over the rival Hungarian noble families. He was crowned with the heavy support of Pope Clement V, which brought Hungary-Croatia into the French orbit for the first time. Today, Pope Clement is remembered primarily for his establishment of the "Avignon Papacy" in France and for his disbanding of the Knights Templar to benefit French King Philip IV (who was deeply indebted to the famous Crusader Order). For the new king of Hungary, the pope's death in 1314 was a blow at a turbulent time in which various noble factions were contesting his rule. Indeed, civil insurrections in Hungary continued into the 1320s before Charles I could consolidate his rule and implement the reforms that would create the stability needed for the future revival of the kingdom.

The Hungarian king had to contend with independent-minded Croatian nobles as well, sometimes indirectly, by supporting one faction against another. This was the case with the 1322 Battle of Bliska, fought near Trogir in southern Croatia. Seeking to check the power of the long-embedded Šubić clan, the Hungarian king supported a coalition created by several Dalmatian noble families against the army of the then-*Ban* of Croatia Mladen II Šubić and his allies. The latter were defeated by the pro-Hungarian coalition led by John Babonić, *Ban* of Slavonia. His allies included the leaders of Krk, Krbava, Šibenik, and Trogir. When King Charles arrived at Knin Castle to make peace months later, Mladen II was apprehended and sent into custody at the royal court in Hungary, where he lived out his days.

With the Battle of Bliska and ensuing Hungarian intervention, the Šubić dynasty lost hereditary rights to power and significant lands and castles. This development broadly benefited other Croatian noble families, like the Houses of Kurjaković, which entered into a marriage alliance with that of Nelipić, as well as the future Frankopan clan in Krk. King Charles nominated another battle ally, Stephen II Kotromanić, as *Ban* in neighboring Bosnia, a strategic, Slavic-inhabited territory valuable for its mining and location on the Balkan land route to Constantinople. In 1330, Ivan Nelipić forced Mladen III Šubić to make peace on advantageous terms after capturing Knin and several Šubić-held lands. Nelipić thus began a dynasty of future counts and local lords that would be a powerful Croatian clan into the 15th century.

The successor to King Charles I, known as Louis the Great (ruled 1342–1382), expanded the Kingdom of Hungary-Croatia well into modern-day Serbia, Romania, Ukraine, and Slovakia. His mother was Queen Elizabeth of Poland, a fact that opened room for a new alliance between two of the most significant Catholic powers in Europe at the time. Louis inherited a rich treasury and further consolidated royal power by changing the ways land grants to nobles could be managed. He also won impressive military victories against Lithuania, Serbia, the Mongols, and the Kingdom of Naples, earning a reputation for toughness, as attested by his willingness to lead troops in close-quarter combat. Louis was also extremely pious (a trait attributed to his mother's influence), and took an active role in Vatican power struggles. He also further consolidated royal control in Croatia, overseeing the military victory over Venice that led to the 1358 Treaty of Zadar, by which the Venetian Republic was forced to cede most of its Croatian littoral possessions to Hungary.

Croatia became crucial again to greater Hungarian stability after 1382 when Louis the Great died without leaving a male heir. Deadly infighting followed before the Hungarian nobility allowed Louis' daughter, Mary, to have her husband (Sigismund of Luxembourg) crowned as king. Well aware of his precarious position, King Sigismund (ruled 1387–1437) gave over half of the Hungarian royal estates to nobles who would support him. In Dalmatia and Slavonia, however, important nobles like Hrvoje Vukčić Hrvatinić (1350–1416) had supported Angevin rivals to the Hungarian throne, and thus became enemies. Hrvoje, who had a marriage alliance with the powerful Nelipić family, was also a trusted ally and advisor of successive kings in Bosnia. However, Hrvoje provoked King Sigismund to invade that kingdom when he supported Ladislaus of Naples, the Angevin relative of the deceased King Louis of Hungary.

Between 1389 and 1392, Duke Hrvoje defeated Sigismund twice, winning the support of most Dalmatian cities for this rival to the Hungarian throne. Ladislaus was crowned as a rival to Sigismund in Croatia, and gave his main ally the title of *Ban*, territories that included several islands and the right to mint coins. However, when King Sigismund defeated the Bosnian army in 1408, Hrvatinić lost his lands, as well as his good standing with the Bosnian King Ostoja. For his own personal interests, the Croat duke fatefully requested Ottoman military assistance against Hungary. The Hungarian army would indeed be defeated at the Battle of Lašva in 1415, but this weakened both Hungary and, especially, Bosnia. The Ottomans quickly expanded their influence and Islamic religion in Bosnia, a development that would have lasting implications and lead to centuries of war.

Indeed, Hungary had been badly embarrassed (and depleted) a few years earlier when a crusade led by King Sigismund to the Bulgarian Danubian port of Nicopolis (modern Nikopol) failed to defeat the Ottoman defenders of the fortress there. The Hungarian king, who personally led a massive force assembled from across Christian Europe, only barely escaped and had to return home by ship, while battle survivors were either massacred, held for ransom, or wandered off toward their homelands. The decisive defeat disheartened Christian Europe, which could no longer stop the Turks. The Ottoman already had overrun much of the Balkans, while also conquering what was left of the Byzantine Empire. In 1453, Constantinople fell to the Turks, and seven years later, so did the successor Empire of the Morea (in the Peloponnesian region of Greece) and of Trebizond (on the northeast Turkish Black Sea coast).

Despite his embarrassing defeat at Nicopolis and numerous plots against him at home, King Sigismund remained a foreign luminary— even being named, in addition to King of Hungary-Croatia, as Holy Roman Emperor in 1410. During his extensive absences from home, Hungary was ruled by Sigismund's most trusted allies. A knightly order with a rather exotic name—the "Order of the Dragon"—this ruling elite had come together following the king's victory in Bosnia over Hrvoje Hrvatinić in 1408. The Order was a sort of Hungarian version of the former Knights Templar and Knights Hospitaller, with its name taken from the famous motif of St. George on horseback slaying a dragon underfoot. The Hungarian victory influenced most Dalmatian towns to switch allegiances from Ladislaus of Naples to Sigismund. He would, however, sell these lands back to the Venetian Republic later on, bringing the Croatian littoral back into their sphere of influence for a few centuries more.

Sigismund's personal battle experience against the Turks at Nicopolis, and subsequent Ottoman gains in the Balkans, convinced him that a new strategy was needed to defend the kingdom's borders. This policy would be continued by his successors into the 16th century. One aspect of this policy was to strengthen Hungary's buffer zone against the Turks in the southern borderlands. Sigismund achieved this by giving large estates to Serbia's King Stefan Lazarević, Mircea I of Wallachia (in modern Romania), and other neighboring states, which would then assist in the common defense. Sigismund also built over a dozen new fortifications along the Danube borderlands.

The second aspect of King Sigismund's defensive policy was to mobilize the ever-increasing Christian refugee populations escaping north from the Ottoman-controlled Balkans and organizing them into military units. Most of them were Serbian and given protection in Hungarian territory in return for fighting the Turks. Hungary also went on the offensive, with famed commander John Hunyadi leading troops deep into Ottoman-held territory in 1443–1444, reaching as far as Sofia (in modern Bulgaria). At the same time, a Vatican-organized crusade— the last such adventure—was defeated by the Turks at the Battle of Varna in 1444. Still, Hunyadi's forces continued to fight the Ottomans in their own newly captured lands, but were finally defeated at the Battle of Kosovo in 1448. The Serbian province had been the site of a more famous battle in 1389 where the Turks defeated Serbian forces, an event traditionally seen as a decisive turning point in the Ottoman conquest of the Balkans. John Hunyadi led one final and somewhat more successful operation in defending the key Danubian city fortress at Belgrade in Serbia. Fresh off the 1453 capture of Constantinople, Ottoman Sultan Mehmed II marched on Belgrade in 1456, but was stymied and forced to withdraw by Hunyadi's 30,000 defenders.

While the Ottoman Empire's continual expansion tends to overshadow such efforts by the Hungarians and their Croatian, Serbian, and other allies, there is no question that the Hungarian-organized resistance slowed the Turkish encroachment by several decades, buying time for Western Europe. Under John Hunyadi's son, King Matthias Corvinus (ruled 1458–1490), Hungary remained on a war footing, with new taxes levied to arm and maintain what was one of the first professional standing armies in Europe. However, despite initially continuing his father's military policy, capturing an Ottoman-held fortress in Bosnia, King Matthias soon learned that Western allies would no longer help against the Ottoman threat. So, while he strengthened

Hungary's fortresses along the southern frontier to keep the Turks at bay, King Matthias attacked rivals in Poland and Austria, attempting to gain Papal endorsement for further anti-Ottoman actions. However, this strategy was counterproductive and unpopular at home, where Hungarian nobles chafed at King Matthias' autocratic rule. Thus, after his death in 1490, they installed a weak successor, Vladislaus II of Bohemia (ruled 1490–1516).

This proved to be a disastrous decision for Hungary's defensive capacities. While the compliant new king reduced taxes and generally catered to the whims of the landed aristocracy, these policies made it difficult to continue funding the army and led to a peasant's revolt. The chaotic situation enabled by weak leadership and aristocratic greed continued after Vladislaus II's death in 1516 when his ten-year-old son Louis II was named king. His noble regents pursued their own interests. The fractious and poorly defended kingdom was an inviting prize for Ottoman Sultan Suleiman the Magnificent (ruled 1520–1566), who captured Belgrade in 1521 and prepared to invade Hungary-Croatia. Thus, at the 1526 Battle of Mohács on the Hungarian Plain, a massive Ottoman army of 100,000 soldiers destroyed a Hungarian army of just 26,000; the young king was among the 20,000 killed on the battlefield. It was the kingdom's greatest defeat since the 1241 Mongol Invasion and led to the partitioning of Hungary between 1526 and 1541 when the Turks invaded Buda.

Despite these defeats in what was called the "Long War" with the Turks, the tenacious defense of the Hungarians and Croats—the last remaining unconquered Christian peoples on the Balkan frontier—preserved Western Europe from Turkish occupation. Because John Hunyadi's defense of Belgrade from Mehmet II had prevented Ottoman expansion in 1456, the city would not be taken until almost a century later. After defeating the Hungarians, Suleyman besieged the Austrian Habsburg Empire's capital of Vienna in 1529 and again in 1532, both times without any success. In fact, it was the brave and improbable defense of Croatian commander Nikola Jurišić at the Siege of Kőszeg (also known as the Siege of Güns) that spared Vienna in the latter campaign. Defending the western Hungarian fortress (also known as Güns in German) with only 700 Croatian soldiers, Jurišić stopped Suleyman's army, which numbered over 120,000 soldiers as it attempted to march toward Vienna. Bad weather and other priorities forced the Turkish sultan to withdraw, thus sparing one of Europe's most important capitals.

This and other mostly unsung efforts by Croatian soldiers in the long war against the Turks shaped broader European history and were indeed recognized by contemporaneous leaders. For example, Pope Leo X in 1519 called Croatia the "Bulwark of Christianity" (*Antemurale Christianitatis*), recognizing the key role Croatian soldiers played in defending Central Europe following the collapse of Bosnia and Serbia. While historians disagree over its exact dates or duration, a so-called Hundred Years' War was waged on Croatian soil between the Turks and Croats, backed by Venetians and Austrians, during the 15th and 16th centuries. This often low-intensity border war, which began with a decisive Turkish victory at the Battle of Krbava Field in 1493, intensified after Suleyman's victory over the Hungarians in 1526. The Turks made inroads across the eastern half of Croatia, capturing Jajce in 1528, Požega in 1536, Klis in 1537, as well as Nadin and Vrana in 1538. The size of Croatia was greatly reduced and it effectively became a buffer state between the Ottomans and Venetian-controlled Dalmatian coast. Ottoman raiding parties and Croatian guerrilla skirmishes occurred intermittently over the century-long period, particularly affecting the easternmost region bordering Ottoman-controlled Bosnia and Serbia. Known as the Croatian Military Frontier, it was frequently attacked and perilous, whereas the regions further west to the coast were safer from Turkish raids.

MEDIEVAL SLOVENIA: FROM THE COUNTS OF CELJE TO THE HABSBURG EMPIRE (1202–1557)

Due in large part to the spirited defense put up for centuries by Hungary and Croatia, the people of the future Slovenian state were largely spared from the degradation of Ottoman incursions. Even from the earlier Middle Ages, their own geographical position influenced a unique national development. For while both the Croats and proto-Slovenes were Slavic peoples, the former was influenced largely by its Serbian, Bosnian, Hungarian, and Venetian neighbors; the Slovenes, on the other hand, were pulled into a Germanic, Austrian, and Italian zone of influence. The cultural and ethnic distinctions created by these divergent experiences created divergent identities between the two Slavic peoples that exist to this day.

In 1204, a core part of the future Slovenian state was ruled by Bernhard von Spanheim. Bernhard was the Duke of Carinthia (ruled 1202–1256), a territory that had been ruled by his ancestors for well over a century by that point. Count Bernhard's relatives fought in the Crusades, and he and his family were active participants in the rival claims to the German throne of different noble families. Under rulers like the Spanheim dukes, Carinthia was fundamentally oriented toward the

Germanic world, and not the Slavic one of the Croats, Serbs, Moravians, or others. Priorities for Bernhard included bickering over control of estates with other landed aristocrats and hosting chivalrous tournaments, jousting, and *minnesinger* (medieval German poetry) readings.

In other (less stereotypically medieval) activities, Bernhard executed a strategic vision for dynastic expansion by taking over key mountain passes linking Carinthia with the March of Carniola (a military zone, called *Kranjska krajina* in Slovene), of which his son Ulrich III became ruler in 1248. The central heartland of today's Slovenia, Carniola provided access to the major transport route linking the Northern Adriatic from Italy to Croatia and Central Europe. Originally created as a buffer zone against the Hungarians and Croats, Carniola was settled with Bavarians but retained its Slovene culture to some extent. By the time of Ulrich III, the March (also called a Margravate) enjoyed special privileges from the Holy Roman Empire for its strategic positioning as the empire's southeastern-most March. In 1273, a dispute with Ulrich's successor, Ottokar, caused German King Rudolf (of the important Habsburg family) to claim Carniola. Although Carinthia and Carniola would change hands several times, this act was used as a precedent in 1364 when the Austrian dynasty's Duke Rudolf IV declared Carniola a Duchy. Soon thereafter, the 1379 Treaty of Neuberg, signed between different lines of the Habsburg dynasty, divided the family's hereditary lands. Carinthia and Carniola were attached to Inner Austrian, ruled by the Habsburg Leopoldian line from its base in Vienna.

These territories were eventually inherited and ruled by the imaginatively nicknamed Ernest the Iron from 1406 until his death in 1424. The tenor of relations between the Habsburgs and Hungary-Croatia at the time was attested by the complex relationship between Ernest and Hungary's King Sigismund. While the latter made Ernest a member of his elite knightly Order of the Dragon, he also unsuccessfully tried to invade Ernest's lands. Ernest's eldest son, Frederick V, would be crowned Holy Roman Emperor in 1452, consolidating power over Austria's growing empire in Habsburg hands. Despite sporadic efforts of Hungarian and Croatian rulers to seize territories that would comprise the future Slovenia, these territories would remain under the control and cultural influence of one of Europe's most powerful dynasties, right until the end of World War I (WWI) in 1918. The first (Royalist) Yugoslavia that was created following the 20th-century conflict represented an experiment based on rationales that, in the case of Slovenia, had little to do with historical continuity.

While the Habsburgs had effective control of Slovenian lands during the Middle Ages, they did grant local administration to local Slavic and Slavic-Bavarian aristocrats, particularly in the 1300s. The most eminent of these were known as the Counts of Celje (in Slovene, *Celjski grofje*), or Cilli. (Celje is a town and eponymous county in today's Slovenia). These local lords were actively ruling Carinthia, Carniola, and parts of the Austrian province of Styria, often retaining power through marriage alliances. With lands comprising much of modern-day Slovenia and spilling over into Austria and Slavonia, the Counts of Celje also supported Hungarian forces attacking the Venetians in Dalmatia, joining the later Crusades against the Turks. As vassals of the Habsburg dukes, they began to rule in 1341 and enjoyed an elevation in status five years later, becoming Princes of the Habsburg-led Holy Roman Empire.

Medieval church records indicate the ancestry of the Counts of Celje can be traced back to at least 1130, and the related dynasty of Sanneck (Žovnek in Slovene) Castle, located on the Sann (Savinja) River in Lower Styria. This geographic location brought the Slovene lords into conflict with different groups than the Croats experienced. For example, to fulfill their duty of supporting the Habsburg Empire, Lord Leopold of Žovnek supported the Habsburgs in the 1278 Battle on the Marchfeld. Further, the lords aided German Habsburg King Rudolf I early in the next century when he was vying with the Austrian Habsburgs and Bohemia for control of Carinthia. Further, a marriage alliance between the Žovnek Lord Frederick and the House of Heunburg in 1322 dramatically increased the Slovenian dynasty's inherited territories. These events further attest how geographic orientation and allegiances to the Habsburgs brought these predecessors of modern Slovenes firmly into the Austrian and Germanic orbit, unlike the case with Croatia.

Indeed, Munich was the location for Frederick's appointment as count and governor of Carniola by Emperor Louis IV in 1341. He was also bestowed with the title of Count of Cilli (a derivation from Celje Castle). Frederick and his descendants amassed over twenty castles and enlarged their territories in the Celje region of modern Slovenia, as well as Styria and Carinthia. As imperial guardians of the March of Carniola, the Counts of Celje administered the Habsburg's southern border with Hungary and Croatia.

Although the purpose of a military March was to provide a defensive buffer zone between Habsburg and neighboring lands, this did not mean that the relationship between the Counts of Celje and Hungary-Croatia was by nature adversarial. Rather, it depended on overarching Habsburg interests, and, of course, those of the other side. When the common interest was, for example, to counter the Venetian expansion in coastal Dalmatia, Celje's Count Ulrich I sent his mercenaries to support Hungary's King Louis I in 1354. Further, through marriage alliances, the Counts of Celje became interrelated with the kings of Bosnia (as were the Croatian nobles) and with the kings of Poland, Hungary, and Bohemia. Such connections provided a stabilizing force in the Habsburgs' relations with these neighboring powers.

Ultimately, it was the common cause of Christendom versus an expanding Muslim Turkish empire that brought the Counts of Celje to their apogee—aided, somewhat, by chance. While fighting on the Danube at the Nicopolis Crusade of 1396, Count Hermann II saved the life of Hungary's King Sigismund in the failed battle for the Ottoman-held fortress. In gratitude, Sigismund granted Hermann the Slavonian Croatian town of Varaždin, in the Zagorje region of northwest Croatia, along with many other lands there. King Sigismund later married Hermann's daughter, Barbara of Celje. Thus, the House of Celje increased its fortunes, while giving the Hungarian royal family a claim for future land inheritance in Slovenia.

The practice of dynastic land inheritance in medieval Slovenia was common and helped avoid military dispute resolution in several cases. The concept of marriage alliances was a consideration in Hungary-Croatia and indeed everywhere in medieval Europe, as it could make or break not only an individual family's fortunes but also shape the identity and borders of whole countries. For example, when in 1418 the noble House of Ortenburg died out, Count Hermann II inherited its large holdings in Carinthia and Carniola, making the Counts of Celje even more powerful. After King Sigismund was crowned Holy Roman Emperor in 1433, he raised the Counts of Celje to the higher level of Princes of the Holy Roman Empire. This move alarmed the Habsburgs, who were well aware of the Hungarian claims on Slovenian territory near the common border. Thus, even though the Turkish threat was more urgent than ever on Hungary's southern flank, the Habsburgs launched a war that only ended in 1443 when the terms of mutual inheritance were agreed formally.

Soon after, the powerful Count Ulrich II (1406–1456) achieved the improbable status of regent to the Hungarian throne when he was given care over the boy-king Ladislaus, son of the Habsburg King Albert II Ladislaus in 1452. Ulrich II had used his family's historic web of marriage alliances (including his own 1432 marriage to Serbian despot Đurađ Branković's daughter Catherine) to justify his claims to Hungary, Bohemia, and Austria. However, Ulrich could not count on any military or political power equaling his ambitions; he was assassinated in Belgrade by the powerful Hungarian Hunyadi family in

November 1456. The overweening ambition that caused Ulrich II's death also extinguished the male line of the Counts of Celje. Ironically, according to the treaty of inheritance, the Habsburgs would swallow all of their territory with Ulrich gone. This event and the transfer of lands that had been granted to the Slovene dynasty by King Sigismund thus brought about direct Habsburg control over large estates in Croatia and Bosnia—a development that would have significant consequences for the future development of the latter countries.

Habsburg control over Hungary-Croatia accelerated after 1526 when Hungarian King Louis II died while fighting the Turkish army at the Battle of Mohács. While the Hungarian nobility squabbled over who should replace Louis, the Austrian Habsburgs and Ottoman Empire competed for ultimate control over the defeated kingdom. After a chaotic dynastic dispute, the Ottomans recognized the claim of the Zápolya clan, which led to their annexation in 1541 of the eastern half of the kingdom, including much of Transylvania. (This province of today's Romania still has a large Hungarian minority dating back to medieval times.)

In the west, the crown of Hungary and Croatia was claimed in 1526 by Austrian Habsburg King Ferdinand I (1503–1564). The half-Spanish monarch based his claim in the dynastic dispute on the fact that the deceased and childless Louis II was his brother-in-law. At the same time, Ferdinand's elder brother, Charles V, was Holy Roman Emperor, administering other Habsburg lands such as Spain. Much of Hungary's barons and all of the Croatian nobles and local clergy supported the ardently Catholic Ferdinand. After an extraordinary Diet (parliament) in the Hungarian city of Pozsony (modern Bratislava, Slovakia), Ferdinand was crowned as King of Hungary and Croatia in addition to his other titles. Ferdinand vowed particularly to uphold the historic rights of the independence-minded Croats, as well as to defend Croatia from the Turks, which gave the Croats some measure of hope for the survival of their people. Ferdinand tried to raise funds for improving the Habsburg armies through an unpopular "Turkish Tax" (*Türken Steuer* in German). Nevertheless, an insufficient tax base in war-ravaged Hungary and weak Austria forced Ferdinand to seek assistance from his brother, the Holy Roman Emperor Charles V. Although Ferdinand was able to defeat his rival claimant John Zápolya at two battles in 1527 and 1528, this conflict provided the Turkish sultan a pretext for attacking Ferdinand owing to his support for the exiled Zápolya.

Suleyman's ensuing siege of the Habsburg capital of Vienna in 1529 forced Ferdinand to escape to Bohemia. However, neither this siege nor a second one in 1532 were successful owing largely to Vienna's strong defenses and the stout resistance of Croatian soldiers at the fortress of Güns. Nevertheless, to end the Turkish harassment, King Ferdinand was forced to sign a treaty with the Ottoman Empire that formally split Hungary into Habsburg-controlled territory in the west and Turkish-held territory in the east and southeast. When Ferdinand broke the treaty on an unexpected succession development and invaded eastern Hungary, Suleyman responded by destroying the city of Buda. Further, he forced the Habsburgs to pay tribute, while also making the new "Kingdom of Eastern Hungary" an Ottoman vassal state. Nevertheless, despite this development and the continual back-and-forth military incursions in the years to follow, the continuation of marriage alliances and hereditary claims meant that the Habsburgs would continue to view all of Hungary and Transylvania as rightfully theirs. The rivalry continued, both in military and political forms, up until both empires were dissolved in the aftermath of WWI.

Even as Frederick was occupied with both the Ottoman threat in Hungary and dealing with the internal Christian controversies of the Protestant Reformation, the Turks continued to ravage inland Croatia. Although Frederick had depended for much of his own kingdom's agrarian needs on Hungary and Slavonia, the Turkish threat greatly damaged these territories' capacity to provide either foodstuffs or taxes. Ottoman incursions in Slavonia continued through the 1540s. In 1547 when a brief truce expired, the kingdom was forced to find new defensive solutions. The Croat General Ivan Lenković created systematic plans for new fortifications in the contested areas, but the Ottomans proved strong enough to seize this key Slavonian town in 1552. The alarmed Habsburgs thus created the Croatian Military Frontier (*Hrvatska Vojna Krajina*) in 1553, with supreme military control transferred to the Austrian General Staff in Vienna. The designated military zone existed through the 19th century, and was settled by poor Orthodox Serbs and Catholic Croats, both refugees and serfs. These people accepted military service against the Turks and gained some freedoms in return. Ironically, the frontline Ottoman troops involved in many of the Muslim battles of conquest were also Christian Slavs press-ganged into the Turkish military after their lands had been conquered.

In 1557, King Ferdinand became Holy Roman Emperor when his brother Charles decided to abdicate. This historic event resulted in the voluntary division of the Habsburg Empire, which would bring Croatia and the future Slovenia even more firmly into the Austro-Hungarian orbit. Frederick and his descendants were given control over the Empire's Central European and Balkan territories, while Charles gave his son, Philip, control over Spain, the Netherlands,

Naples, Milan, and Spain's colonies in the Americas. This territorial divestment divided the Habsburg lands into clear zones of influence as a veritable world war continued between the forces of Christendom and Islam, as Habsburg generals, admirals, and missionaries vied with the Ottomans for influence and supremacy across a global theater stretching from the Philippines to Malta to South America. It is in this larger context that the development of Croatia and Slovenia must be understood heading into the 17th century.

5

From the Defeat of the Ottomans through the Age of Enlightenment (1557–1805)

TURNING THE TIDE AGAINST THE OTTOMAN TURKS (1557–1699)

By the mid-16th century, Croatia remained in a decades-long tug-of-war between the Ottoman Empire and the Austrian Habsburg Empire—a semifrozen conflict in which large pitched battles were more the exception than the norm. Both of these great powers of the day were often reluctant to engage in open hostilities, preferring short-term peace treaties due to challenges on numerous other fronts. Nevertheless, much of today's Croatia remained disputed or was incorporated into different zones of influence; the so-called Kingdom of Croatia (centered around Zagreb) and Kingdom of Slavonia were but small outposts of independent Catholic-ruled territory in comparison to Croatia's bygone medieval apogee.

By 1573, much of the Dalmatian hinterland and formerly Croat Bosnia had been seized by the Ottomans, and a deep, semicircular expanse of territory bordering the Adriatic coast, Ottoman Bosnia, and Austrian-allied Croatia and Slavonia was classified as a military march, or borderland, by central planners in the imperial court at Vienna. In 1553, the Croatian Military Frontier (*Hrvatska Vojna Krajina* in Croatian) officially came into existence. Run directly from the Austrian high command, the Military Frontier was a constantly shifting territory that remained under the nominal jurisdiction of the Christian empire through the late 19th century. Frequently attacked by brigands and Turkish raiding parties, this precarious place was settled first by Serb and Croat peasants. In exchange for providing military service and remaining loyal to the Habsburg monarchy, these immigrants were granted freedom from serfdom. The Croatian and Slavonian Military Frontiers merged near the confluence of the strategically significant Una and Sava Rivers.

One long-term outcome of the "Hundred-Year War" with the Turks was indeed a new ethnic mixing in border areas of today's Croatia, Bosnia, and Serbia. In addition to the indigenous Serbs and Croat peasants inhabiting the areas that became part of the militarized zone, Austrian authorities resettled other willing peasants, as well as professional soldiers and other necessary personnel, from around the empire. These included Slovaks, Czechs, Ukrainians, Germans, and Rusyns. While the descendants of such border-dwellers have long since been incorporated into the larger local populations, some minority groups remain in this wide Balkan area (particularly in the northern Serbian province of Vojvodina to the east of Croatia) to the present day.

Population engineering was, however, the easy part as far as outfitting the Military Frontier was concerned. The greater issue was how to pay for it. In 1578, a special event was convened to assign responsibilities for the defensive effort. Known as the Congress of Inner Austria, it was held in the town of Bruck an der Mur in the Austrian province of Styria, near modern Slovenia. Important decisions reached here included a new obligation for Styrian nobles to fund the Upper Slavonian section of the Military Frontier. At the same time, aristocrats from elsewhere in Austria, and the Slovene counts of Carniola and Carinthia, were charged with financing the Croatian Military Frontier, which effectively served as a security blanket for Slovene and Austrian populations.

Despite its relative insulation from the Turkish threat, Slovenia had been occasionally ravaged (particularly in the south) during the previous two centuries of Ottoman–Habsburg wars. The Turks destroyed prosperous Slovene towns like Vipavski Križ and Kostanjevica na Krki, attacks that were not only damaging on their own but which also threatened the Austrian Empire's control of the land route to Italy, north of the Adriatic Sea. The Slovene nobility thus understood that their own defense lay on the Croatian frontier, and local and imperial forces worked quickly to stave off the threat posed by Ottoman expansionism.

The decisive battle that began to turn the tide in the long war took place in 1593 at Sisak in today's central Croatia. Overlooked by a castle, the town was strategically located at the confluence of the Kupa, Sava, and Odra rivers, just thirty-five miles southeast of the capital of Zagreb. Defending the city was considered vital for preserving both river traffic and the relatively little that remained of the Croatian kingdom. (The triangular fortress of Sisak, where the city's defenders were garrisoned, remains the town's major tourist attraction today.)

The Battle of Sisak exemplified the full complexity of the Austrian Empire's Balkan presence in the late 16th century. It was fought by a joint force of Croat, Austrian, and Slovenians under the command of ethnically Hungarian Croatian Ban Thomas Erdődy and Austrian General Ruprecht von Eggenberg. Their mission was to end the Turkish siege of Sisak Castle, where an outnumbered local garrison had been left under the charge of Croat commanders Blaž Đurak and Matija Fintić. Despite being outnumbered, the imperial forces launched a surprise attack on the besieging Ottomans on June 22, decisively defeating them after thousands of retreating Turks drowned in a river, with the remainder fleeing after setting their store of gunpowder alight.

The result was immediately significant because it marked the Turks' third recent failure to capture the key fortress of Sisak and thwarted their advance toward Western Europe, where the fame of the operation's leaders soon spread. Indeed, von Eggenberg was promoted and obtained several other victories against the Turks soon after, while Ban Erdődy was lauded by Pope Clement VIII and subsequently knighted by the Spanish King Philip II into the Order of Saint Savior. For his part, Andreas von Auersperg, the Habsburg field commander of troops from the Duchies of Carniola and Carinthia, became known as the "Carniolan Achilles" in Europe following the Battle of Sisak. Although the latter was a Protestant, Pope Clement sent him a personal letter to express his gratitude for saving Central Europe from the threat of an Islamic invasion.

By the end of the 16th century, the Croatian Military Frontier was also becoming known as the Karlovac Frontier (after the name of the central Croatian city, located between Zagreb and Rijeka on the Adriatic coast). From the 1630s, the Upper Slavonian Military Frontier was known as the Varaždin Frontier, after the name of another important

Croatian city. While the Military Frontier was ultimately controlled at the level of the emperor, practically speaking it was most often administered at the level of the Austrian Archduke's War Council, located in the city of Graz.

The War Council took several overlapping decisions to strengthen the Frontier's defenses, for which the previously agreed system of subventions from the nobility was no longer sufficient. In addition to the existing (but expensive) mercenary units that had been employed in previous campaigns, the military leadership encouraged the general local population to oppose the Ottomans and continue the Christian presence in the border regions by granting them the status of free peasants. The last vestiges of local control over border zones were also erased in 1627 when administration of the Military Frontier was transferred from the Croatian Sabor to the Habsburg War Council. This significantly diminished the power of the Croatian Ban and parliament, but it also put the responsibility for achieving military objectives and defense squarely in Austrian hands. (The Habsburg authorities would enjoy full authority over these regions until the Military Frontier system was officially ended in the late 19th century.)

In 1630, a second significant reform affected the Military Frontier with the Turks, Habsburg Emperor Ferdinand II proclaimed the *Statuta Valachorum* (Vlach Statute), an edict which was meant to legally define the status of the so-called Vlach settlers—primarily, war refugees from areas seized by the Ottomans. While many of these newcomers were indeed Vlachs (Arromanians, Latin people closely related to modern Romanians), the blanket definition of the Vlach Statute also included a fair number of Croat and Serb refugees. With the Vlach Statute, the Austrian Empire defined the terms of military obligations of the newcomers, as well as the rights to internal self-administration they could expect to have under Habsburg rule. In this respect, the Austrians were more generous (that is, more pragmatic) than the disempowered Croat kingdom would have been, in that they allowed the large Serbian population that settled Croatian and Hungarian areas of the Frontier to preserve their Orthodox Christian faith in a predominantly Catholic country. In return, the Serbs became spirited fighters, with the entire fighting-age male population, eventually becoming soldiers for the Habsburgs, and not only against the Turks.

After the Battle of Sisak, the Croatian Military Frontier also became more expensive to maintain because it slowly grew in size as the European powers began to roll back the Turkish advances. The Frontier soon stretched from the Adriatic Sea across Croatia, Hungary, and Romania. While the Age of Exploration had been well underway since the late 15th century, with the new maritime powers of Britain, France, Spain, Portugal, and Holland colonizing the most distant shores, the Ottomans stubbornly clung to their ultimate aspiration of taking Western Europe. However, in attempting to do so, they came into direct conflict with not only the Habsburgs but also Poland, and eventually the Russian Empire. This was too big of a challenge across too wide a front, and, given its challenges on other fronts from other powers too, the Ottoman Empire ultimately failed in its land invasion of Europe.

The final major showdown occurred in 1683 when war broke out between the Habsburg and Ottoman Empires. Seeking to achieve the dream of capturing Vienna that had eluded Sultan Suleyman the Magnificent in 1529, the Ottoman Grand Vizier (Regional Governor) Merzifonlu Kara Mustafa Pasha set off with an army of roughly 200,000 men in early 1683 from Edirne in distant Thrace, marching through the Balkans and to the outskirts of Vienna in July of that year. The Grand Vizier was an accomplished commander who had won several battles on the Ottomans' European fronts, and was besieging a city protected by only 15,000 Austrian soldiers in a garrison led by Commander Ernst Rüdiger Graf von Starhemberg. He had been appointed by the Holy Roman Emperor, Leopold I, who himself fled the city with his court for the safety of Passau in Bavaria.

While no military hero, Emperor Leopold did at least forge an alliance to defend Vienna, known as the Holy League, consisting of the Habsburg Monarchy, the Holy Roman Empire, the Papal States, the Venetian Republic, and Poland-Lithuania. The last of these was the major player in the alliance, with Polish King John III Sobieski appointed general commander of the relief force. Sobieski (1629–1696) was a respected leader and veteran of many successful campaigns against the Turks (and other enemies) in his long career. His arrival at the head of a sizable Polish contingent of infantry and famed "winged Hussar" heavy cavalry troops brought new hope to the Viennese defenders, who had been busy trying to locate and disarm explosives planted by the Ottomans, who had already managed to blow up some of the outer city walls. The defending citizens under von Starhemberg were in fact preparing for urban combat as the late-arriving allies hurried to get organized.

The Polish force under King Sobieski crossed the Danube northwest of Vienna on September 6, where they met up with imperial forces and German auxiliary troops from Saxony, Bavaria, Baden, Franconia, and Swabia. Their ranks were swelled by Zaporozhian Cossack troops from Polish-controlled parts of Ukraine. Other key leaders of allied forces were led by Charles V, Duke of Lorraine, who had crucially defeated the Ottoman Hungarian vassal Imre Thököly at Bisamberg, just three miles from Vienna, the previous month. The Christian allies enjoyed another stroke of luck when they sent a successful spy mission to Kahlenberg, the wooded mountain south of the capital where the Turks had announced their presence by lighting large bonfires. From this mission, the allies were able to deduce Mustafa Pasha's attack plans for the following morning.

Thus, early on 12 September, the Ottomans attacked and were met by stiff resistance on three fronts, in what would be known as the definitive Battle of Vienna. First, some of the German forces prevented the Turks from reaching the city, while Charles of Lorraine led the imperial army on the Ottoman's left flank. Soon after, the Ottoman right flank was under attack from Sobieski's Polish infantry. Despite multiple Ottoman counterattacks, the Holy League troops captured several key fortified villages. The final hours of the battle was a tense race against time as Mustafa Pasha held back elite troops for a final storming of the city; however, the Viennese discovered and disarmed the explosives that the Turks had intended to use for destroying the city walls. This allowed sufficient time for Sobieski's Polish infantry to make headway against the Ottoman right flank. On the opposite flank, Charles of Lorraine was advancing as well; his forces arrived within sight of the central Ottoman camp in time to see the Polish Hussar assault, led by King Sobieski; at 18,000 horsemen, it remains the largest cavalry charge in history, which forced the Ottomans to flee the battlefield.

The salvation of Vienna made Sobieski and his comrades heroes across Europe, and was one of the biggest turning points in European history. The Turkish defeat led to the slow but steady retreat of Ottoman power southward from Central Europe and part of the Balkans. In the years after the battle, the Habsburgs recovered much of Hungary and Croatia. The long war finally ended in 1699, with the Treaty of Karlowitz, signed in Sremski Karlovci in modern-day Serbia. Among the territories returned to the Habsburg Empire by this treaty were the regions of Lika, Kordun, Banija, lower Slavonia in Croatia, Syrmia, Bačka, Banat, and Pomorišje in Serbia, and Transylvania in Romania. Yet, while the Ottomans had been forced to cede these territories, the Habsburg Empire did not abolish but rather expanded the Military Frontier. Maintaining central control over the area not only prevented local *bans* from challenging the emperor but also preserved the abundance of military forces that could be drafted into service in case of future Turkish raids. This preservation of the Military Frontier after the 1683 Battle of Vienna kept the empire's Balkan flank well defended, but it also slowed the development of the individual countries of Slovenia, Hungary, Croatia, Serbia, and Romania that would emerge in the 19th century.

PIRATES OF THE ADRIATIC: THE *USKOCI* BETWEEN AUSTRIA, VENICE, AND THE OTTOMANS (1522–1669)

Croatia's Early Modern history was not, however, limited to a simple war between the forces of imperial Islam and Christianity. On the margins of this greater conflict emerged unusual and memorable populations such as the *Uskoci* or Uskoks (plural of the Croatian word *uskok*, meaning "the one who ambushed"). Originally composed of Serbs and Croats driven out of their homes in Bosnia and Croatia by the Turks, the Uskoci began their long and infamous reign on the Dalmatian coast as mercenaries for the Austrians, and were associated particularly with the coastal town of Senj, protected by mountains and (from 1567) the Nehaj Fortress. The Uskoci are notable in Croatian history not just as colorful, swashbuckling brigands but also because their exploits gave them an outsized role in history—though never more than a few thousand men, the Uskok pirates played a role in major clashes between rival empires, attaining positions of rank and power, while sparking conflicts involving not only the Habsburgs, Ottomans, and Venetians but the more distant Spanish, Dutch, and English as well. Today, they are remembered in popular history and even in the name of one Special Forces unit of the Croatian Army known as the Commando Uskok Company (*Komando uskočka satnija*).

Uskok irregulars in the Habsburg Army originated from the early 16th century and inhabited inland and coastal Dalmatian areas, increasing in number as Ottoman expansion in Bosnia forced Serbs and Croats living there to flee westward. Early on, bands of Uskoci waged guerrilla campaigns against the Ottomans; they presented a dual threat by being both expert mountain fighters and sailors, rowing swift boats along the coast and sometimes along rivers inland to launch their attacks. The Hapsburgs resettled many of these refugees in the walled town of Klis, located inland just northeast of the important coastal city of Split. Further north along the coast, the Habsburgs had since 1522 been nominally in possession of Senj, a naturally defensible coastal stronghold on the Military Frontier, surrounded by rugged mountains and forests. Both places became known for their large Uskok populations.

Because of its strategic location, Klis Fortress was long-sought by the Turks. It safeguarded the path through the mountains that led to the riches of coastal Dalmatia, cities like Split and the islands. The first notable Croatian Uskok leader, Petar Kružić (died 1537), commanded Senj and Klis Fortresses. Because he protected Klis (and thus Split) from the Turks, Habsburg Emperor Ferdinand I turned a blind eye to the Croat leader's frequent piracy. *Knez* Kružić was also immensely popular among his countrymen for his military achievements. Klis had been under constant siege from the Ottomans since the second decade of the 16th century, and they appeared poised to capture the town in February 1524. However, Kružić arrived in time from Senj, and despite having a somewhat smaller force, managed to crush the Turkish army and preserve the town's freedom until his death in 1537. The surrender of Klis soon after forced the Uskoci to escape north to Senj. This created a unique population of locals, new fighters, and increasing numbers of refugees from other towns and villages in northwestern Croatia. In fact, as Senj's reputation for piracy grew, other outlaws from around Christendom flocked to it, piling up new wealth from the Uskoci's piracy at sea and land. Even the local Catholic Church enjoyed favors from the plunderers, such as the Franciscan and Dominican monastic orders, who received endowments from local chieftains.

Senj was a natural redoubt for pirates because of its unique geography: mountains and forests protected it from land attacks, while the shallow and often stormy bay was unsuitable for large naval galleys to enter, let alone drop anchor in. By contrast, the Uskok swift boats were more easily protected and could navigate small inlets and estuaries. With these advantages and little arable land to live from, the Uskoci increased their attacks on commercial ships, seizing not only gold and silver but other then-valuable commodities from the Ottoman East, such as silk, cloth, and spices. By 1540, however, these activities had become a major headache for Venice. Trying to preserve its former position as unquestioned guardian of the seas, Venice made a treaty in that year with the Ottomans, promising that the latter's merchant fleet would be safe in the Adriatic. Nevertheless, even when escorted by Venetian galleys, the commercial ships were still often attacked. Worse for the Venetians, the irritated Uskoci sought to make good for their losses by attacking the Venetian-held Croatian islands of Krk, Rab, and Pag, while using Venetian-administered areas in Dalmatia as launching pads for attacks against the Ottomans.

While Venice did not appreciate such behavior and vowed to crack down on the pirates, any such action was risky because it might antagonize the Habsburgs—the nominal rulers of the Uskoci and often thankful for their military services. As a land power, Austria had a long inland frontier to defend and relatively little access to the sea. The territories that they did possess, such as Senj and increasingly Uskok-populated ports northwards in Istria and today's Slovenia, provided a crucial outlet to the Adriatic, which was otherwise dominated by Venice.

One particularly renowned Uskok leader, Ivan Lenković (died 1569), rose to the rank of general in the Croatian Habsburg army. The construction of Nehaj Fortress in Senj is attributed to him. (The Uskok legacy is still celebrated every summer inside the fortress, during the now tourist-town's festivities.) Aside from helping the Austrians oversee and organize the Military Frontier with the Turks, General Lenković was particularly renowned for a specific battle that captivated Christian Europe. As the Ottoman-Habsburg Wars continued to rage, both sides took back territory from the other—often within short spans of time. For example, the strategic Klis Fortress was recaptured in April 1569 by a Croatian noblemen from Split, further up the coast, prompting Ottoman Beg Mustafa besiege the fortress with a large army. Although outnumbered roughly ten-to-one, General Lenković and his uskok relief forces harried the Turks, granting the city a two-month reprieve. Although eventually being forced to withdraw and dying soon after being wounded in battle, Lenković was heralded for his bravery in Habsburg Austria and throughout Europe, adding to the Uskok phenomenon that would live on in folk songs and legends. The Uskoci added further to their heroic reputation by destroying a Turkish army that had, in 1592, invaded Croatia specifically to capture Senj. However, even though the large Turkish force initially succeeded in laying waste to Uskok villages outside of the fortified town, it was defeated and dispersed the following year by local Uskok guerrillas.

Nevertheless, by the turn of the 17th century, the Venetians had become desperate to solve the "Uskok problem" once and for all because the centuries-old reputation of Venice as guardian of the Mediterranean was in question: with these Croatian pirates harassing Ottoman, papal, Venetian, and other Italian ships, foreign emissaries were frequently grumbling to the doge and his ambassadors about their unfulfilled responsibilities. This led directly to a continual escalation of tensions that climaxed in open war between Venice and Habsburg Austria, a conflict sometimes referred to as the "Uskok Wars" due to the ill will between both powers due to the continual piracy in the Adriatic. The conflict was presaged by grisly tit-for-tat attacks; for example, after the Venetians captured an Uskok fleet and displayed the pirates' severed heads in St. Mark's Square, the Uskoci massacred the crew of a Venetian ship, reportedly flavoring their food with the blood of the unfortunate Italians.

In 1615, Venice took action against the Uskoci when Archduke Ferdinand of Styria refused to do so. Thus began a ruinous, and largely unnecessary, war fought in the area north of the Adriatic that comprises the modern-day borderlands between Slovenia and Italy. Remarkably, the fighting extended into the Alps and even involved Dutch and British mercenaries (on the Venetian side) and support from Spain's Habsburg leaders, the Croats, and Slovenes on the Austrian side. Particularly fierce fighting was encountered in the Gorizia Hills area of western Slovenia, as well as around the Austrian-held town of Gradisca (now in Italy).

Ultimately a peace treaty was agreed in late 1617. According to the treaty, the Uskoci were to be expelled from their stronghold of Senj (and other fortified towns), their ships destroyed, and their bands broken up. The next couple of decades saw large-scale migrations of Uskok families, though not all to one place. Interestingly, some Uskoci were resettled in the Croatian interior, while others moved northward to today's Slovenia. In the latter case, their name became synonymous with the *Uskoken Gebirge*, a mountain range bordering the province of Carniola; this area today is called Žumberak. The Uskok refugees were also settled in the neighboring Slovenian provinces of White Carniola and Kostel. In the 1630s, the Habsburgs granted lands and other privileges to keep these somewhat unpredictable subjects content.

Of course, there was always the option of serving on the Frontier against the Ottomans, which some former pirates did. Though in their heyday the Uskoci pirates attacked vessels indiscriminately in their continual hunt for wealth and sustenance, it is worth noting that these fighters did follow to some degree an "Uskok Code," by which they were ultimately defending a common Christianity against the Islamic Turkish threat. Thus history records, well after the main period of Uskok activity, some of these Slavic brigands in high positions of power in the ongoing fight against the Turks, and even on the side of the Venetians. Such was the case with Stojan Janković Mitrović, a Serbian Uskok who lived from roughly 1636 to 1687. As the commander of a special Balkan detachment, he fought for the Republic of Venice from 1669 until his death in 1687. One of his major campaigns was the war against the Ottomans in Venetian Crete. (Following a lengthy siege, the Venetians ended up losing that island, which they had held since 1204, and a good deal of their domination of the Mediterranean.)

In fact, thousands of Uskoci whose legacy is now largely forgotten played a role in distant battles for imperial Christian causes over their almost two centuries of existence. One significant example was the crucial 1571 Battle of Lepanto, in which a Croatian Uskok fleet helped the

Holy League navies of the Spanish and Austrian Habsburg Empires and the Venetians to defeat the Ottomans. Considered Europe's largest naval battle since Classical Antiquity, the engagement was fought in the Gulf of Patras in Greece; the victory cemented Emperor Philip II of Spain's image as the preeminent defender of Catholicism in Europe. This was particularly important for the Habsburgs (of Austria as well as Spain) as a new schism within the church—the Protestant Reformation—was threatening the power of the pope, Catholic rulers, and indeed changing the whole system of traditional alliances in Western Europe.

THE PROTESTANT REFORMATION AND DEVELOPMENT OF THE SLOVENIAN NATION (1517–1583)

As one of the most significant events in European history, the Protestant Reformation unsurprisingly had a large impact on Croatia and, especially, Slovenia and their unique cultural and religious paths of national development. It can be said with certainty that the introduction of a new Christian "option" that transcended the long-existing duality of Orthodoxy and Catholicism in the Balkans accelerated the differentiation of peoples that, while neighbors sharing similar languages and customs, began to evolve in different ways because of the new internal competition for Catholic hearts and minds (the Reformation had much less of an effect on Orthodox countries, which except for Russia and parts of Romania were under Ottoman control anyway).

The Reformation occurred because of gradual disagreements within the Catholic Church, the rise of science and critical thought, and the formulation of questions that had previously been banned—such as the inherent infallibility of the pope. The man most associated with the Reformation is German theologian Martin Luther, who published his influential "95 Theses" in 1517 as a form of scholarly challenge to the Vatican. Luther particularly objected to the pope's right to sell "indulgences," or official dispensations for sins committed, to wealthy individuals. In the background, there is no question that the failure of European armies like Austria, Hungary, Croatia, and Poland to defeat the Ottomans in the last crusaders of the mid-15th century also played a role in damaging the prestige of the pope and his preferred rulers.

Luther's protest was not the first such challenge to the Vatican's authority. Movements had begun in previous decades but never quite received widespread support. Though some (like the Czech and the Hussites under Jan Hus in Bohemia) were seen as a threat and dealt

with harshly by the Habsburg authorities, they did get some papal recognition, unlike the case with the Lollard movement in England and
the Waldensian reformers in Italy and France. Thus, Martin Luther
was indeed speaking to a large European audience, which was perhaps ready for change or at least to question some of the established
dogma from Rome. However, his success was to a large part due to his
ability to put forth more nuanced argumentation that was both aca-
demically sound and had application in daily life. In this way, he was
able to demonstrate to the common (and often, illiterate) peasantry of
Europe how his new religious offering was more beneficial than the
traditional ways, as embodied by the Catholic Church.

The arguments put forth by different Protestant leaders varied based
on their ideals and areas of special interest. Luther criticized the sale of
indulgences on theological grounds, arguing that the pope's authority
could not possibly extend over purgatory (the spiritual realm between
heaven and hell, in which souls not fit for the former were left to lan-
guish, according to doctrine). All Reformation leaders emphasized a
distinction between law and gospel, faith in Jesus as crucial to receiving God's forgiveness, and especially total reliance on scripture as the
source of doctrine. Some went further, questioning the need for saints
and advocated that priests be allowed to marry.

All these radical ideas were too much for the Vatican, and the
Lutherans were condemned in the Pope's 1521 Edict of Worms. Under
it, all citizens of the Holy Roman Empire were banned from supporting Protestant innovations. The Vatican went further in defending its
interests by supporting the Counter-Reformation, which began in 1530
with a spirited defense of Catholic beliefs and included the Council
of Trent in 1545. In all of these efforts, a key role was played by the
Jesuit Order (also known as the "Society of Jesus") from 1540. This
influential Catholic order would go on to periods of great influence
followed by a purge, and eventual reinstatement, with their influence
continuing to this day (in 2013, Pope Francis became the first elected
Jesuit pope in history).

However, it is important to remember that Luther and his followers
did not perceive their ideas as being anti-Christian, or particularly revolutionary; they considered their work more of a restoration of what
Christianity had been meant to be from the time of Jesus, rather than a
reformation that fundamentally changed the religion. While over the
centuries the various Protestant denominations have fundamentally
divided the Christian world, with some being seen as excessively liberal and even supporting secular beliefs, the original reformers of the
16th century based their arguments on close examinations of the Bible.

This reliance on scripture and language had a direct impact on the linguistic development of Europe as more Bibles and commentaries on Christian matters were published than ever before. Slovenia experienced this much more than Croatia, where the spread of Protestant evangelizers was limited and met with mistrust. Unlike the Croats, Slovenes were to a large extent geographically protected from the constant existential threat of the Islamic Ottoman Empire. This reality had a historic impact on maintaining a defensive religiosity in "front-line" countries like Croatia, Serbia, and Romania, whereas relatively insulated nations in Central, Northern, and Western Europe lived under conditions in which their religion was not grounds for their execution at the hands of the "infidel."

At the time of Martin Luther, the Slovene-populated lands included Carniola, Gradisca, Gorizia, Carinthia, and today's Inner Austria and Styria. However, by that time, most Slovenes were subjects of the Habsburg Empire—one of the bastions of Catholicism in Europe. Nevertheless, the Reformation brought new ideas and new arguments, which had to be translated into new languages. For this reason, Protestantism became a major reason for the production of more books in the vernacular, proto-Slovene language. Seeking to convince local populations across Europe about the rightness of their argument, the Protestants reasoned that both the academic class and the peasantry would benefit from having, and being able to share, knowledge of their views in their own language. Such works would be more easily accessible to them than writings and masses in Latin, which the Catholic Church still used primarily, despite the fact that Latin was no longer spoken or understood widely.

It is thus no surprise that the first Slovene-language books were written by the country's main Protestant evangelizers and their followers. While essentially liturgical and theological in subject, these works used a vocabulary and grammar close to the spoken word of the day, which would become the example for a standardized Slovene language. The creation of a unique language helped establish a new sense of Slovenian identity that both differentiated them from their Italian and Austrian neighbors and distinguished their language from closely related South Slavic languages like Serbian and Croatian, as well as from Western Slavic languages like Czech, Slovak, and Polish.

In this light, the key figure of Slovenian literacy and culture was Primož Trubar (1508–1586). As Slovenia's main Lutheran reformer, he was the founder and first leader of the Lutheran Church in Slovenia. Trubar was also the author of the first books in the Slovenian language on religious matters. This was even more important as the age of the printing press was, by Luther's time, less than a century old in Europe, and Trubar's was the first Slovene-language book to come off of a printing press. Trubar and his supporters based the Protestant Church in Slovenia in the Duchy of Carniola. However, the Austrian Habsburgs joined the papacy's Counter-Reformation from 1530, implying that the new faith was suppressed, and leaving only a small Lutheran following in the Prekmurje region in the east.

Trubar, who was a native of Carniola, was schooled in Croatia (at Rijeka, from 1520 to 1521), before continuing on to Salzburg and then Trieste for advanced studies. Here he came into contact with famous Humanist thinkers, like the Dutch scholar Erasmus, who would have a tremendous influence in the West on the perception and pronunciation of the Ancient Greek language. In 1527, Trubar became a priest and was assigned to his Slovenian homeland but continued his education in the capital of the Habsburg Monarchy, Vienna. However, Trubar's deepening interest in Protestantism did not go without notice, and he was expelled from Ljubljana in 1547.

This experience gave Trubar the impetus needed to put down his preaching to text, which he did while exiled in Rothenburg in Germany, where the Reformation had been somewhat more popular. There he wrote the first two books in Slovene, which were then printed that year in Germany. During his lifetime, Trubar wrote more than twenty books in the Slovenian language (as well as two others in German). His achievements also included being the first person to translate sections of the Bible into Slovene. In keeping with similar Protestant movements elsewhere, he also managed a South Slavic Bible Institute located in Urach, near Tübingen in Germany. The institute's work was meant to encourage more active participation between ecclesiastical thinkers of the Balkan region, and particularly to spread Protestantism among the Orthodox populations there.

In this respect, Trubar had some success. He cooperated with a Serbian Orthodox monk and scribe Jovan Maleševac (died 1562), who was acquainted with Slovenian culture, having lived for a time in the Habsburg province of White Carniola. In 1561, the two cooperated on a project to print religious works in the Cyrillic alphabet—the alphabet that had been used in Serbia, Macedonia, Montenegro, and Bulgaria following the evangelization works of Saint Cyril and Saint Methodius in the 9th century. To assist, a second Serbian monk, Matija Popović, was commissioned. Humorously, the German Protestants referred to the Serbian Orthodox monks as *uskokische Priester* ("Uskok priests," in German)—a term that referred more to the refugee status of these churchmen from Ottoman-controlled territory than to any predilection for piracy they could have had. Nevertheless, the amusing nickname reveals again the extent to which Central Europe viewed its neighbors from the northwestern edges of the Balkan Peninsula in the 16th century.

With Trubar, the two monks worked for five months at the Cyrillic printing press in Urach, where they proofread the New Testament, as well as works by Martin Luther. While these literary endeavors did not succeed in making any significant inroads for Protestantism in Serbia, the activity of common linguistic cooperation for a shared purpose (in this case, Christianity) would prefigure later acts of linguistic cooperation for a different one (ethno-nationalism and linguistics) by Slovenes, Croats, and Serbs in the 19th century. Thus, Trubar's initiatives remain relevant for both their historic role in developing the Slovene language and consciousness, and as an early example of the convergence of interests and cooperation between South Slav peoples that would shape much of the 19th- and 20th-century Balkan events.

Another important early Slovenian Protestant was Adam Bohorič (c. 1520–1598), a preacher who also contributed to the development of the national language by writing the first Slovene-language grammatical textbook in 1584. In fact, the book used the first Slovene alphabet (called the Bohorič alphabet,

A historic bust depicts Adam Bohorič (1520–1598), one of the most important figures in the development of Slovene literacy and nationhood. An early supporter of the Protestant Reformation in Habsburg-ruled Slovenia, Bohorič devised a revolutionary alphabet that bears his name and wrote the first Slovene grammar, thus expediting the nation-building project and South Slavic education in general. (Kar Wai Chan/Dreamstime.com) after its creator), which remained in use up to the 1840s. A third great contributor to the development of Slovene language and culture, Sebastjan Krelj (1538–1567) was a highly educated Protestant church-man from the Duchy of Carniola. He served under Primož Trubar, working for the leading Lutheran in Slovenia as a preacher in Lju-bljana, where he became superintendent of the Carniolan Protestant Church in 1565. Although he died of disease at an early age, the poly-glot philologist Krelj had a major impact on the direction of linguistic and philological developments in the later 16th century and thereafter. Along with knowing a host of modern and ancient languages, Krelj carefully distinguished the dialects spoken in Slovenian and Croatian lands—in subregions such as Istria, the Vipava Valley, and Lower Car-niola. This work was expanded upon by Jurij Dalmatin (c. 1547–1589), the Slovene Lutheran minister who completed the first full transla-tion of the Bible into Slovene in 1583, printed using the new Bohorič alphabet.

The Habsburg Counter-Reformation was carried out across all Slovenian-speaking lands, resulting in the expulsion of Protestants, intimidation, book-burning, and restrictions on even speaking the local Slavic dialects. The one area largely spared from this fate was the eastern region of Prekmurje, ruled as it was by Hungary; the Hab-sburg's joint empire tolerated certain forms of Protestantism among the Hungarian nobility, such as Calvinism, in the name of preserv-ing political stability. Since they too were Protestants, the Hungarian Calvinists generally did not persecute the Slovenian Lutherans under their control in the border region. Despite the excesses of the Counter-Reformation, the literary and cultural legacy created by Trubar and his clerical comrades would live on to the present day.

CROATIA, SLOVENIA, AND THE REIGN OF
EMPRESS MARIA THERESA (1664–1780)

During the period of constant war with the Ottomans, from the 1553 implementation of the Military Frontier onwards, a much-depleted Croatian kingdom endured, though its territory was much lessened than it was at its medieval height. The noble families that had been accustomed to ruling Croatia (if under the ultimate control of Austria) had lost much of their ancestral lands to the Turkish and Venetian occu-pations. The constant emergency situation on the constantly changing border of the militarized zone left large areas deserted, making the country a place for Christian refugees and potential vagabonds, such as the Uskoci.

The buffer zone of refugees and settlers—not only Serbs and Croats from Bosnia but also Germans, Hungarians, Czechs, Slovaks, and Ukrainians—had the unexpected (but predictable) negative effect of creating an ungovernable mass united only by their poverty. With feudalism and the absence of a firm hand of the former domestic aristocrats who had dealt with ground realities in more stable medieval times, the Austrian Empire was faced with an often ill-tempered and rebellious rural population. For example, in 1573, a peasant revolt broke out in northern Croatia and Slovenia, leading to the public execution of peasant leader Matija Gubec and thousands of other rebels by the imperial authorities. Heavy-handed reprisals like this kept the peasantry in line, though it hardly made them devoted subjects. For the Croats, Slovenes, and others living in the border areas, it was a case of accepting the lesser of two evils by accepting Austrian rule. Across the Ottoman Empire, the Turks were well-known for forced Islamicization of conquered populations (as in Bosnia). Those who refused to convert faced the possibility of having their children seized, the boys for the Sultan's elite Janissary corps of soldiers and the girls for the imperial harems.

As the tide started to turn against the Ottomans in the 17th century, Croatian hopes rose that their kingdom might be restored to somewhat of its former glory. However, they were disappointed by Vienna when Emperor Leopold failed to capitalize on the Austrian army's partial victory over the Turks at the Battle of Saint Gotthard on August 1, 1664. In this decisive contest, Croatian and Hungarian forces under local noblemen aided the combined armies of Germany, France, Hungary, and the Habsburg Empire. This victory prevented a large Ottoman army from retaking fortresses and towns in Croatia and Hungary that had been recently seized by local fighters. However, these local lords were enraged when Leopold chose to sign a quick and pragmatic treaty with the Turks (known as the Peace of Vasvár) in 1664, which provided for a twenty-year truce but allowed the Ottomans to keep control of large areas of Hungary, Transylvania, and Croatia. In truth, Leopold was more concerned with bigger issues, such as a rivalry with France over the line of succession in Habsburg Spain; the empire thus chose stability and a status quo on the Balkan border over expanding and regaining its territories there, much to the consternation of the Croat and Hungarian nobles who had supported the Austrian Empire in the four-year war.

These disenfranchised aristocrats decided that overthrowing Emperor Leopold would somehow secure their personal interests. Their so-called Magnate's Conspiracy (or Zrinski-Frankopan

Conspiracy, after its main protagonists) was poorly organized, and Hungarian Count Wesselényi unrealistically tried to gain military aid from various nations, including France, Sweden, Poland, Venice, and even the Turks. Ironically, it was the Ottoman court that tipped Leopold off to the plot in 1666. In reality, the aristocrats were not seeking a national liberation but rather personal power (as their negotiations with the Ottomans indicated; they were prepared to give the Turks total control of all Hungary in exchange for enjoying personal fiefdoms there). Nevertheless, Leopold did nothing as his agents deemed the plot as unserious.

It was only in 1670, after printed calls for a general insurrection in Hungary began to appear that the Habsburg authorities cracked down. The main instigators (Hungarian Count Ferenc Nádasdy and Croatian counts Petar Zrinski and Fran Krsto Frankopan) were executed on April 30, 1671, and roughly 2,000 other local aristocrats (most of who had nothing to do with the plot) were detained. The position of *Ban* was discontinued in Croatia, and both countries came under direct Habsburg rule. Thus, a plot that never actually materialized benefited the Habsburgs, who centralized administrative power locally, establishing an absolute monarchy. Among other victims of the crackdown were Hungary's minority Protestant populations, whose churches were burned down across the country by the authorities.

This experience left Croatia more obedient to the Austrians over the decades to come. The Croatian elite thus supported Emperor Charles VI's Pragmatic Sanction of 1713, which ensured that (as had been the custom in Habsburg Spain) a female descendant could rightfully inherit the throne. This was a major issue because since the death of his brother in 1711, Charles was the only surviving male Habsburg, but lacked any children of his own. The issue of succession in an increasingly complex Europe, with its colonies spread around all corners of the earth, had caused a bitter war over Spain, as well as much diplomacy, the ultimate victor of which was arguably England. By the turn of the 18th century, the English had cemented their position as world trading leader, relegating the Dutch, Ottomans, and Venetians to a secondary class, while the decline of the Holy Roman Empire led to increasing power among different states in Germany.

In this context, Croatia and Slovenia had a minor but still notable role in the greater political complexities by supporting Charles VI's Pragmatic Sanction of 1713. At that time, the Austrian Habsburg Empire also controlled parts of Hungary, Croatia, the Kingdom of Bohemia, the Duchy of Milan, the Kingdom of Naples, the Kingdom of Sardinia, and the Austrian Netherlands. However, France, Prussia, Bavaria, and

Saxony broke their agreement after Charles' death in 1740, contesting the legitimacy of his daughter Maria Theresa (1717–1780) to become empress. This sparked another pan-Continental conflict, the War of the Austrian Succession (1741–1748), in which Maria Theresa ultimately prevailed. Although her father had left her unprepared for the task, Maria Theresa proved to be a capable ruler and enjoyed a long and successful forty-year rule.

Croatia saw some benefits from her accession since its major nobles had supported both the 1713 Pragmatic Sanction and the allies of Maria Theresa in the 1741–1748 war. The Croatian nobility slowly recovered some of their privileges, and, with the steady traction of the Ottomans, their lands. Maria Theresa also took special interest in Croatian matters, making several reforms, including changes in the Military Frontier's administration, as well as tax relief. In 1767, she also reinstated some degree of home rule by founding the Croatian Royal Council (*Hrvatsko kraljevinsko vijeće*) to govern Croatia and Slavonia. While originally based in Varaždin, the Royal Council was later moved to Zagreb. In 1776, Maria Theresa also gave the then-free city of Rijeka to Croatia. In addition to being the leader of Austria, she was also the Holy Roman Empress (her husband, Francis of Lorraine, was thus the Holy Roman Emperor), and was personally a very devout Catholic. These Habsburg rulers thus appreciated the loyal support of Croatia as it was a strongly Catholic nation. With the spread of various branches of Protestantism over the past century-and-a-half, numerous wars had been fought and political intriguing carried out due to the Catholic–Protestant divide, having an imperial possession that remained a stalwart supporter of the Vatican strengthened the empress' position.

THE ENLIGHTENMENT IN CROATIA AND SLOVENIA (1695–1805)

In parallel with the empress' reign and the gradual restoration of Croatian state institutions and territory, Croat and Slovene thinkers were deeply involved in the new intellectual ferment then sweeping Europe: the Enlightenment. This 18th-century phenomenon involved new breakthroughs and innovations in the natural sciences, technology, mathematics, philosophy, the social sciences, literature, and the arts. It combined the earlier Italian Renaissance's fascination with the cultural achievements of ancient Greece and Rome with the new spirit of questioning ingrained beliefs and institutions that pervaded the Protestant Reformation.

The Enlightenment succeeded due to its public and decentralized nature. The movement had no leader—a common zeal for knowledge and truth took the leading role—and thinkers met and exchanged ideas at scientific academies, literary salons, and even coffee shops. Crucially, their works enjoyed a wide audience because of the rapid increase in the number of printing houses in Europe. This allowed for not only the creation and circulation of new books but also the inauguration of scientific journals, ideological pamphlets, and literary magazines. Whereas the Church, kings, and emperors had previously held a tight grip on the dissemination and approval of ideas, the new decentralization of thinking in the Enlightenment era challenged the established authorities. This, in turn, created ideal conditions for new forms of political thought that would manifest across Europe—including in Croatia and Slovenia—in the following century when the concept of the nation-state with roots in ancient history became a driving factor in European politics and, especially, in the Balkan region.

Those Croat and Slovene intellectuals who participated in the Enlightenment were heavily influenced by the French view: that is, of a world in which reason comprised the basis of knowledge, in which the ideals of individual liberty, progress, secular governance, and religious toleration were promoted. For its part, Slovenia's participation in the Enlightenment owned first to preferable conditions; the Slovene lands were at peace and economic growth occurred. Further, the mixed Italian-Slovene port city of Trieste became a "free port" in 1718, bringing new economic and intellectual opportunities. The administration of the Habsburg Empire under Maria Theresa was favorable to Slovene interests. With economic growth, a new bourgeoisie class developed, as elsewhere in Europe. The physical location of Trieste on the historic main route between Italy and Central Europe and the Adriatic coast made it an ideal place for the exchange of new ideas from all directions.

In other parts of Slovenian-inhabited Habsburg lands, the Enlightenment took on a specifically literary characteristic and involved active participation of not only the bourgeoisie but also bonded workers and especially the peasantry. While German would remain the predominant language of cultural transmission, governance, and education long into the 19th century, Slovenes during the Enlightenment re-embraced their own language and culture in a romanticizing literary movement that drew on a mythologized view of local legends and history.

Known as *bukovniki*, the work of these thinkers was the continuation of local practices begun by peasants during the Habsburg Counter-Reformation, in which crypto-Protestants transcribed banned religious texts by hand. Over time, this activity came to include the transcription of nonreligious books such as folk tales, poetry, literary works, and others. Prevalent in parts of Carinthian, Carniola, and Styria, the Slovene *bukovniki* movement expanded the reader base and active interest in Slovene literature. The first major contributor to Slovene literature in the Enlightenment, Marko Pohlin (1735–1801), was an enthusiastic supporter of Slovene as a literary language and wrote the first modern grammar book of the language (*Kraynska grammatical*, or Carniolan Grammar). Although Pohlin's efforts to modernize the 16th-century grammar of Protestant preacher Adam Bohorič did not catch on, his work inspired fellow Slovenes to look more favorably on their own language and its literary potential.

As elsewhere in Europe, the Enlightenment in Slovenia benefited from the patronage of wealthy aristocrats. Chief among these was Sigmund Zois Freiherr von Edelstein (1747–1819). Generally referred to as Sigmund Zois, this Carniolan nobleman based in Ljubljana donated heavily in the later 18th century to the research and creative works of Slovene intellectuals (the so-called Zois Circle in Ljubljana). Sigmund Zois was well situated to fund such an endeavor; his father had been a wealthy industrialist from Lombardy in Italy, who married into the Kappus von Pichelstein family. This noble Carniolan clan had owned and operated a profitable iron mine and foundry since medieval times. Sigmund enjoyed a broad education at home and abroad. This included studies in natural science with Gabriel Gruber (1740–1805), an expert in architecture, hydrotechnology, and mechanical engineering. Gruber, who was contracted to build a canal that would minimize urban flooding in Ljubljana, also built a grand mansion that exists today (as the Slovenian National Archive).

Sigmund Zois had wide intellectual interests and, after inheriting his father's fortune in 1777, left business matters up to his family and became a full-time patron of the Slovenian Enlightenment. One of his close collaborators was Balthazar Hacquet (c. 1739–1815), a Carniolan of French background who gained knowledge of human anatomy after serving as an imperial war surgeon. His subsequent work as a professor of anatomy and surgery in Ljubljana introduced Slovenia to new medical knowledge emerging elsewhere in Europe, as well as to chemistry and chemical analysis. Like many other Enlightenment figures, Hacquet had wider interests: he studied the ethnography and languages of the South Slavs, the geology and botany of Carniola, and is also credited as being the first person to explore the Julian Alps.

From the early 1780s, eminent members of the Zois Circle met at the wealthy aristocrat's Ljubljana mansion. Uniting the various subjects that were discussed was a common belief in liberal humanism. Among the luminaries contributing to the Slovenian Enlightenment here were Jesuit priests Jurij Japelj and Blaž Kumerdej, who together published the Bible in Slovene. They based their work on the 16th-century translation of Protestant preachers Jurij Dalmatin and Adam Bohorič (but did not adopt Pohlin's linguistic innovations). Their work established a basis for the standard modern Slovene language. For his part, Kumerdej enjoyed several royal appointments during the reign of Maria Theresa, and later expanded the teaching of Slovene across the country and helped develop its philological basis.

Other leading members of the Zois Circle included Anton Tomaž Linhart (1756–1795), author of the first Slovene-theatrical work (a comedy that was actually an adaptation of an existing German play). Despite being Czech by descent, Linhart notably also wrote the first history of Slovenes as a distinct ethnic group in two German-language volumes. This work prefigured trends in European historiography and politics in the following century. In the area of verse, Valentin Vodnik (1758–1819) was an educator and Zois Circle author renowned as the first Slovene-language poet. He also edited the first Slovenian newspaper, the short-lived *Lublanske novice* (*Ljubljana News*) from 1797 to 1800.

The Enlightenment in Croatia had a somewhat different flavor and geographical center owing to its divided historical fortunes: between an eastern inland that had for centuries been a conflict zone with the Turks, and an Adriatic coastal zone where wealthy cities flourished under the relative protection of the Venetian Republic. Although that polity was defeated in 1797 and finally abolished in 1808, throughout the 18th century the Venetian cities of Dalmatia, which had for centuries enjoyed a high level of development and education, became the natural points of contact with Western European Enlightenment concepts and innovations. Debating societies and colleges were opened, while theater performances in Croatian and Italian were held in coastal cities like Dubrovnik, Zadar, and Rijeka, as well as islands like Hvar and Korčula.

In this light, Dubrovnik enjoyed a natural advantage because it was already well known to Western Europeans as a destination and cultural capital. Indeed, the works of French Enlightenment thinkers like Montesquieu mentioned Dubrovnik, where numerous plays by Molière were translated and performed. The city also inspired Western European authors then beginning a new genre of travel literature; in the contrast between Italian-style aristocracy in the Ragusan Republic and the rugged mountains and traditional villages of the interior, they realized the imagined Jean-Jacques Rousseau's idealized "man in his natural state." Enlightenment travelers like the Venetian Alberto Fortis explored and wrote about the people and landscape Dalmatian coast, while praising the highly cultured nobles of Dubrovnik, comparing the city favorably with Italian cities of the Enlightenment era.

There was a clear connection between these trans-Adriatic neighbors. The children of wealthy Ragusan merchants studied in Venice and Rome (or even Paris), often under the guidance of Jesuit priest-scholars. The most eminent Croatian students sometimes remained abroad permanently, the most significant being Ruđer Josip Bošković (1711–1787), who left the city for Rome after basic education and continued his studies under the Jesuits, eventually becoming a priest in their order. A brilliant mathematician, physicist, and astronomer, Bošković achieved previously unaccomplished scientific feats, such as proving that the Moon has no atmosphere and computing planetary orbits. He was also a forefather of modern atomic theory.

The Croatian Enlightenment fueled a tremendous increase in literary output as well. One of the great contributions to Croatian language and literature during the 18th century was made by native Dalmatian Joakim Stulić (1730–1817), a lexicographer who began work in 1760 on what would be the largest dictionary of the old Croatian dialects ever published. Although it was not published until 1801, his 4,700-page, trilingual (Latin, Italian, and Croatian) dictionary remains an invaluable resource of approximately 80,000 words gleaned from over 100 authors and the oral tradition of daily life and folk tales from Croatia.

In Dubrovnik itself, reactions to the Enlightenment differed. The city was already home to a sophisticated Renaissance literary canon, such as the works of Marin Držić (1508–1567), a rebellious author of lyric poetry, pastorals, and comedies like *Dundo Maroje* (*Uncle Maroje*), still considered classics on a high European standard today. Although Ragusa was a republic, local authorities tended to be conservative, enacting bans and censoring speech from time to time on sensitive issues. Two examples were the 1782 ban on debate over religion, and a ban on theater performances in 1783. Unsurprisingly, the Church-influenced local government was scandalized by the hedonistic poems of young aristocrat Ignjat Đurđević (1675–1737), even expelling him temporarily from the city. His verse, characterized by longing and love, was better received in Venice; however, in 1728, Đurđević published the long romantic poem *Uzdasi Mandaljene pokornice* ("Sighs of Repentant Magdalene"), along with his *Pjesni razlike* ("Various Poems").

A rather more modest poet of the Enlightenment was Franciscan monk Andrija Kačić Miošić (1704–1760) from Makarska on the Adriatic coast. A descendant of a prestigious and long-established Croatian clan, Kačić Miošić penned one of the most popular works of the Enlightenment and National Revival period that followed it, a folk history of the Slavs told in verse, and relying on the (largely imagined) history of them by the 16th-century Ragusan author Mavro Orbini and Pavao Ritter Vitezović. This 1756 work, *Razgovor ugodni naroda slovinskog* ("A Pleasant Conversation of Slavic People"), was a simple yet comprehensive book; Kačić Miočić hoped to spread Enlightenment ideals and national pride, while also raising the literacy rate among the peasantry. This work decisively popularized the Shtokavian dialect, influencing its later selection as the basis for the standard Croatian language.

In his research on Slavic history, Andrija Kačić Miošić had also been influenced by another important Croatian Enlightenment writer, Pavao Ritter Vitezović (1652–1713), who was himself also an admirer of Mavro Orbini and his historical imaginings. Vitezović was born in the Uskok capital of Senj, where his father was a Habsburg soldier; his upbringing in this town famous for its independence and piracy no doubt affected his views as a historian, linguist, and cartographer. Vitezović was also a diplomat who had Senj's interests at the Habsburg court in the turbulent decades preceding the Uskok Wars. He would later also fight for the Austrians against the Ottomans in Croatia.

These affiliations put Vitezović more in the Austrian rather than Italian sphere of Enlightenment activity. Thus, while he studied under the Jesuits in Zagreb and at their Illyrian College in Rome, Vitezović was ultimately influenced by the German historian Johann Weikhard von Valvasor, who he encountered while studying in Slovenia. Vitezović was also German by descent. Nevertheless, he became devoted to the history of the Slavs, who he equated with the Croats. He made the pseudohistorical argument that Croatian territory stretched from the Adriatic to the Black and Baltic Seas; while this argument was made to justify Habsburg expansionism in southeastern Europe, it would later feed into the ultranationalist concept of a "Greater Croatia" encountered in WWII, when a Nazi puppet regime ran the country. In the early 18th century, however, such ethno-nationalist theories were very novel and romanticized concepts.

6

From National Awakening through World War I (1805–1919)

CROATIA AND SLOVENIA IN THE WAKE OF NAPOLEON BONAPARTE (1793–1820)

The Enlightenment of the 18th century, which did so much to stimulate intellectual activity and cultural development in Croatia and Slovenia, also caused significant turbulence for these countries, and indeed, all of Europe and its imperial colonies abroad. While the American Revolution had proved that armed insurrection could in fact lead to a peaceful democratic republic, the subsequent revolution it sparked in France was more explosive.

The combination of ideological ferment and years of resentment against royal privileges by the peasantry led to the famous "storming of the Bastille" by commoners in July 1789, and culminated when King Louis XVI and his wife, Marie Antoinette, were beheaded in January 1793 following the decree of a provisional authority. These turbulent events, which included the establishment of the First French Republic, shook Europe to its core. Monarchs and aristocrats in other countries became increasingly uneasy, lest they suffer the same fate, and other European populations who felt similarly oppressed as the French peasantry began to feel that their own national awakenings could be realized only through new kinds of governance.

However, the Enlightenment that sparked the French Revolution had a darker side; whereas it succeeded in producing a more or less peaceful democracy in the new United States, nestled between a vast ocean on one side and largely unexplored wilderness on the other, the situation in France was fundamentally different, surrounded as it was by other countries with their own independent interests. Even before the death of Louis XVI, the new Republic was at war against Prussia, Austria, Great Britain, and the Dutch Republic in November 1792, causing counterdeclarations of war against France from the Holy Roman Empire, Portugal, and other states.

The French Revolution's violent aftermath presented the perfect opportunity for a strong and autocratic leader to step in and assert control. This man, of course, was the flamboyant would-be ruler of Europe, Napoleon Bonaparte (1769–1821). A military genius who rose quickly in the ranks after 1793, he led numerous historic campaigns against foreign adversaries and became Emperor of France in 1805, ruling until 1814 when allied monarchic forces from around Europe united to defeat him. While France reverted for a time to a status of kingdom, the geopolitical results of Napoleon's military campaigns and his spreading of Enlightenment ideals deeply affected other countries including Slovenia and Croatia, politically, socially, and culturally.

One of the victims of Napoleon's success that directly affected Croatia was the Venetian Republic, already fading by the time of his ascendancy. In 1797, the Adriatic territories became disputed territories as France expanded. The fall of the Venetian Republic occurred in the same year after French invasions of the Italian peninsula and multiple failed Austrian counteroffensives, led from Austria and Slovenia into Italy. The city of Venice was itself driven by different religious and international factions. On 12 May, the Grand Council met for the last time; the doge somberly announced the end of the Venetian Republic from a balcony to a mixed and cheering crowd. Renamed as the "Provisional Municipality," Venice was peacefully annexed and occupied by Napoleon's troops—the first foreign soldiers in Venice's long history to occupy the city.

However, despite the peaceful transfer of power in Venice itself, the extinguished republic's Croatian coastal provinces initially refused to accept the new reality. In Trogir, pro-French locals saw their property attacked and looted by pro-Venetian residents, while the French consul himself was assassinated in Šibenik. In Dalmatian and Istrian ports, whole fleets refused to follow French orders. This led Napoleon (who was more concerned about establishing a French presence in the formerly Venetian islands of Greece's Ionian Sea, bordering the Ottoman Empire) to follow a policy of pragmatism in the upper Adriatic. Thus, he decided to hand these cities to the Austrians. The latter were largely welcomed by the local Croatian inhabitants.

Nevertheless, by 1805, these Croatian territories were retaken by France. In a very interesting and historically significant decision, they became known as the Illyrian Provinces. For thousands of years, these territories had had nothing to do with the ancient Illyrians; this name drew specifically on the historic romanticism cultivated by Croatian, Serbian, and Slovenian intellectual elite of the previous century, who sought (as elsewhere in Europe) to trace their origins to ancient civilizations that had inhabited their territory. Between 1805 and 1813, the future Slovenia was almost entirely included in the Illyrian Provinces despite the fact that little of this land had ever been considered part of the Illyrian civilization in ancient times.

As an autonomous province of the French Empire, the Slovene-inhabited, northernmost part of the Illyrian Provinces existed with its capital at Ljubljana. French rule here was short-lived, but it did lead to a new awareness of Enlightenment values and a desire for new freedoms and reforms, especially among the peasantry, chafing under the age-old Habsburg feudal system. Napoleonic rule introduced into Slovenia concepts such as legal equality, equal taxation, separation of powers between Church and State, and so on. But Napoleon's rule also included compulsory military service, meaning that young Slovene men could be drafted into the French army to join in the emperor's increasingly ambitious campaigns throughout Europe.

As Napoleon's many enemies began to get the upper hand in August 1813, Austria declared war on France. Austrian General Franz Tomassich led his forces into the Illyrian Provinces, restoring all the Slovene-inhabited lands to the Austrian Empire. With Napoleon's final defeat in 1815, the Habsburgs secured the Croatian as well as Slovene lands. Although the Venetians were no longer in the game, a sizable Italian population remained on the coast; they would remain there until WWII. The division of Croatia that ensued followed previous examples of territorial control. While Dalmatia and Istria came under the direct rule of Vienna, capital of the Austrian Empire, inner Croatia and Slavonia (including Zagreb) were from 1816 under the allied Kingdom of Hungary. This arrangement would lead to problems in the decades to follow and had partially historical roots: on the Military Frontier of Slavonia, there was a tendency for Croat and Austrian military men to fraternize in secret societies such as the first Masonic lodges of Croatia that flourished from the 1770s until 1795 when they were banned by the empire. Croatia's historic preference for Austria over Hungary, which had a very singular language and culture, would be significant in influencing alliance formations—from the 18th century through to the current day.

THE NATIONAL AWAKENING IN SLOVENIA (1820–1850)

Buttressed by the newfound weight of Enlightenment values in general and Napoleon's sudden reforms in particular, Slovenes began to look with new eyes on their political and cultural identity and, indeed, their broader Slavic heritage. The concept of a unique Slovene nationality, which had gradually been created through the labors of intellectuals in the Protestant Reformation and Enlightenment of the preceding centuries, began to manifest. The idea of a unique political unification of the Slovenes to match their newfound cultural feelings grew. This was witnessed not only among the intelligentsia; from the 1820s through the 1840s, Slovene songs, literature, and folklore became more popular among all portions of society. Philologists collected folk songs in mountain villages, the way a natural scientist might collect butterflies. This aided the ongoing steps toward a standardization of the Slovene language from its numerous regional dialects.

Most popular of all was the Romanticist poet France Prešeren (1800–1849), who influenced the course of Slovene linguistic and cultural progress in his own lifetime, and who would later be upheld as one of the country's great authors in 20th-century Yugoslavia, with his works now translated into many languages around the world. Despite his short lifespan, Prešeren left a large oeuvre including the first Slovene ballad and a long epic poem; filled with themes of personal melancholy, a homeland tragically oppressed and unrequited love, his poetry had both a personal appeal and national resonance among an increasingly educated populace looking to escape the centuries of subjugation under the Austrian Empire. His stirring descriptions of beautiful places in the Slovene countryside, like Lake Bled, added to a new sense of national pride.

France Prešeren and his work thus played an important role in Slovenian identity formation and, indirectly, in political events. Although he occasionally wrote in German, he was primarily a Slovene writer and—like his Enlightenment-era forerunners—believed strongly in its merits as a world literary language. In this, he was a direct follower of the Enlightenment-era priest and poet Valentin Vodnik, who personally encouraged Prešeren in his writing, and who also had previously pioneered the concept of Slovene as a respectable literary language. This was particularly important as it would lead Slovenians to preserve their own variant of a Slavic language from the (essentially identical) languages now referred to nationalistically as Serbian, Bosnian, Croatian, and Montenegrin.

Prešeren thus disagreed with the proponents of a pan-South Slavic language, an idea supported by some Slovene intellectuals working together with a (much larger) group of Croatian and Serbian linguists. (The latter, often associated with the so-called Illyrian Movement, will be discussed in more detail in the following text.) Indeed, though he was of Carniolan background and identified himself thus, over time the poet embraced a broader Slovene identity—setting an example for other literati to follow, thus helping to shape the national identity.

Another important influence on Prešeren was his friend and literary colleague, Matija Čop (1797–1835), one of the most important Slovene linguists. With knowledge of an astonishing nineteen languages, and frequent updates on the latest developments in Western European literature, he was a valuable contributor to the works of other writers of his time. Like Prešeren, Čop was a strong believer in a Slovene literary language and national identity. After he tragically drowned in the Sava River, Prešeren dedicated his epic poem *Baptism on the Savica* (*Krst pri Savici*) to his deceased friend. The work (still performed today) is notable for the time in its depictions of the proto-Slovene Slavs as victims of violent Christian persecution, introducing readers to ancient Slavic gods and goddesses while depicting the Church in a decidedly unusual light.

THE ILLYRIAN MOVEMENT AND THE CROATIAN NATIONAL AWAKENING (1830s–1860s)

A complex combination of phenomena came together in the first third of the 19th century, leading to the birth of a popular movement, often referred to as Croatia's "National Awakening." In the big picture, this movement was enabled by aspects of preceding movements, such as the linguistic and scholarly perspicacity of the Protestant Reformation, and the fascination with ancient culture and big ideas that had propelled the Enlightenment. When mixed with a sense of romantic nationalism, this movement blossomed and took on political aspects as well; Croat intellectuals were reacting to similar movements in neighboring countries that threatened their own. Thus, the apparent attempts at the Germanization and Magyarization of Croatia, led by forces in Germany, Austria, and Hungary, provided additional urgency for the Croatian thinkers to form a solid national identity in a land where people had previously identified themselves primarily with the region in which they lived.

The common thread that united these thinkers turned out to be something called "the Illyrian Movement," in reference to the ancient Roman province of Illyria and tribal society that had preceded it, partly on the territory of the modern Croatia. Particularly because of the romanticizing aspects of Croatian nationhood and the long-lost Illyrian civilization created by Enlightenment-era intellectuals (including some from Western Europe), Napoleon was inclined to refer to his former Venetian Adriatic lands the "Illyrian Provinces" at the turn of the 19th century. This decision would have formidable consequences as it both gave the Illyrian Movement a tangible geography and a public prominence in the romantic Enlightenment mind—one that was becoming increasingly nationalistic, with political ambitions, in the first third of the century.

Looking back at this movement from the 21st century, understanding the motives and inclinations of these Croatian thinkers may seem a bit mysterious, especially as modern-day Albanians, living well south of Croatia, have now become the main "claimants" of ancient Illyrian heritage. As with all retrospective perceived continuities of past civilizations with modern nations, any ethnic connection between the Illyrians and modern-day Croats, Albanians, Serbs, or others is notoriously difficult to prove. The constant migrations and intermingling of cultures and ethnic groups, as well as the rise and fall of empires and invading forces, made the Balkans a particularly diverse region in Europe. This fact, ironically, reified the nationalistic and political tendencies of all ethnic groups that sought to show their "ethnic purity," from Slovenia in the northwest down to Greece in the southeast.

However, in the 19th century, the Romanticism that developed in Croatia, Slovenia, and elsewhere in the Balkans was not just driven by local populations. In fact, Western European intellectuals sought to get to the source of what, in their view, lay at the basis of modern European values as expressed by 18th-century Enlightenment thinkers. This primarily meant ancient Greece and Rome but also included other civilizations like the Egyptians, Thracians, Illyrians, and others. A famous example of Romanticism driving Western action during the National Awakening period was the British poet Lord Byron, who idealized the ancient Greeks in his works while visiting Greece during its revolution against the Ottomans in the 1820s. When the Greeks proved incapable of governing themselves following the assassination of the first postindependence leader Ioannis Kapodistrias, a bewildered Bavarian King Otto, sent to rule over the formerly Turkish province, was surprised that the Greeks he met did not in any way resemble the heroic ancients of his schooling. While Otto renamed the streets of Athens after famous Classical Greek figures, he also sought to build wide boulevards and orderly neighborhoods in the style of his native Munich.

Western institutions such as the Vatican had used the allure of ancient historic civilizations as a means of identifying and organizing their flock in the Balkans. For example, from the 1600s, the Church operated the so-called Illyrian College in Rome, catering to visiting Catholic scholars of Croatian, Slovenian, and Albanian backgrounds. The early historiography of Croatia and the Balkans, uncritically received and very easily spread, combined legends with truth and partially accurate information together with pure guesswork disguised as authoritative knowledge. The long-term effects of this were major because these early chronicles influenced the developing historiography in both Western Europe and the Balkans, partially driven by Church scholars (Catholic and Orthodox, respectively). The general accumulation of histories—often mutually exclusive and confused—informed the developing differentiation of nation-states. This process would result, eventually, in war along ethnic lines in the 19th and 20th centuries.

However, before that, the Croatian (and Slovenian) national awakenings that were driven by a romantic look back at ancient predecessors such as the Illyrians were curiously guided by an overall uniting principle that brought them in touch with neighboring Serbia, Bosnia, and Montenegro—the homeland of other Yugoslavs (literally, "South Slavs"). The future country known as Yugoslavia that encompassed these countries (and Macedonia) were united, in the minds of Romanticist thinkers, by shared historic kinships but, more demonstrably, by language. The fact that these peoples spoke essentially the same language became a uniting factor for thinkers of the National Awakening period; ironically, it would become an acute point of conflict in the following century, with enduring results for nation-building in the Balkans.

The concept of a Croatian language and culture as separate and distinct from neighboring states, but at the same time inclusive of all the diverse regional characteristics within the country, was promoted in the 1830s, as were the ideas of unique Slovenian and Serbian languages in those countries. Intellectuals such as Ljudevit Gaj (1809–1879) in Zagreb associated with the Illyrian Movement promoted the goal of a common Slavic language reflecting the common identity of the South Slavs, working closely with other Croatian linguists as well as philologists in Slovenia and Serbia.

Gaj's greatest contribution was the creation of a standardized Latin alphabet that adopted it in place either together with or instead of Cyrillic in 1835 (the Croats and Slovenes are the only South Slavic nation in the later camp). Gaj was drawn to the idea by the suggestion of another Croat scholar, the previously cited Pavao Ritter Vitezović. The latter had proposed that the ideal Croatian alphabet should use just one letter for every sound in the language. Gaj took this idea and partially based his new orthography on the Czech alphabet of Protestant reformer Jan Hus. Gaj's alphabet is still used in Bosnia, Croatia, Montenegro, and Serbia (though the latter countries interchangeably use Cyrillic).

In 1850, following years of intellectual cooperation, Croat supporters of the Illyrian Movement realized their goal of a joint linguistic standardization with their neighbors to the east, working with Serbia's most noted linguist, Vuk Stefanović Karadžić (1787–1864) and his supporters. Karadžić also believed in the "one sound for one letter" principle, but applied it to the Serbian Cyrillic alphabet, which differentiated it slightly from other Cyrillic alphabets like Russian, Bulgarian, and Macedonian. Karadžić made great contributions to Serbian literary culture, publishing folk tales, New Testament translations, and the first Serbian dictionary. He agreed with Croat linguists that the southern Shtokavian dialect would become the basis of the Serbo-Croatian language. This result was strongly influenced by the preference for Shtokavian expressed by Croat and Serbian writers of the preceding Enlightenment period. However, a view that would acquire momentous political ramifications in future was Karadžić's contention that all speakers of the unified language were originally Serbs by ethnicity.

Although of a poor and rural background at a time when literacy was low, Karadžić managed to get an education. He was influenced by the tumultuous First Serbian Uprising (1804) against the Ottoman Empire, and the subsequent defeat of the partially liberated Serbia in 1813. In Vienna, Karadžić published Serbian folk songs that won acclaim from French, German, and Russian writers (among others), including Goethe, Grimm, and Pushkin. In Vienna, he would also meet and cooperate with Slovene philologist Jernej Kopitar (1780–1844), who shared his enthusiasm for South Slavic language reform. Kopitar had great influence among the Austrian intelligentsia as he worked for the empire and was able to get support for the Serbo-Croatian project (on the other hand, his ideas were opposed in his native Slovenia, where the idea of a Slovene high literary language championed by Čop and Prešeren in the 1830s). According to a legend, Karadžić admired Kopitar until the literal end, standing over his deathbed in 1844.

In Croatia itself, leading intellectuals like Ljudevit Gaj, father of the Croatian alphabet, began to publish newspapers and journals from the mid-1830s, specifically naming and associating with the grand concept of a shared "Illyria" among the South Slavs. This somewhat odd association had to do with an obsession for unifying regional differences of speech and place, a phenomenon that was common across Europe at the time of national awakenings. Since Croatia lacked deep ancient roots, the idea of Illyria—a concept similar to the more tangible and simple Yugoslavia to come—was the name Gaj and his followers chose. In newspapers with names like *Ilirske narodne* ("Illyrian folk newspapers"), Gaj published mixed texts written in all the dialects of South Slavic languages (including the Venetian-Slavic *Dalmatico* of Dubrovnik and the coastal towns); this was done with the hope of appealing to readers from all over the lands of "Illyria," a semimythical, semiterritorial entity.

Interestingly, some of the most prominent "Croatian" figures in the Illyrian Movement were not actually from Croatia. One such person was Vatroslav Lisinski (1819–1854), a composer born as Ignatius Fuchs into a German-Jewish family. However, he Slavicized his name, became important in the Illyrian Movement, and was renowned for composing the first Croatian-language opera, *Love and Malice* (*Ljubav i zloba*). A similarly unique example was Stanko Vraz (1810–1851), a writer born in Styria with the Austrian name Jakob Frass. He similarly changed his name in keeping with his nationalistic preferences. As the first Croatian professional writer, Vraz wrote original poetry and also collected folk poems from around Slovenia and Croatia, while pioneering the art of the travelogue about his country, and had a particular influence in the Slavonia region of inland Croatia (then under Hungary). Vraz also translated international literature into Croatian, and was well known for his work in Slovene as well. In an example of the movement's neighborly character, his *Illyrian Folk Songs Sung in Styria, Carniola, Carinthia and the Western Part of Hungary* became the first Slovene-language work to be published in Gaj's Latin alphabet.

A moment of interest in the history of the movement, which saw the convergence of the academic and the political, was the so-called Vienna Literary Agreement (*Bečki književni dogovor*) of 1850. It was signed between prominent cooperating (and competing) philologists from the South Slav lands in an attempt to reach an agreement over the different alphabets and dialects they had championed. It was attended by several prominent Croatian scholars, while Vuk Karadžić was the main Serbian signatory. Although it did not bind anyone to follow its conclusions regarding a unified language at the time, it would be referenced in the following century as a historical precedent for the Yugoslav concept of the Serbo-Croatian language that became the official language of that country (and which still is essentially the case today, despite small regional differences).

The Austrian government had a political rather than academic interest in bringing rapprochement to the Slavs living in and beyond its imperial borders; these populations were perceived as both a form of power projection against the Ottomans and a check on the ambitions of other rising nationalist movements (notably, the Hungarian one) that threatened the cohesion of the empire. Thus, in a broad, background sense, it can be said that the concept of Yugoslavism came to be partly from Vienna.

POLITICAL RAMIFICATIONS OF THE ILLYRIAN MOVEMENT ON CROATIA (1832–1878)

By the early 1830s, the enthusiasm that earlier and contemporary scholars had converted into works of popular scholarship and literature had become a political topic of importance, partially in reaction to the attempted "Magyarization" (Hungarian nationalism) of inland Croatia. The prime political voice in this struggle was Janko Drašković (1770–1856), a writer, politician, and veteran of the late-18th-century Austrian-Turkish war, who also had a considerable impact on the cultural infrastructure and involvement of women in the Croatian National Awakening.

Drašković became politically important with his 1832 Croatian-language political treatise, written in reaction to the 1830 official demand to implement the Hungarian language across the Kingdom of Hungary—something opposed by all Slavic peoples. Between the years 1832 and 1836, Drašković presented Croatian at the Diet (parliament) in Pressburg (the German name for the modern-day Bratislava, Slovakia, at the time, part of the Austrian Empire). Along with the rights of the common people, Drašković was representing the interest of a Croatian nobility that felt disenfranchised (as had so often been the case since 1102 state union with Hungary) by the pretensions of Budapest. In this respect, Drašković was serving as a defender of Croatian landed aristocrats. But in doing so, he was able to gain wider political and financial support for developing the cultural infrastructure of the Illyrian Movement in Zagreb and across Slavonia. For example, Drašković's efforts led to the creation of the so-called Illyrian Reading Club in 1838 in Zagreb, and the National Theater in the same city two years later. The "Illyrian Foundation" (*Matica ilirska*) was another cultural center of the movement that he helped to found. It published Croatian literature of earlier generations, self-translating their various dialects into the mutually agreed štokavian dialect of the Illyrian Movement.

Drašković also emphasized the role of women in this movement, who had largely been ignored in earlier periods. In particular, he began by circulating the new cultural and nationalist views among influential women of upper-class backgrounds. Drašković also stressed the importance of developing Croatian national sentiment through education of women and the youth in general. In texts he entreated "the noble-minded daughters of Illyria" and was the driving force behind the creation of a "Society of Female Patriots" in Zagreb. Thus, even if it was done for largely political and pragmatic purposes, these initiatives marked a kind of female emancipation not seen at the time in neighboring Balkan countries to the east and southeast.

In 1840, Drašković's cultural activities became overt with his establishment of the Illyrian Party, which from 1843 would become known simply as the National Party. This was because the nationalistic movement was starting to alarm the Austrians (with, of course, some propagandistic help from the Hungarians). In the same year, Austrian Chancellor Metternich (1773–1859) forbade the use of the name and symbols of Illyria in public. Nevertheless, this edict did not really affect the cultural aspects of the movement, and was perhaps an overreaction: while its views were certainly nationalistic, neither this party nor others in Croatia called for full independence from the empire; rather, they envisioned a power-sharing arrangement with the Hungarians that would limit the Magyarization aspirations of the latter in Croatia.

In 1848, this view was affirmed when Drašković attended a session of the Croatian Sabor, where he called for an independent Croatian government—within, however, a joint parliament with the Hungarian Kingdom. Nevertheless, broader nationalistic stirrings were clear as a year earlier the Sabor had unanimously voted that its working language be changed to Croatian from the traditional (but rather archaic) Latin. At the same time, broader revolutionary activities within the entire Austrian Habsburg Empire were beginning to cause changes that would have profound implications for not only the empire but also for the entire balance of power in Europe.

FROM REVOLUTION TO THE AUSTRO-HUNGARIAN COMPROMISE (1848–1870)

From spring 1848 through November of the following year, the Austrian Empire was rocked by several internal revolutions of various sizes and characters. However, they did not result in a single sweeping revolt such as the American or French revolutions had; to a large extent, this was due to the overwhelming ethnic diversity and mutually exclusive goals of those taking part, as well as their general identity (prominent intellectuals and students rather than well-armed, unified militias).

By 1848, the Austrian Habsburg Empire was home to a diversity of peoples who would later go on to create numerous modern states in central and eastern Europe. These populations included Germans, who increasingly sought a common homeland, and Hungarians, whose new nationalism was bolstered by the historic view of a coequal status in the empire. Of course, the empire also included Slovenes and Croats, groups that included citizens of the former Venetian Republic in Dalmatia, Istria, and the northern Adriatic Slovenian and Italian coastal towns. Austria also included Poles, Czechs, Slovaks, Ukrainians, and those Romanians and Serbs from lands not yet fully liberated from the Turks.

The revolutionary spirit even spread to Slovenia, which the Austrians had always tended to take for granted as something akin to cousins. But in 1848, a significant political and grassroots movement arose, calling for a United Slovenia (*Zedinjena Slovenija*) within the Austrian Empire. Although the Slovene activists did not take up arms, their entreaties for more independence and the unification of all Slovene-speaking lands were a direct result of the Illyrian Movement and the brief Napoleonic occupation a few decades earlier that had introduced Western Enlightenment values.

Due to its larger size and more assertive population, Croatia took on a much bigger role in the revolutionary period. The main Croatian leader at that time was Ban Josip Jelačić von Bužim (1801–1859), a nobleman whose father had served as a field marshal at the Turkish Military Frontier in Slavonia. A well-educated man, Jelačić was also a military commander who also served for Austria on that frontier and steadily rose through the ranks, becoming a major-general and then field marshal. He also played an important role in the defense of Croatian (and imperial) interests, leading a Croatian military expedition into Hungary to help suppress the Hungarian Revolution of 1848. The Austrians allowed the Ban to govern Croatia and Slavonia under the Ban's Council (*Bansko vijeće*). This also allowed for an elected parliament, the Croatian-Slavonian Diet. While the Austrians distrusted the motives of Jelačić—who indeed supported an independent Croatia that would also include Dalmatia and Istria—they recognized that Jelačić was a faithful subject whose government promised unconditional loyalty to Emperor Franz Joseph and the Austrian cause. He was thus a useful counterweight against Hungarian independence movements. Today, Jelačić is considered a Croatian national hero (though his legacy is, of course, less exalted in Hungary and Austria).

Jelačić proved his loyalty by invading Hungary, which had established a breakaway government, in September 1848. Following an initial defeat in the Battle of Pákozd, the Croatian general made a strategic detour to Vienna, where he helped suppress a revolt before returning (with Austrian and other reinforcements) to Hungary, occupying Budapest by January 1849. Jelačić, who by this point had been named general commander of imperial forces, then suffered a series of defeats in spring battles and was ordered by Frank Joseph to recoup and retreat to Slavonia, passing through towns like Osijek, Sremski Karlovci, and Vukovar. However, later in the spring of 1849 he returned to the offensive, along with Austrian troops, winning and losing battles in southern Hungary before finally being recalled to Vienna to discuss plans. He returned to Croatia soon after where he was greeted as a national hero who had saved the country and empire from Hungarian hegemony.

Despite Croatia's substantial contribution toward saving the Austrian Empire, it soon suffered from the side-effects of new restrictions placed on Hungary, where an Austrian was appointed king. Nevertheless, Jelačić supported a new Imperial Constitution in March 1849 that cracked down on anti-Austrian newspapers. In 1851, the autocratic Baron Alexander von Bach was enthroned in the Kingdom of Hungary, and was supported by Jelačić, who despite his Croatian patriotism allowed the gradual Germanization of the country—a process that would have lasting importance in future.

When Bach's absolutist regime fell in 1860, a somewhat larger, though still subservient political entity eventually came into being: the Croatian-Slavonian-Dalmatian Vice-regency Council (*Kraljevsko namjesničko vijeće*) under a Ban based in Zagreb. In politics, the independence movement was taken up by new parties like the Party of Rights (*Stranka prava*), founded by politician Ante Starčević (1823–1896) in 1861. Starčević originally studied languages and theology, but instead of becoming a priest he became a lawyer and then an activist within the Illyrian Movement. He was first elected to the Sabor on the party's nationalist ticket in 1861, and would be re-elected until his death, between intermittent periods in prison, as a supposed enemy of the Austrian regime. He is widely considered a pivotal figure in the development of Croatian nationalism.

Other parties in Croatia included the pan-South-Slavic People's Party (*Narodna stranka*), also known as the Illyrian Party. It was cofounded by Bishop Josip Juraj Strossmayer (1815–1905), a well-educated Catholic churchman who had powerful connections and had served from 1847 to 1859 as the official vicar at the Habsburg court. In Croatia, he also founded the Yugoslav Academy of Sciences and Arts in 1867 and refounded the University of Zagreb seven years later. Although Strossmayer was greatly respected in the Sabor, he was unable to win desired concessions from Hungary in the binational settlement sought in the mid-1860s. His legacy includes the addition of a potent Catholic nationalism that would assert itself frequently in the national consciousness, especially during WWII and the Yugoslav secessionist wars of the 1990s.

The increasingly separatist moves in Croatia, Slovenia, Hungary, and other lands under Habsburg control have to be understood in the context of the gradual ebb of Austrian power under Emperor Franz Joseph's long reign, which finally came to an end with the empire itself, in WWI. For example, Austria was defeated and lost territory in Italy in 1859 during the Second Italian

Bishop Josip Juraj Strossmayer (1815-1905), immortalized in a statue in Croatia, was a pivotal figure during the 19th-century age of National Awakening. In 55 years as a bishop, Strossmayer opened or supported numerous schools, monasteries, and churches and championed education and national development. (Zatletic/Dreamstime.com)

War of Independence. The Austrian defeat in the Austro-Prussian War of 1866 led to the Peace of Prague, which was concluded on Prussian rather than Austrian terms, thus allowing the former to lead the Unification of Germany.

Such losses put increasing pressure on Vienna to accommodate Hungarian demands in a compromise. This occurred in 1867 with the creation of the Austro-Hungarian Empire—the so-called Dual Monarchy.Tensions between Croat and Hungarian nationalists were temporarily alleviated by this decision, though fundamental administrative and legal issues were not solved by a separate binational agreement in 1868. According to this, Hungary would—as in days of old—be responsible for nominating the Ban of Croatia, while Hungary would also receive 55 percent of all tax revenues. Adding insult to injury, Hungary would also gain authority over Croatia's most important Adriatic port, Rijeka. In most other respects, however, the Kingdom of Croatia was made autonomous in internal matters, such as local administration, the church, schooling, and the judiciary.

CROATIA AND SLOVENIA IN THE PREWAR YEARS (1870–1914)

In the decades before WWI, the history of Croatia and Slovenia became affected by new forces from west and east that changed the traditional balance of interests. First, from the west, was a newly unified Italian state that looked with great interest at the formerly Venetian, partially Italian-populated Croatian Adriatic towns. From the east was the growing prominence of Serbia, which had largely driven out the Turks with little external assistance and established a kingdom. Because of the pan-Slavic ideology that earlier academics had supported, the concept of some sort of joint state between the two nations was envisioned by some. However, between them lay mountainous Bosnia, still an Ottoman possession, and home to a Croat minority, Bosnian Muslims (Bosniaks), who had been converted by the Turks in medieval times, as well as large numbers of Serbs. This ethnic diversity would become a source of conflict at several points during the 20th century.

Against this background, some political parties like the People's Party reacted by supporting a more traditional, pro-Hungarian policy. But this led to internal schisms as in 1880 when a breakaway faction created the Independent People's Party (*Neodvisna narodna stranka*). Ban Khuen Hedervary, the Hungarian-appointed local leader of the time, became a target of the increasing tensions in 1903. Two years later, the Independent People's Party united with an influential new political force, the Croat-Serb Coalition (*Hrvatsko-srpska koalicija*). This alliance became the strongest political grouping in the prewar years, working additionally with the Party of Rights, the Independents, and the Radical Party.

The Croat-Serb Coalition became a significant force in Croatia during the late Austro-Hungarian Empire. This was due partly to ideology but also due to its leadership. Like all Croatian parties before it, the coalition did not seek full independence but rather self-rule within the empire for Croats in Croatia-Slavonia and Dalmatia, along with some degree of cooperation with Serbia. The cofounder of this party, Frano Supilo (1870–1917), was among the most skillful and pragmatic of all Croatian politicians; however, his sense of idealism would later be disappointed by a perceived Serbian desire to dominate the party (and future state), relegating the Croats to a secondary status.

Like the nationalistic Party of Rights, Supilo believed in a self-ruling Croatia, but he took a broader and more nuanced view of the concept of pan-Slavism that would feed the idea of the future Yugoslavia, which fundamentally rested on prior activities of the Illyrian Movement. Supilo (who was also a journalist) could influence public opinion across Croatia, which proved valuable for nation-forming against the forces of the old guard. For example, when Austria attempted to cling to its Adriatic possessions through elections (a coalition of the pro-Italian Autonomous Party and Serbian coalition) in the 1880s, he changed public opinion in the key port town of Dubrovnik toward a more Croatian nationalist view. Supilo became particularly active on the coast, working as the Party of Rights' leader in Rijeka and all Dalmatia in 1900, five years after joining that party.

Supilo's somewhat romantic view (but one definitely shared by the intelligentsia) considered Croats, Serbs (and later, Slovenes, too) as three peoples from the general South Slav tribes of old; thus, not three nations, but three components of one Yugoslav nation. Some pan-Slavists also considered Macedonians and Montenegrins as part of this nation. Linguistically, unity was the strongest between Croats, Serbs, Bosnians, and Montenegrins, who basically spoke the same language with regional dialect and differences in accent. This homogeneity was evident not only to intellectuals but also to the common people, as the languages of others in the region—including Turks, Hungarians, Austrians, and Italians—were completely different from one another and from the Slavic languages. These distinctions as evidence of nationalist chauvinism were evident to all of society in some high-visibility situations, as in 1906–1907, when the Hungarians tried to impose their language officially on certain Croatian train lines, sparking a strong reaction from Croats.

These political developments in Croatia and growing unrest generally in Europe's late nation-building period can be understood within a much larger context of events in central and southeastern Europe that affected the Austro-Hungarian (and other) empires. The simplistic and oft-cited explanation for WWI was that an unhinged Bosnian Serb, Gavrilo Princip, shot an Austrian royal, causing Austria to respond militarily. Yet, while there is overtly some truth to this, the assassination of Archduke Franz Ferdinand in 1914 was simply the event that sparked an already flammable situation.

Austria's 1908 annexation of Bosnia-Herzegovina (a former Ottoman possession which it had occupied since 1878) had been a direct provocation to the Kingdom of Serbia, its Russian allies, and the dying Ottoman Empire, which had ruled Bosnia for centuries. However, the Ottoman Empire—then, in a similar state of decline—had been continuously diminished by rebellions and protests in the southern Balkans and Greece for over two decades. In 1908, the internal "Yong Turks" revolution led by Mustafa Kemal, the future Ataturk (founder of the modern Turkish state) was also launched with the aim of creating a reformed and democratic Ottoman Empire. In 1912–1913, the Balkan Wars saw Serbia, Montenegro, Bulgaria, and Greece declare war on the Ottomans. They rapidly seized large amounts of territory from the Turks, which also fueled internal brinksmanship as well as concern from major European powers. Austria's 1914 declaration of war against Serbia was thus an indirect response to Serbia's enlargement and the fear that its Russian allies could, on a separate eastern front, threaten Austria and its German allies.

Adding to this turbulent and fluid situation in the Balkans were the divergent interests of other European powers, such as the British, French, and Russian Empires, as well as Germany, Italy, and the Ottomans. At that time of late imperial Europe, the most powerful countries were still bound by a somewhat antiquated alliance system, which meant that a declaration of war by one power would automatically trigger rival declarations of war. Given the abundance of European colonies on all other continents, such a system could, in the worst case, result in a world war, which is exactly what happened in 1914.

CROATIA AND SLOVENIA DURING WORLD WAR I (1914–1918)

The so-called (rather optimistically) Great War killed over 160 million people between military campaigns and disease, such as a massive influenza outbreak in 1918. The war was fought between two sides: the Triple Entente (Great Britain, France, and the Russian Empire), later referred to as the "Allied Powers," and the Triple Alliance (Germany, Austria-Hungary, and Italy) later known as the "Central Powers." Both sides drew in different, smaller powers ranging from the Turks to the Japanese. The Italians, however, largely stayed out of the larger conflict and later switched sides.

The final result of the war in 1918 saw victory for the former (though Britain lost some territories in part, such as Ireland) and defeat for the latter, with the momentous result of the dissolution after centuries of the Austrian-Habsburg Empire and the Ottoman Empire soon after. These power changes would have direct implications for the future political orientation of Croatia and Slovenia, and indeed for all peoples of the Balkans. World War I is often referred to as the war that ended the European imperial system (though it did not quite do that in all cases). Its major outcomes were the fall of the Russian tsar in the 1917 October Revolution, which led to Communism under the Soviet Socialist Republic, and the entrance of the United States (a late entrant into the war, on the side of the Entente) as a global power. The 1919 Paris Peace Treaty also created the League of Nations, designed to end future wars, which was the direct forerunner to today's United Nations.

The conflict officially began on July 28, 1914, when Austria declared war on Serbia, exactly one month after Gavrilo Princip assassinated Franz Ferdinand, presumptive heir to Franz Joseph, in the Bosnian capital of Sarajevo. In Croatia, the nationalistic Party of Rights expressed their hostility to Serbs and commemorated the assassinated archduke. Vienna responded at first by encouraging anti-Serb riots in Bosnia, Croatia, and Slovenia, forming Bosniak Muslim militias against Serbs, and imprisoning approximately 5,500 prominent Serbs, about half of whom died in jail. Thus, while the initial reaction to Ferdinand's assassination in Vienna itself was one of indifference, the harsh Austrian reaction—and involvement of Croats, Bosniaks, and Slovenes—had a profound effect on the Serbian consciousness and awareness of how imperial forces could manipulate its neighbors against them. (This did not even include Hungary to the north, which had long been an enemy desirous of Serbian territory.) In the end, Austro-Hungarian forces had to impose curfews and intervene as Croat nationalists burned Serb houses and shops and attacked civilians everywhere from Slavonia to Dalmatia. This unprecedented behavior would have ominous ramifications for conflicts to come.

The assassination caused a political crisis when finally Austria issued an unacceptable ultimatum to Serbia. Ultimately, this resulted in the triggering of the alliance system as Serbia called on its allies to defend it. When Austria invaded Serbia, an initial Serbian victory forced the Austrians to withdraw, but only temporarily. The following second invasion was also inconclusive. In fact, it was only with the support of Vienna's faithful Croat and Slovene force, and especially Bulgaria's declaration of war on Serbia on October 12, 1915, that allowed Austria (and Bulgaria in the south) to occupy the Serbian kingdom. This forced the Serbian army to escape southwest in winter, crossing the mountains of Albania amidst snowy conditions and surrounded by hostile brigands.

Nevertheless, the core of the Serbian army made it to the Ionian coast, where they took shelter on the Greek island of Corfu, before being transferred to the northern Aegean city of Thessaloniki, where they spent much of the war along with British, French, and Russian troops in a stalemate situation against the German-allied Bulgarians, who occupied Macedonia and the corridor that led northward to Serbia, Hungary, and Austria. Thus, the day after Bulgaria's capitulation to the Entente on September 29, 1918, fearful leaders in Vienna called for an immediate peace treaty.

For Croats and Slovenes, the war was a traumatic event, in which soldiers were forced to fight on the Italian, Serbian, and Russian fronts. Except for those (like the Party of Rights) who thought that the Austrian Empire was the best guarantor of Croatian semi-independence, conscription to fight against their neighbors—who also composed part of the ruling government—was futile. During the war, Croatia itself was not invaded, but it did experience a military government in which freedoms and dissent were outlawed. Food shortages and (in 1918) an outbreak of influenza added to the difficulties of civilian life.

Croatia was also a victim of foreign intrigue in WWI as Austria thought it could still control Dalmatia as it had long done. At the time, the Serbs and Italians from across the Adriatic also sought this strategic region containing vital ports. Italy switched sides and joined the Entente Allies in 1915 by signing the secret London Pact. This treaty supposedly guaranteed that Italy would be allowed to annex large parts of Dalmatia after the war as a reward for leaving the German-Austrian coalition. The formerly Venetian territory still had notable Italian population; Italy had always considered the Croatian coast part of its "near abroad."

Italy had already seized portions of Albania, which had actually been created for the first time in 1912 by agreement between itself and the Austrians, with blessings from the Vatican. Albania was another component in Italy's near abroad that had strategic value. By November 6, 1918, as the war was winding down, Italian troops seeking to take advantage of the London Pact clause landed in Dalmatia and took several important towns, such as Šibenik. Whatever Croatian resistance existed was ineffective as by the war's end Italy had seized all of the Dalmatian coastal territory allotted by the treaty with the Entente. Admiral Enrico Millo became the self-declared Italian governor of Dalmatia.

All in all, the general experience of the war hardened divisions between the Slavic populations. It increased the Serbian perception that, whereas Serbia had liberated itself from the Ottomans with precious little assistance, the Croats and Slovenes had for centuries been servile vassals of the Austrians and thus not deserving of respect as sovereign peoples. Serbia, which had suffered more casualties per capita than any other country in the war, became the major power in the postwar country known as the Kingdom of Serbs, Croats, and Slovenes (in which Montenegrins, Macedonians, and the then-minority Albanians of Kosovo were also included). The groundwork for this political formation had been laid by the so-called Yugoslav Commission, based in London and endorsed by influential Croat politicians like Supilo, who had fled to England after the 1914 assassination of Franz Ferdinand. This "first Yugoslavia" would survive until WWII.

Because of its general insulation from conflict during the war, Croatian politicians and intellectuals had plenty of time to ponder and argue over what their future state should look like. In the early years, when some hope lingered regarding the Austro-Hungarian Empire's survival, autonomy within a reformed empire was considered. There were also pro-Yugoslavist factions that looked toward a union with Slovenia and Serbia, either within or out of the empire. Some politicians believed that only a unified Croatia consisting of Slavonia, Dalmatia, and the rest of the coast could survive as an independent state.

In the end, despite the considerable anti-Serb sentiment, as seen in the demonstrations of the early part of the war, Croats soon began to take the idea of a state union with the Serbs seriously. This was largely due to their fear of an Italian coastal invasion in winter 1918. Thus, a decree for unification was read out on December 1, 1918. Notably, this occurred without the approval of either the National Council or the parliament. Thus began a new chapter in the country's history: an uncertain entity known as the Kingdom of Serbs, Croats, and Slovenes.

7

The First Yugoslavia and World War II (1918–1945)

FROM THE YUGOSLAV COMMITTEE TO THE KINGDOM OF SERBS, CROATS, AND SLOVENES (1915–1918)

The origins of the 1918 Kingdom of Serbs, Croats, and Slovenes (the first Yugoslavia) are to be found in the complex and violent events of the previous decade. Due to Austria's 1908 Bosnian annexation, the Balkan Wars, and WWI, borders and polities across the region remained in a state of flux. The central Balkan position of Serbia reoriented Croatia and Slovenia, for the first time in centuries, from a worldview shaped by Austria, Italy/Venice, and Hungary. This was very significant in that it drew Slovenia and Croatia away from their "Western" focus and more toward a Balkan one. This was beneficial for the interests of the Allied governments, as perhaps a strong Yugoslav state could serve to check the future ambitions of the Germans and Austrians in the Balkans, a region which the Austro-Hungarian Empire had considered its "near abroad" for centuries.

The long-term effects of this development for Slovenia and Croatia would be a slow process over the 20th century of alternating opportunities to increase control over Balkan affairs and to retract to the countries' traditional Western orientations. Ultimately, the latter would prevail over 19th-century pan-Slavic ideals, and the two countries achieved total independence in the wars of the 1990s. But well before then, in the aftermath of WWI, it still seemed possible (and even preferable) that a pan-Slavic state could come into being. As behind every war lies some amount of covert diplomacy, the origins of Yugoslavia were both characterized by negotiations carried out behind the scenes while the fighting was still ongoing, and by the goals of the Great Powers of Europe.

Some strategic planners in Great Powers such as Britain considered a South Slav polity as a desirable outcome after the war from as early as 1915, the year after the so-called Yugoslav Committee began working from London and Paris. Diaspora figures from Croatia, Slovenia, and Serbia were most enthusiastic about the Yugoslav ideology. Like the revolutions of the Enlightenment a century earlier, however, this ideology was largely orchestrated by a small intellectual and sociopolitical elite, not the majority of local populations. This would be one of the major background reasons for the eventual failure of both the first and second Yugoslav states.

Croat émigrés in the European diasporas were significant in the forming of the Yugoslav Committee, which held its initial meetings in 1914 and became official in April 1915. In fact, Croat intellectuals have been credited with starting the Yugoslav Committee: Frano Supilo (1870–1917), Ivan Meštrović (1883–1962), and Ante Trumbić (1864–1938). Supilo was a journalist and activist whereas the latter two were a politician and sculptor, respectively. (These figures, and especially Meštrović, would have a lasting place in the Croatian national consciousness that remains to this day.) They were all longtime critics of the Austro-Hungarian rule over Croatia. Organizing in 1914 out of Florence, Italy (where Supilo had fled following the outbreak of WWI), they resolved to create a political lobby for the creation of a state in which Slovenes, Croats, and Serbs would be equals, drawing on the similarities of their language and cultures.

Their largely Croat-backed Yugoslav Committee was formally created in April 1915 in Paris. However, the headquarters of the Committee would become London, given Britain's leading role in the Entente forces. Ante Trumbić was chosen as the president. As a lawyer and former mayor of Split, he had considerable diplomatic experience, which would become useful when negotiating with the royalist Serbian government to establish the new country. As of 1915, the Committee was still a small group, comprising less than twenty members. Many of them were from Dalmatia, and had concerns over Italy's desire to seize former Venetian coastal towns and islands with Italian populations. For this reason, they saw a larger Yugoslav state as a protective counterweight to protect their own interests. Thus, a British-orchestrated secret treaty of 1915—which would have political ramifications just a few years later—promised to achieve concessions from Italy to Croatia, if the former would drop out of the war and thus stop its support for Germany and Austria.

As the opposition movement grew stronger and the Austrian-German alliance began to falter, diaspora groups became more important. The Committee formed offices in Switzerland, Russia, the United States, and South America in addition to its bases in London and Paris. It worked together with the United Yugoslav Youth, a group formed in 1914 in Vienna, declared illegal by the Austrian authorities. Although organized originally by Croats, therefore, the Committee and its related diaspora groups all had considerable cooperation and participation of Serb, Bosniak, Montenegrin, and Slovene activists.

The inevitable diversity of interests represented by all these different sides with a single (or, at least, similar) language would tax the ability of Croat negotiators. The most important figure with whom they had to contend was Nikola Pašić (1845–1926), the leader of the People's Radical Party and eight-time prime minister of the Kingdom of Serbia and then Yugoslavia. Influential in Serbian politics and foreign diplomacy for four decades, Pašić was an astute disciple of the school of *realpolitik*, working both with and against the new Yugoslavist movement to preserve the interests of Serbia. The fast-paced, shifting events of the war (such as the Russian Revolution implementing communism in February 1917) constantly shifted the equilibrium in a negotiating process where the Serbian politician-in-exile was at odds with the wishes of the Serbian royal family.

In the end, Nikola Pašić and Ante Trumbić became the main signatories of the so-called Corfu Declaration, by which the first Yugoslav state was envisioned. Signed on July 20, 1917, it was created following several months of discussion (with oversight from British and French representatives) on the Greek island of Corfu, to which the retreating Serbian army had been evacuated during the terrible winter of 1915–1916. The Declaration envisaged a State of Yugoslavia as a parliamentary monarchy under Serbia's Karađorđević dynasty. In addition to then-modern innovations (such as women's right to vote), the Declaration specified equal rights for the three constituent nationalities.

The Corfu nation-builders also specified that equal rights would be given to the different religions, and that the Serbo-Croatian language be coequal in both Latin and Cyrillic scripts.

At the same time, Pašić, in particular, had to take steps behind the scenes to reassure the Allied powers—and the Serbian royal family—that the Yugoslav Committee would not be the official representative of the envisioned state at postwar peace treaties. The controversy surrounding the whole venture led to mutual mistrust and disavowals (Supilo had already left the Committee the year before the signing), which was to be expected given the native rivalries between and within the Serb, Croat, and Slovene political and social structures.

As WWI came to an end, both major populations vied for power. In Zagreb in October 1918, Croatian leaders declared the State of Slovenes, Croats and Serbs. Essentially continuing the previous decades' tendencies toward Croatian nationalism, the unrecognized country essentially comprised Croatia and the Serbs and Slovenes who had lived in it and under the now dissolved Austro-Hungarian Empire. However, the state lasted only thirty-three days before agreeing to join the Kingdom of Serbia in the form of a joint state that the Yugoslav movement had envisioned.

The fatal flaw in this arrangement was the miscalculated balance of power between two large entities (Croatia and Serbia), which both vied for political leadership and an overlapping territory (Bosnia) that had long hosted minorities from both communities, as well as a Muslim Bosniak community left over from Ottoman times. Many Serbs (whether pan-Slavists or not) looked with outright contempt at Slovenians and Croats who had lived out the war under Austro-Hungarian occupation (or even been recruited by them into fighting) while Serbia had been destroyed by the Axis forces, with over 1.1 million soldiers alone killed.

Indeed, the surreal nature of the divergent experiences of the war was exemplified by the "Yugoslav Club" of some prominent Croat and Slovene politicians that met freely during the war, even at the imperial court in Vienna. This was because, as during many previous times in history, Catholic Croats and Slovenes wanted merely to gain more rights within the empire rather than secede from it entirely. Croat politicians like vice-Ban Vinko Krišković negotiated with Austro-Hungarian leaders to try and win concessions—but never to cause undue upset. Following the death of Emperor Franz Joseph in November 1916, some Croat and Slovene politicians proposed the so-called May Declaration, by which the empire would be reorganized on a trilateral basis. This option did not succeed, however. Lacking any experience of having achieved true independence, Croat and Slovene leaders did not have the capacity to imagine it.

As such, there were—even beyond the larger Serbia-Croatia tensions—problematic relations within the Croat and Slovene Yugoslav movements. The May Declaration of 1917 promulgated by Croat politician Anton Korošec and other "Yugoslav Club" members amenable to Austrian rulership was not acceptable to Ante Trumbić and others from the Yugoslav Committee. For Croat and Slovene nationalists who would have preferred continued subservience to Austria rather than a joint state with Serbia and Montenegro (which also included Serbian-occupied Macedonia and Kosovo), the new political reality of December 1918 was a bitter pill to swallow. But the first priority, once the new state had been created, was establishing its new borders. For Croats and Slovenes, this meant particularly dealing with the Italians and Austrians at the subsequent rounds of negotiations that followed.

DRAWING THE BORDERS OF THE NEW STATE (1918–1922)

While border negotiations between the future Yugoslavia and Italy had been underway, secretly and then overtly since 1915, the question of Slovenia and the anticipated borders with Austria was not reached until the very end of the fighting. Despite having traveled and fought in a perilous circle from Serbia to Greece and back again, the Serbian army continued north (with the assistance of Slovene irregulars), taking the war to the Austrians who had originally started the hostilities by invading Serbia. The main region of contention was Lower Styria and Lower Carinthia, inhabited for centuries by both Slovenes and German-Austrians.

Following the Slovenes' November 1918 capture of Maribor and parts of Lower Styria, guerrilla leader Franjo Malgaj continued the fight in Carinthia through June 1919, supported by the Serbian army. They even managed to occupy the city of Klagenfurt (in today's Austria), but were forced to relinquish it due to the terms of the 1919 Treaty of Saint-Germain. A referendum was held elsewhere in southern Carinthia (in October 1920), with most of the population voting to remain in Austria. Yugoslavia did, however, receive Slovene provinces around Dravograd and Guštanj and the Slovene-inhabited Prekmurje region (in the Treaty of Trianon of June 4, 1920). This was notable in particular, as it had been ruled by Hungary for over a millennium at that point.

For Croatia within the new kingdom, the future of the Adriatic coast was of prime interest. The presence of large Italian-speaking populations in many coastal towns and islands was a potential threat, in Croatian thinking, as the Italians could try to claim these areas in the future. While it had already dropped out of the war, Italy did have an interest in what it considered, since Venetian times, as its own "Adriatic near-abroad." Thus, when the end of the war was in sight, in March 1918, Ante Trumbić began negotiations with the Italian representative, Andrea Torre, and signed an agreement that local democratic votes would guide the future borders. Similar to other Croatian coastal populations, most Dalmatians voted to join the Kingdom of Serbs, Croats, and Slovenes.

However, both this backchannel negotiations and the Treaty of Versailles, which officially ended the war on June 28, 1919, ultimately angered Italy because they violated earlier Allied promises. The secret London Pact of 1915, drawn up at a moment when the Allies were keen to find an incentive for Italy to cease its alliance with Germany and Austria, had promised Italy large pieces of Dalmatia, Istria, and Slovenia after the war. Were such terms to be honored, Croats and Slovenes would not be left with much of a state. In the end, the London Pact was declared void at Versailles, in part due to disapproval from the U.S. president Woodrow Wilson. Receiving little support from its French and British allies either, Italy suffered political crisis and public anger at the Treaty of Versailles. This lack of a result directly abetted the rise to power of fascist dictator Benito Mussolini three years later.

To mollify the Italians, the new Yugoslav government sought a compromise with the Treaty of Rapallo, signed on November 12, 1920 in Italy. However, this result would also prove controversial, as almost 500,000 Croats and Slovenes suddenly found themselves living inside the Kingdom of Italy's expanded territory. The prime Italian objective (other than the Dalmatian and Istrian coast) was the narrow northern Adriatic strip of land formerly ruled by Austria, and parts of the Slovenian Alps. In the end, Italy received some of western Carniola, and much of Inner Carniola, along with several other Slovenian municipalities. Italy also received the entire northern Adriatic coast, though it gave back the island of Krk. However, Italy was given the important Dalmatian coastal city of Zadar and the islands of Lastovo and Palagruža. As for the much-coveted coastal city of Rijeka (Fiume in Italian), this Italian-majority settlement was declared a "free city" and shared. Unsurprisingly, these concessions to Italy increased Croat and Slovene suspicions that the central government in Belgrade was not committed to their interests.

This manifested soon enough when important Croat leaders like Ante Trumbić, who had negotiated on Yugoslavia's behalf in Paris, voted against the new 1921 constitution. The renegade parliamentarians, chiefly from Slovenia and Croatia, claimed that the constitution gave Serbia too much power. They protested against the way internal territorial administrative divisions were being devised, regarding these as anomalous with traditional Croatian entities. However, to a large extent the problem again lay in the fact that Croatia had so often been subdivided and the subject of power-sharing before and during the Austro-Hungarian imperial rule. The situation was even more complex in mountainous Bosnia, and the former Turkish military frontier that surrounded it, from Slavonia to Dalmatia. Both Serbs and Croats (not to mention, the Muslim Bosniaks) had large populations in these regions, guaranteeing that no one would be satisfied with any administrative solution. It was in this context that an increasingly tense rivalry between local political parties, involving even assassinations and coups, would begin. Unhelpfully, all European powers unhappy with the Versailles Treaty were quietly rearming in anticipation of the next opportunity to settle scores.

STJEPAN RADIĆ AND NEW POLITICAL EXPRESSION (1921–1928)

The sudden change of political and social orientations for Croats and Slovenes following WWI created a generation of political leaders who were particularly prominent in guiding national interests during the interwar period. In the creation of a joint South Slavic state, one could find not only the idealism of the post-Enlightenment romanticism and the perpetuation of a historic tendency toward maximalist aspirations within a larger political entity, but also new ideologies and issues such as workers' rights, education reform, and overall social betterment.

While various Croatian politicians exemplified each of these, the most important for the latter was Stjepan Radić (1871–1928), the ill-fated leader of Croatia's main political party, the Croatian Peasant Party or HPSS (*Hrvatska seljačka stranka*). Raised in a village near Sisak in the then Kingdom of Croatia-Slavonia (under the Austro-Hungarian Empire), Radić was a charismatic figure who was capable of uniting Croats from the peasantry and working classes to support some of Croat's nationalist goals—while at the same time downplaying the role of the Catholic Church, unlike the more conservative Croatian politicians of the day.

From his student days, Radić made a reputation for himself as a nationalist. He criticized the Hungarian Ban of Croatia during a ceremony commemorating the 300th anniversary of the Battle of Sisak and received a short prison sentence. More dramatically, Radić and fellow students burned the Hungarian flag during the October 1895 visit of Austro-Hungarian Emperor Franz Joseph to Zagreb. While not as significant as the Sarajevo shooting of Franz Joseph's heir in 1914, this symbolic event was a considerable embarrassment for local authorities and Radić was once again imprisoned. He was also expelled from the University of Zagreb, and thus resumed his studies in France after travels in Russia and Prague, graduating in 1899.

This period was characterized by increased Hungarian chauvinism at the level of the Banate, which had effects like the increased indebtedness of the peasant class, manipulated divisions between local Croats and Serbs, and popular distrust of the urban elite. Such results created the conditions for something new—a viable populist movement that catered to both the social complaints of turn-of-the-century Europe and the background nationalist character of previous revolutions. Stjepan Radić, together with his brother Antun, was able to appeal to this voter base through their new Croatian Peasant's Party (created in December 1904). This gave the young activist the opportunity to participate in public life more than as an activist. The party was represented in the Sabor and in 1920, when internal discussions were going on about Croatia's future orientation, Radić played an important role.

Given the options available in Croatia at the time, Radić's agenda was perhaps too complex, especially considering that his voter base was neither well educated nor politically experienced. He supported the peasantry and their right to private property, therefore opposing communism (increasingly so after the Russian Revolution of 1917), though his party was not overly concerned with the urban poor. He was a devout Catholic, but unlike some other parties he denounced the interference of the church in politics. While he championed Croatian nationalism and self-determination, Radić also sought to preserve the rights of Serbs and stood for a nonviolent solution to national problems.

By 1923, his party was Croatia's largest and most influential in the entire kingdom after the Serbian Radical Party. Serbian prime minister Nikola Pašić, and also the autocratic-minded King Alexander, grew increasingly concerned about the Croat party's potential for destabilizing the country as a whole. This suspicion increased after Radić made three well-publicized trips to England, Austria, and the new Soviet Union to highlight the status of Croats in the Kingdom of

Serbs, Croats, and Slovenes. Following his trips (which lasted a full year), Radić was arrested for meeting with communists and imprisoned. While soon freed, he was arrested again in January 1925 after the king declared his party a threat to national security. Predictably, this only increased Radić's popularity, leading to a large electoral majority in the following parliamentary elections. This resulted in the release of Radić and his peers, as well as an unlikely coalition with the rival Serbian Radical Party, and the recognition of the king's authority. However, this power-sharing arrangement ended just over a year later with the death of the elderly Radical Party's leader, Nikola Pašić in December 1926.

Although relegated to the opposition, Radić quickly returned to the national scene by cooperating with a former foe (the representative of Serbs in Croatia, Svetozar Pribićević of the Independent Democrats). Their new coalition was significant in that it unseated the long-dominant Serbian Radical Party. Nevertheless, considerable resentment lingered against Radić for his past acts of filibustering and blocking motions in parliament, which was seen by rival politicians as essentially blocking any legislation.

The new government brought attention back to controversial Croatian interests, such as the 1925 Treaty of Nettuno, which stipulated that Italians be allowed to settle freely in Croatia. This proposition outraged Croats (and especially in Dalmatia and Istria), who considered it a form of colonization by Italian strongman Benito Mussolini. However, by summer 1928, Belgrade's parliament had still not ratified it; when they finally did—by a single vote—tensions were already at boiling point due to the assassination of several Croat politicians in parliament by a Montenegrin member of the Serbian Radical Party, Puniša Račić, on June 20. One of the targets was Radić, who died several weeks later in hospital. Although he had been warned that an assassination attempt was imminent, Radić had decided to continue with his job undeterred. After the melee, Račić walked calmly out of the building. Although he was arrested, his sentence was shortened, angering Croats who already suspected that Račić had been acting on behalf of the king or the government, or at least Serbian nationalist elements.

Historians have long put question marks around Radić and his general role as a moderating force in Croatian politics. Had he not been assassinated, some maintain, the fatal division between Serbs and Croats may have been prevented or at least not allowed to become so extreme. The animosities would finally explode in WWII. Today, Stjepan Radić is considered a national martyr and one of Croatia's most respected historical figures, with schools, streets, squares, and other public spaces named after him across the country, among other commemorative aspects.

KING ALEXANDER'S YUGOSLAV AUTOCRACY AND THE RISE OF CROAT MILITANTISM (1929–1934)

The assassination of Croat parliamentarians, followed by the possibility of Italian resettlement plan by treaty, inflamed tensions between Croatia and the central government in Belgrade. The main actor in shaping subsequent developments was King Alexander Karađorđević (1888–1934). The king had a clear understanding of the situation, but did not make the decisions necessary to gain the results he sought. Early on in the crisis, he told Pribićević that Croatia could be allowed its independence if it meant preserving the rest of Yugoslavia as a whole. The king considered the prospect of a peaceful separation, but for several reasons decided against doing so. Alexander gave the country more time, but the Slovene Catholic priest he had appointed as prime minister in late 1928, Father Anton Korošec, could not stop the internal conflict, such as deadly rioting in Zagreb that accompanied a celebration of the ten-year anniversary of the kingdom in December. In retrospect, cutting Croatia loose at that point might have been the best decision. However, the king chose differently.

On January 6, 1929 (Orthodox Christmas Eve), seeking to restore order and diminish the factionalism and ethnic tensions gripping the country, King Alexander suspended the constitution, dissolved parliament, abolished political parties, and declared an absolute monarchy. He renamed the country as simply "Yugoslavia," hoping to further diminish the internal tribalism that had prevented national unity. While Croats and Slovenes were quick to declare the king's actions as pro-Serbian, many Serbs did not approve of them either. What really angered many Croats were the new internal administrative divisions King Alexander ushered in. He reduced them from thirty-three existing *oblasts* to nine new *banovinas*. Of these, Slovenes were in the majority in only one, the Croats, in two. The Bosniak Muslims were in minority all across Bosnia, while the Macedonians were not acknowledged at all.

Further, the new borders deliberately did not conform to historical ones, and were given topographical or otherwise nonethnic names in keeping with the king's ultimately futile effort to minimize ethnic tensions under a joint "Yugoslav" identity. The king even went so far as to invalidate the use of Serbia's millennium-old Cyrillic alphabet out of a "modernizing" zeal for using the Latin alphabet solely. Due to the widespread opposition all of these innovations incurred, Alexander relented to advice from his French and Czech allies, and agreed to reinstate a revised constitution with political parties allowed. However, the way in which this was done angered many even more (particularly Croats), further inflaming tensions. Ironically, King Alexander even tried to help the peasantry—that cherished electorate of politicians like Stjepan Radić—by preventing the banks from seizing their assets in cases of unpaid loans. But it was too little, too late.

In January 1931, the murder of Croat intellectual Milan Šufflay by Serb nationalists became an international cause célèbre, with the likes of Albert Einstein calling for an investigation. Šufflay went further than many who had simple daily-life gripes with their neighbors by writing works that insinuated Croats and Slovenes were intellectually and morally superior to Serbs and others east of the Drina River, which he located specifically as the dividing line between Western civilization and the exotic East, by invoking the former division of the Roman Empire into western and eastern halves. Notably, during one of his previous arrests for stoking tensions in the 1920s, Šufflay's defense lawyer had been Ante Pavelić, who would go on to become Croatia's most notorious Nazi collaborator in WWII.

By 1932, Yugoslavia was on the edge of civil war, with various terrorist groups active, assassinations and acts of violence pervasive, and general dysfunction. In September of that year, Alexander was disappointed to see his former friend, Ante Trumbić—the first president of the Yugoslav Committee—muse that Croatia would be better off as an independent country, in an interview in England. Calls for ethnic federalization became more widespread. The elder Croatian politician's call became more explicit on November 7, 1932, when he and Radić's successor at the Croat Peasant's Party, Vladko Maček, proclaimed the so-called Zagreb Points, demanding a Yugoslav Federation, if not total independence. This concept was soon copied in similar declarations from Slovenes, Bosniak Muslims, and the Hungarian minority of Serbia's northernmost Vojvodina region.

In the bigger picture, this fractious country was also stuck at that moment by different possible outcomes on the European stage. King Alexander was warned by his French allies in early 1933 that the newly empowered Nazi power in Germany had the potential to be very dangerous—which would certainly prove true—and the king thus sought to formulate alliances that would mitigate any future threat from Germany and Austria. With Serbia's other traditional ally, Russia, lost under communism, Alexander considered making a new Balkan Pact that would include Yugoslavia, Romania, Greece, and Turkey. However, nothing serious came of it, and stoking internal instability became increasingly tempting for foreign powers, such as Mussolini's fascist government in Italy.

Indeed, the Italians upped their support for breakaway terrorist groups in Croatia due to their own territorial pretensions in the eastern Adriatic. The major entity they supported was the Ustaše, an ultra-nationalist terrorist group that carried out assassinations and sabotage attacks in their quest for Croatian independence. Italy provided weapons and logistical support for the group's actions, such as the Velebit Uprising in November 1932, which served to increase support for a violent resolution to the national question among the peasantry. King Alexander was quite aware that foreign powers supported Croat irredentism and frankly told Mussolini, through an intermediary, that the only way to destabilize Yugoslavia would be by assassinating him.

That is precisely what happened on October 9, 1934, when King Alexander and French foreign minister Louis Barthou were shot while riding in a motorcade in Marseille, France. They were killed by Vlado Chernozemski, a Bulgarian agent of the Internal Macedonian Revolutionary Organization (VMRO), a semisecret militant group that had operated since the 1890s seeking to secure Macedonian independence. The murder of the Serbian king and French foreign minister was also significant for being one of the first assassinations ever captured on film. The VMRO had worked on the plot, partly in Hungary, with support from their Croatian confreres, now led by former lawyer Ante Pavelić. Ironically, the assassinations occurred on a state visit after which the French government would ideally pressure Mussolini into stopping his support for Croatian separatists.

NATIONALIST ORGANIZATIONS, GREAT POWERS, AND THE ROAD TO WORLD WAR II (1934–1941)

Much of the political disturbances and militant activities associated with them derived from the larger Balkan context of the prior century's revolts against the belated Ottoman Empire. All the groups that were involved with assassinations, terrorism, infrastructure disruption, ideological dissemination, and so on were very similar in most areas of the first Yugoslavia and beyond.

For example, the legacy of broad social infiltration (at first, secret) of the public sector, the military, private business, and cultural associations for nationalist goals went back at least to Greece's late-18th-century Philiki Etaireia (Society of Friends), a quasi-Masonic

Enlightenment-era militant group that started the Greek war of independence against the Turks (1821–1829) under the slogan "freedom or death." The slogan was picked up primarily by Orthodox nations (the Greeks, Bulgarians, and Macedonians in the 19th century, and by the Serb Chetniks in the early 20th century). Catholic Balkan nationalists tended to have different insignia and mottos, as will be seen. But they did have from the beginning a tendency toward secret fraternization, too; for example, Croat military officers of the 1770s–1780s stationed on the Ottoman Military Frontier (and more widely in Slavonia) participated in short-lived Masonic lodges, along with mostly Austrian military officers. The tendency toward nationalist development based on relationships with Great Powers alliances and "sponsoring" states can be seen everywhere from diaspora agitators for Croatian independence in the United States to the use of former ruling terrain for the planning of assassinations (as, for example, Hungary, where the Bulgarian and Croats trained for the assassination of the Serbian king in 1934).

Ironically enough, the ill-fated king (and his dynasty) had only been empowered due to a secret, military-sponsored spate of assassinations in 1903 that had ended the then-ruling, pro-Austrian Obradović dynasty. The dynastic change from a pro-Austrian to a pro-Russian and pro-French one was one of the main background drivers for WWI, though it is frequently forgotten considering the rather more colorful event of Franz Ferdinand's assassination at the hand of Gavrilo Princip—a member of a nationalist youth movement called "Young Bosnia" and the mysterious "Black Hand" secret society of anti-Austrian Serb nationalists. The case of Puniša Račić exemplifies the kind of character in the Balkans of the time. This Montenegrin parliamentarian famous for assassinating Stjepan Radić in 1928 had been a longtime member of the Serb nationalist group, which had branches across Yugoslavia and which provided everything from social and cultural activities to arming militias, engaging in battles with Bulgarians in Macedonia, Albanians in Kosovo, and rivals in Croatia and Bosnia, where they claimed to be supporting the Serb population from the rival ethnic groups and authorities perceived as a threat to local Serbs.

While the Chetniks were closest with the Serbian Radical Party and the royal dynasty, the Ustaše was the most significant Croat organization, having some overlap with supporters of the Party of Rights. They derived from this long tradition of Croat nationalism, first against the Hungarians and Austrians, then against the Serbs, but were particularly stirred to action by the assassination of Stjepan Radić in summer 1928. Nationalist anger over the shooting helped the group attain critical mass, so that when King Alexander declared monarchical rule in January 1929, the Ustaše were officially formed under Ante Pavelić. The name of the group derived from the Croatian word *ustati*, meaning "rise up." The word also had military connotations, having been used as part of a rank title in the late Habsburg Imperial Croatian Home Guard, and in German-allied units in WWI.

By April 1931, the group was known in full as the *Ustaša—Hrvatska revolucionarna organizacija* or UHRO (Ustaša—Croatian Revolutionary Organization). Two years later, it became known as the *Ustaša—Hrvatski revolucionarni pokret* (Ustaša—Croatian Revolutionary Movement). For historians and generally, the organization is referred to variously as Ustaša, Ustaše, Ustasha, Ustashe, and so on.

The Ustaše remains more controversial than any other Yugoslav paramilitary and ideological group from the wartime period because of its Nazi ideologies of racial superiority, fascist practices and alliance with Hitler and Mussolini during the war, and murder of hundreds of thousands of Serbs, Jews, Roma (gypsies), and anti-fascist Croats. The Ustaše was also heavily supported by the Vatican and rabidly pro-Catholic, weaponizing the chauvinistic anti-Orthodox views of Croatian intellectuals against their neighbors to the east. The legacy of the group's activities is still alive and remains a political issue in Croatia and abroad. As will be discussed further below, both the Ustaše's practices of rule (in the so-called Independent State of Croatia, a puppet regime of Nazi Germany) and of postwar escape (fleeing and rejoining forces in South America, aided by the Catholic Church) constitute the darkest chapter in the country's history.

In Slovenia, by contrast, the resistance movements of the mid-1930s were rather mild. This was partly because the postwar treaties, and Mussolini's later anti-Slovene activities, had dramatically reduced the country's size and population, and therefore its ability to launch any meaningful opposition. Between Austria and Italy, much of the historic Slovene lands had been annexed, with roughly one-quarter of ethnic Slovenes finding themselves within these countries by the mid-1930s. Additionally, it can be said that the Slovenes' historically risk-averse prudence, something that separated them from for their Balkan countrymen, also convinced many that resistance would be futile. Thus, no major uprisings occurred in Slovenia until WWII. Further, during the decade preceding it, Slovenia was Yugoslavia's richest and most industrialized region, even boasting a nascent tourism industry around picturesque destinations like Lake Bled.

Nevertheless, in the Slovene-populated areas under the control of fascist Italy, conflict (ongoing since 1918) continued into the prewar years. Italian dictator Benito Mussolini had made no secret that he viewed the Slovenes and other Slavic peoples as an "inferior" race; he regarded the Slovenian-populated north Adriatic littoral as a hindrance to his quixotic dream of a restored Roman Empire. After Italy's military occupation of coastal areas, and then the Treaty of Rapallo in 1922, low-level conflict began as Mussolini launched an Italianization program on Slovenes in the education and cultural realms. This occurred not only in Slovene-populated areas of modern-day Italy but also in ones that were recovered after 1945 and remain today in Slovenia, such as Idrija, Ajdovščina, Vipava, Kanal, Postojna, and Pivka. For the Italians, the arching northern Adriatic coastal route—a crucial transport corridor and center of urban life since antiquity—was important, not only for nationalist nostalgia but also because control of it would connect their forces directly with the bigger prize—the formerly Austrian- and Venetian-controlled coastal cities of Croatian Istria and Dalmatia.

Tensions were considerable from 1918 in places like Trieste, the key coastal city with a large Slovene population. It became a prime target of the Italian Black Shirt fascist groups, who burned the Slovene *Narodni Dom* (National House), eventually forcing many to relocate to the other side of the border. Printed orders from the Italian authorities prohibiting the use of the "Slav language" sparked anger, as did the proliferation of fascist ideologies and police repression. By the late 1920s, official Italian policy went so far as to ban families from naming their children with Slovene or Croat names as well as marking the tombstones of their deceased with their original names. Needless to say, by that point the use of the Croatian and Slovene languages in areas under Italian control had already been banned in everything from newspapers and public transport to politics and the courts.

While there were no resistance movements or secret organizations in Slovenia comparable with those in Croatia, Serbia, or other Balkan states, resistance elements did exist in the 1920s and 1930s, acting chiefly around the hotly disputed areas like Trieste and the littoral. Clashes were frequent, with the Italian authorities and fascist street groups vying with Slovene informal groups. The best-known was the militant anti-fascist TIGR (an acronym for the Slovene-populated regions of Trst/Trieste, Istra/Istria, Gorica, and Reka). This guerrilla movement, in full known as the Revolutionary Organization of the Julian March—TIGR (*Revolucionarna organizacija Julijske krajine*), remained active throughout the 1930s and into WWII. Although numerically less significant than other Yugoslav movements, TIGR is considered to have been one of the first anti-fascist organizations in interwar Europe.

By the late 1920s, the TIGR mainly consisted of nationalist Slovene, and some Istrian Croat youth supported discreetly by the Yugoslav military and outside powers like Great Britain, which sought to check Mussolini's Adriatic ambitions. The members mainly came from Trieste and its surroundings, the Karst Plateau, Inner Carniola, and the Tolmin region, as well as Croatian Istria. The two main aims of the group were propagandizing and education (carried out in regions like Gorizia) and direct confrontation with the Italian authorities in the border areas, Trieste, and police and military zones. In the former locale, TIGR's alliance took on a nationalist-religious tone as it worked with the secret Catholic network around Christian Socialist conspirators like Janko Kralj (1898–1944), a lawyer and center-right political activist, and Catholic priest Virgil Šček (1889–1948). The latter branch of TIGR was soon carrying out attacks on individual members or supporters of Italy's National Fascist Party, while assassinating a small number of border guards, police, military personnel, and occasionally civilians—as with the 1930 firebombing of a fascist newspaper's office in Trieste. Inevitably, these attacks sparked further reprisals from the Italian police and kept the cycle of animosities continuing.

The last and most important group for future developments was the Yugoslav Communists. Just as nationalist groups like the Ustaše in Croatia paralleled the concomitant rise of fascist political parties and groups like the Nazis in Germany and Fascists in Italy, the Yugoslav Communist Party—officially banned since the end of WWI—was part of an ideologically opposite movement that increased in popularity partly in reaction to the Great Depression of the 1930s, and partially as an antidote to the kinds of mutually exclusive nationalist platforms put forth by their rivals. The communists were also fiercely antimonarchical, a position which made them clear enemies of the Serbian royal family and government. Hence, its main congresses and many of its activities were conducted elsewhere in Europe.

Although it was out of power during the 1920s and 1930s, the Communist Party was keen on gaining it, struggling only with the chronic question of whether Yugoslavia should remain a unitary state, a federation, or dissolve into independent countries. Numerous contradicting and dissenting views led to repeated upheaval, expulsions, and course changes. Further, the party's decisions had to be approved by Moscow (through the Comintern, the Soviet organization for interaction with international communist parties and states). This factor brought yet another great power into the equation regarding the future of

Yugoslavia. In truth, however, throughout the 1920s the Soviets often viewed Yugoslavia as impossible to salvage as a single entity for the purposes of communist revolution, due to the difficulty of reconciling the different ethnic and religious factions in the country, not to mention bringing them to support an ideology with which they had no previous experience.

This was evidenced in 1929 when Yugoslavia's exiled Communist Party leadership encouraged peasants to start an uprising after King Alexander's declaration of an absolute monarchy in January 1929. The call received a tepid response and only resulted in the killings or arrest of the party's main leaders within Yugoslavia, and the dismantling of its party structure. However, after the king's assassination in 1934, conditions improved for the party, and a reconciled objective with the Comintern, which also allowed for cooperation with a broader base of leftist groups, led to a tenfold increase in party membership by 1935. Most importantly, the Yugoslav Communists and the Soviet Union also agreed that Yugoslavia should remain a unitary state, albeit a federative one without a king, ruled instead by Soviet-style communist dogma. To be successful, the Communists needed the right kind of leader.

JOSIP BROZ TITO AND THE ASCENT OF THE PARTISANS (1921–1934)

The party received that leader in the form of Josip Broz (1892–1980), commonly known by his nickname, "Tito." He would go on to become the single most important person in Yugoslav history, and indeed one of the world's most remarkable statesmen of the 20th century. This larger-than-life figure seemed to live a life of nonstop action, adventure, and danger. Numerous legends of his life (some spread by Tito himself) would sustain a cult of personality that outlasted his death in 1980. To win the opportunity to achieve such a stature, Tito first had to guide his Communist militant group (the Partisans) to a successful resistance against both foreign enemies (the Nazis and Italians) and domestic rivals (chiefly, the Ustaše and Chetniks) in WWII. While Tito's activities and legacy will be discussed further below and in the next chapter, some background is necessary to understand this remarkable figure and his role in the context of his time.

Son of a Croat father and Slovene mother, Broz was born in Kumrovec, a village in the Zagorje region north of Zagreb, during the late Austro-Hungarian Empire. When WWI broke out, he was drafted into the Austrian army. While Broz quickly ascended in the ranks, he was

soon wounded in battle and taken prisoner by the Imperial Russian Army. Taken back to Russia, where he was assigned to a labor camp, Broz got a firsthand view of the February 1917 Russian Revolution, even taking part in some internecine struggles after somehow being "converted" to Communism.

After the war, the young Croat returned to Yugoslavia by way of Vienna, accompanied by his new (and pregnant) Russian bride, Pelagiya Bolousova. He joined the newly established Communist Party, which fared well in the 1920 election, gaining the third-most votes. However, the party was prohibited when one of its members, Alija Alijagić, assassinated the interior minister, Milorad Drašković, on August 2, 1921—another example of how Balkan political movements across borders were, with little exception, characterized by violence during the period.

Josip Broz (1892-1980), known better by his adopted nickname "Tito," began his career as a communist conspirator and culminated it as a WWII resistance leader and international statesman as president of communist Yugoslavia. Of mixed Croat-Slovene origins, Tito was a towering figure in 20th-century world politics, rebuilding a war-ravaged country and making it a leader of the Non-Aligned Movement, putting Yugoslavia in a uniquely influential position between East and West during the Cold War. (Library of Congress)

The ensuing government crackdown on communists meant that Josip Broz and his comrades often used multiple code names and monikers. He used several, by 1938, settling on "Tito" exclusively. This was his favorite nickname because (as he would state later in life) it was common in his native Zagorje region, and because several famous Croats from earlier times had also been named Tito (ultimately, a derivation of the ancient Christian Saint Titus). Tito was trained in mill work and engineering, but lost his job due to his political activism. In 1925, he relocated to the Croatian coastal town of Kraljevica, where he got work at a shipyard; this provided gainful employment for Tito and his wife, as well as further opportunities to introduce his fellow workers to communist ideology. Tito continued losing jobs as his agitation among metalworkers and others in the labor unions continued, eventually leading to his arrest in 1927. However, while awaiting trial, the party ordered Tito to go incognito and continue his propagandizing among the labor class.

During this period, he also showed nascent political skills, for example, in a February 1928 party meeting, Tito was able to elevate his own status in Zagreb while condemning factionalism and nationalism, and winning support from Moscow to approve personnel changes with the party's national leadership. However, the fiery activist could not stay out of trouble for long and was arrested in November 1928. With his wife choosing to leave him along with his son and return to Russia, Tito devoted himself completely to the revolution. In prison, he met a fellow communist (the Serbian Jew Moša Pijade, who helped spread the prohibited political doctrine among the other prisoners). Tito remained in jail until May 1934 and was placed under heavy police surveillance thereafter. By the time he had left his hometown of Kumrovec for Zagreb, the aspiring revolutionary found that much of the party's central committee had fled to Austria due to political persecution. He successfully escaped across the border to Vienna. However, he was soon ordered by Communist Party superiors to turn back to Slovenia, where he was to participate in a secret party conference in Ljubljana; there Tito first met Edvard Kardelj (1910–1979), a young Slovene communist who would go on to become a close friend and collaborator in postwar Yugoslavia.

Tito's ascent to the leadership of the Yugoslav Communist Party was aided by King Alexander's crackdown on the party as it led to the deaths of most of the higher leadership within the country. Therefore, when King Alexander was assassinated in Marseilles on October 9, 1934, the exiled party central committee determined that Tito should return to Vienna, which he did by traveling on one of his many forged passports. However, as the Austrian government opposed communism, Tito and his comrades relocated to Czechoslovakia.

He was soon promoted within the party by its Soviet leadership, the Politburo, and dispatched to Moscow to inform the Soviet government about revolutionary activities underway in Yugoslavia. It was at this time that Tito began to make important connections among the most influential representatives of the world communist movement.

He was selected by the Soviets as an official of the Comintern, and given a leadership role for the dissemination of communist ideologies in the Balkans, along with other Yugoslav Comintern officials already in Moscow, such as his friend Kardelj, the party's secretary-in-exile Milan Gorkić, Vladimir Ćopić, and the Bulgarian communist leader Georgi Dimitrov. Tito expanded his international party contacts at this time, while speaking at events on topics like trade unions, studying military tactics with Soviet military instructors, and traveling widely across the Soviet Union.

In Moscow, Tito even found time to remarry, falling in love with an Austrian communist, Johanna Koenig (known among the activists as Lucia Bauer). Luckily for Tito, he was soon sent back to Western Europe to recruit volunteers for anti-fascist causes like the Spanish Civil War, right at the time when the notorious Soviet secret service, the NKVD, was carrying out internal purges of many international party branches; several prominent Yugoslav Communists like the thirty-three-year-old Gorkić were killed by the Soviets. This episode revealed Tito's cutthroat nature as he himself is believed to be the one who informed the NKVD that Gorkić could not be trusted. Just as the purges allowed Soviet leader Joseph Stalin to eliminate any threat to his overall rule, the death of Gorkić helped Tito take control of the Yugoslav Communist Party for himself.

WWII: THE INDEPENDENT STATE OF CROATIA AND THE PARTISAN VICTORY (1941–1945)

All of this activity and direct support from the Soviet Union would make Tito's Partisans the most effective and ultimately the victorious resistance movement in the impending war with Nazi Germany. The Yugoslav government, which had been trying to stay neutral due to the country's precarious position, was forced to sign a treaty of alliance with Germany in early 1941. However, a British-supported military coup d'état soon reversed that decision, giving Hitler a pretext to declare war and thus help his Italian allies, who had already launched Balkan operations against Albania and Greece. Thus on April 6, 1941, Nazi Germany invaded Yugoslavia, defeating the country's army within ten days. The attacks included an aerial bombing of Belgrade, which left 20,000 dead. Hitler's Hungarian, Italian, and Bulgarian allies were quick to sweep in from the north, northwest, and southeast, carving the country into pieces quite similar to the WWI occupation.

The few scattered resistance groups were divided between the ideas of fighting the occupiers to restore a united Yugoslavia, or to ethnically divide it into independent states. This ultimately worked in the favor of Tito's communists, as they were the only ones seeking to preserve a unitary state while presenting an ideology that was not seen as excluding different ethnicities. The controversial royalist government, and its military, had been considered to be dominated by Serbs and Serbian interests, which was one of the factors that ultimately led the Allied powers to give up support for the Serbian Chetniks, which scaled back their operations after savage German reprisals against civilian populations made that resistance futile. This left only Tito's Partisans as a main hope for defeating the Axis in Yugoslavia.

Nevertheless, Hitler was easily able to invade the failing country and quickly established puppet regimes, such as the Independent State of Croatia, often referred to by its Croatian-language abbreviation, NDH (*Nezavisna Država Hrvatska*). Led by the fascist Ustaše "Supreme Leader" *Poglavnik*, Ante Pavelić, the NDH was the site of some of the worst atrocities of WWII. Over 100,000 Serbs, Jews, Roma, and anti-fascist Croats died in twenty-two concentration camps on the territory, most infamously, Jasenovac, where the degree of torture horrified even the German Nazis themselves. The NDH was announced on April 10, 1941 by Slavko Kvaternik, deputy leader of the Ustaše, while awaiting Pavelić's return from Italy.

Ante Pavelić (1889–1959), who could generously be described as a sociopath, had long dreamed of an independent Croatia along the lines of racial purity. He became increasingly radical in his political activities after 1929 to the point that he was forced to leave Yugoslavia. He was warmly welcomed by Mussolini in Italy, where he established the Ustaše in 1930. Pavelić expanded support for a fascist-supported overthrow of the Yugoslav government, and helped organize the assassination of Yugoslav King Alexander in 1934. His admiration for Adolf Hitler combined elements of ethnic chauvinism and nationalist "purity," with the added dimensions of a fierce Croatian Roman Catholic identity and anti-Serb outlook. Pavelić and his Ustaše collaborators were also notable for their anti-Semitic views.

Backed by German troops who annexed northern Slovenia, and Italian troops who invaded the Adriatic coast, the ultranationalist dream of a "Greater Croatia" was briefly achieved. At its height, the NDH included most of modern-day Croatia and Bosnia, parts of modern-day Serbia and Slovenia, as well as Croat-inhabited parts of Dalmatia, Istria, and Međimurje. Repeating the historical pattern, Croatia enjoyed independence within a dependence on a larger imperial structure. This led to the predictable excesses of authoritarianism and chauvinism characteristic of puppet states. *Poglavnik* Pavelić was quick to please Hitler; just weeks after the NDH's establishment on April 10, 1941, his government proclaimed a sweeping series of laws that banned any anti-NDH activities, removed all nonsympathizers from the civil service, and forbade some Jewish commercial activities. Pavelić's decrees were made in the context of Hitler's Aryan racial purity ideology. By late May, all Jews in the NDH were ordered to wear yellow identification badges; one month later, Pavelić decreed that Jews be sent to concentration camps such as Jasenovac. However, with his most hated population being the Serbs, Pavelić also gave Jews and others the opportunity to convert to Catholicism and fight for the NDH.

The NDH lasted for only four tumultuous years, but would fight until the end, getting supplies from Germany until the last months of the war with new aircraft. The major reason for its failure—aside from terrorizing all of its minority populations—was the fact that it never had the manpower or means to effectively control its suddenly enlarged territory. At the war's beginning, the Ustaše had only 12,000 members. The government's somewhat humiliating treaty terms with Mussolini (which involved the supreme leadership of an Italian king of Croatia, who never stepped foot in the country) included limiting their naval and military capacities while preventing the NDH from having naval control over its coast. (This changed after Italy capitulated in late 1943.) Further, the NDH's racial purity laws that had thinned the ranks of the civil service meant that important administrative functions were taken over by Ustaše members lacking any competence to execute their functions.

The inability of the Croat fascist authorities to achieve a seamless transition to a pacified independent state was also due to constant gamesmanship and the diverging goals of Mussolini, who sought to annex the Adriatic coast, and Hitler, who wanted to quickly put down resistance in the Balkans to free up troops for his anticipated invasion of the Soviet Union. Hungary, which also sought to recover its historic hegemony over Croatia, was another factor on the Axis side that caused concern. In this vacuum, the Ustaše carried out systematic torture and murders of mainly Serbian civilians on NDH territory, with the goal of eliminating the historic Serb populations from Croatia and Bosnia. Pavelić was taking the advice of Hitler on how to guarantee that an ethnically pure Croatian state should best be achieved. The plan also saw the forced deportation of many Croatian Serbs to Serbia.

The excesses of the NDH, initially not well known outside of Yugoslavia, were attested not only by Nazis, but the atrocities sanctioned by Pavelić and his commanders also irritated Hitler because they resulted in increased support for the Partisans and other resistance groups, which meant that German troops were bogged down in Croatia—which itself could not supply soldiers, as had been planned, for the eastern campaign. Thus, in September 1942, Hitler requested Pavelić join him for a meeting after which the Ustaše's most zealous lieutenant, Eugen Kvaternik, was replaced by the slightly more moderate Jure Francetić. Although Kvaternik and his family were relocated to Slovakia, the same pattern of repression continued in the NDH throughout the war.

The conduct of the Axis war in Yugoslavia was hindered by both the weak capacities of the Italians and Ustaše forces and by geography. In 1941 and early 1942, the German-led forces overseeing the NDH army sought a quick victory over the Partisans by encirclement. However, Tito's forces were able to escape both times and regroup, aided by the mountainous and difficult fighting terrain of the region—Bosnia, Sandjak (a region in Serbia), and Montenegro—in which they operated. Thereafter, the Partisans tended to avoid large-scale battles in favor of guerrilla tactics. The presence of Spanish Civil War veterans on the communist side aided in this, as did the technical background of Tito and his colleagues, which helped the insurgents to hinder the occupying forces by blowing up bridges, downing communications lines, and otherwise disrupting the logistical systems upon which their armies relied. The Partisans were able to "liberate" large areas of territory, allowing supply drops and the infiltration of Allied intelligence officers.

The Partisans' visible resistance activity and ability to spread ethnically inclusive communist rhetoric in the territory they controlled rapidly increased public support for their cause. This and their (relatively greater, compared to the Chetniks) battlefield sacrifices at confrontations with the Germans like the 1943 Battle of Neretva and Battle of the Sutjeska allowed Tito to present his group as the only long legitimate opposition force. When Mussolini was overthrown and Italy bowed out of the war in September 1943, the Adriatic zones Italy had controlled were divided between German and NDH control. However, despite the Ustaše's control of the Croatian state, the majority of Partisan members by that time were already Croats and Slovenes by background. WWII in Yugoslavia was, thus, very much a series of fratricidal conflicts within a world war.

Tito won Allied diplomatic support at the December 1943 Tehran Conference, at which Churchill, Stalin, and Roosevelt agreed to back the Partisans in Yugoslavia. The larger goal of promoting anti-Nazi resistance in Yugoslavia was meant to distract German troops from their Eastern Front with the Soviet Union, and from France, where the Allies were planning to land the following spring, in what would be the June 1944 Normandy Landings (D-Day). The Partisans continued to distract Germany with guerrilla raids into spring of that year when Hitler unsuccessfully tried to have Tito assassinated in his encampment in the Bosnian mountain town of Drvar during a fierce air and land battle in late May.

At the same time, Allied air forces finally began to engage the Croat and German ones, making it almost impossible for the latter to harass the Partisans from the air as they had been doing since the occupation began. This allowed Tito's forces to liberate ever larger stretches of territory and increase the number of civilians supporting their cause. In total, some 800,000 men and women joined the Partisan ranks in units stretching from Slovenia to Macedonia, making Tito's army the largest and most successful of all anti-Nazi resistance groups in Europe during WWII.

With the likelihood of a Partisan victory growing, the exiled Serbian royal family called on Yugoslavs to accept Tito as their leader in fall 1944, even as Romania and Bulgaria switched sides against the Germans. These developments allowed the Partisans, with Allied help, to liberate Belgrade in October 1944. By year's end, they controlled much of Yugoslavia, with the exception of parts of Serbia, Bosnia, and the Independent State of Croatia, from which German divisions hoped to leave as soon as possible. But to broaden his appeal, Tito promised amnesties to all Yugoslavs who would join his side, including Chetniks and Ustaše, a pragmatic move that would not always be honored later on.

However, as the war began to wind down and the realities of a postconflict reconciliation set in, many questions were still left unanswered. The Allies had recognized Tito as the legitimate ruler of a unified Yugoslav state—though what sort of state it would be and where its precise borders would extend both remained to be determined. As a man of Croat-Slovene ancestry, Tito had a personal connection with these territories, which affected his cumulative decision-making for the newly unified Partisans of all Yugoslavia. Tito was determined to take back Trieste (and as much of Slovenia as possible) from the Italians, which had repercussions for others in his ranks. For example, some Macedonian Partisans who protested that their own anti-Bulgarian campaign should be continued across the border to liberate Macedonian-populated areas of Greece were taken aside and shot as examples to other potential dissenters.

The importance of establishing "facts on the ground" for Tito in Croatia and Slovenia was apparent by his final strategic advances. A wave of Partisan armies attacked westward throughout Bosnia and northern Croatia in April, reaching Zagreb after a bloody battle near month's end. With NDH and German forces in retreat, Partisan armies also seized the Croatian Littoral, taking control of the Adriatic islands. A task of specific urgency for Tito was in the contested north Adriatic strip, where his forces beat the Western armies to Trieste by a single day, reaching the city on the ideologically significant May 1. The following day, the Soviet Red Army captured the German capital of Berlin, essentially ending WWII.

In Yugoslavia, scattered battles continued into the early summer of 1945 as the Partisans consolidated their control and, in many cases, engaged in reprisal killings of perceived traitors and Nazi collaborators from all ethnicities. By fall, the country—newly reorganized as a socialist federation—held its first elections. Unsurprisingly, Josip Broz Tito was elected as the country's first prime minister. A new era for Croatia and Slovenia was about to begin.

8

The Yugoslav Communist Experiment (1945–1990)

ORIENTING YUGOSLAVIA IN THE POSTWAR ERA (1945–1954)

Unlike previous conflicts, WWII resulted in a radical transformation in global political orientations and international governance structures. The United Nations (UN) was created as an organization that would have significantly more clout than its failed predecessor, the League of Nations, and the balance of power as a whole tipped away from traditional European states, which saw their empires diminish yet further, for the first time. The concept of international justice and genocide was incorporated in regards to the war crimes trials of Nazis involved with the Holocaust, and all other combatant countries looked to prosecute—and reconcile with—their own internal hostile forces.

But above all, the postwar world was divided into two opposing camps: the West, led for the first time by an outward-looking United States, and the communist bloc led by the Soviet Union. This so-called Cold War between the two nations would last for almost sixty years and result in further alliances, such as North Atlantic Treaty Organization

(NATO) in the Western case and the Warsaw Pact in the Soviet one. In this larger context, many other countries (often, disadvantaged ones in the developing world) became the site of violent proxy battles, economic or military, between the two great powers.

However, for Yugoslavia, the Cold War would for many years be highly beneficial. As a statesman, Tito had good instincts, preserving cooperation but also independence between the rival superpowers. Over the following three decades, Tito's East-West balancing act would gain him prestige as the leader of the Non-Aligned Movement (a group of countries claiming a sort of neutrality and middle ground between the American and Soviet superpowers). Following earlier events and cooperation with leaders of countries like India and Indonesia, Tito hosted a 1961 conference of heads of state in Belgrade, increasing Yugoslavia's role in the movement.

Before gaining such prestige, of course, Tito and his victorious comrades had to consolidate their rule and rebuild Yugoslav—a country that, like many other in Europe, had been devastated by WWII. Yugoslavia consisted of six socialist federal republics (Serbia, Croatia, Slovenia, Bosnia and Herzegovina, Montenegro, and Macedonia), as well as two autonomous provinces of Serbia, Vojvodina to the north on the Hungarian border, and Kosovo to the southwest, on the Albanian border. As prime minister of a one-party communist state with a ceremonial presidency, Tito was ironically able to assume the powers of an actual monarch that had eluded the country's erstwhile ruling families. In this regard, post-war Yugoslavia remained authoritarian in nature but was also more functional. Bolstering hope for the post-war future was a strong state propaganda effort made through media and public displays of various sorts, aimed at reifying the validity of the new regime and its benign intent toward citizens of all ethnicities. In this, Tito continued to play on the Partisans' wartime strength by minimizing ethnic divisions and identifying all citizens as equal members under a single ideology,

Like the Serbian royals whose palaces were among the many properties he confiscated in the name of the state, Tito ruled from Belgrade. With the main Yugoslav parliament and the military located in Belgrade, Yugoslavia was still oriented toward the needs of its largest population, the Serbs. However, unlike Yugoslavia's previous incarnation, the communist version had a strong Croat and Slovene influence owing to Tito himself, and his party confidante and leader of the Slovene Partisan wartime resistance, Edvard Kardelj (1910–1979). Born in Ljubljana, Kardelj was a journalist, intellectual, and a major figure in the Communist Party of Slovenia even before the war.

Slovenes had played a limited role in the resistance, and Kardelj being a trusted comrade of Tito's helped lead them. Slovene Partisans were active mostly on the Italian Front and later elsewhere in Yugoslavia; after the war, the Yugoslav delegation that negotiated with Italy over disputed border areas in Slovenia (the so-called Julian March) was thus led by Kardelj. He led the diplomatic team that reached an agreement on the Slovenia and Croatia border issue at the 1946 Paris Peace Conference. Yugoslavia received only the northern part of the Gorica region, while the western part was given to Italy. Yugoslavia also won back most of Istria and Rijeka, though Trieste itself was declared a "Free Territory," temporarily administered by a dual military occupation.

Indeed, while Slovene Partisans had occupied Trieste in May 1945, Tito allowed temporary control of the area to be shared between his forces and the British and American armies. Although Italy had abandoned its alliance with Germany and left the war in 1943, tensions still ran high locally as both the Italians and Slovenes of the Julian March were concerned about their futures. Adding to the typical postwar uncertainties was the emerging East-West dynamic of communism versus capitalism. Indeed, as soon as Hitler's Germany had been defeated, the main priority of the Western Allies was in slowing the spread of communism from Eastern Europe. In this context, the Slovenes of the Julian March were the major victims, as were the native Italians of Croatia and Slovenia, many of whom left Tito's Yugoslavia. The U.S.–British military administration included Trieste (in modern-day Italy), Pula (in modern-day Croatia), and modern-day Slovenian areas like Gorica, the Soča Valley, and most of the Karst Plateau.

The "Trieste Question" was not resolved until 1954 when the city was awarded to Italy. Although Yugoslav leaders before and after that deal claimed to have won various concessions and recognitions of minority rights from the Italian government and international community, the final loss of Trieste (and the other Slovene territories previously seized by Mussolini) was a bitter disappointment for Slovene nationalists. Tito's decision to not push too hard in disputed border points in Slovenia and Macedonia reflected his awareness of limits; the new leader of a country with postconflict challenges did not wish to go sparking new conflicts with more powerful forces.

While this prudent policy exemplified Tito's approach to territorial conflicts, his approach to ideological and political ones was more aggressive. The most significant, and perhaps the most daring, example of this was Tito's famous "break with Stalin" in 1948. The decision of the Yugoslav leadership's decision at that time to become less aligned with the Soviet Union's ideological and political authority. Soviet leader Joseph Stalin, undisputedly one of the major world leaders at war's end and leader of the communist bloc, saw Tito as somewhat of an unpredictable nuisance prone to acting too independently. Stalin was alarmed, for example, that Tito's troops would shoot down U.S. transport planes occasionally during the Trieste military occupation period, while Tito's military support for the communist side in the Greek Civil War (1946–1949) was a headache for Stalin in his bigger-picture negotiations with Britain and the United States over postwar Europe.

From the beginning, Tito had regarded himself as having relatively greater leverage in dealing with Stalin than other Eastern Europe leaders because the Soviets had played a relatively lesser role in liberating his country compared to others. This add-on success of the Yugoslav Partisans strengthened Tito's belief that his country should remain more independent from the Soviet Union in the future. Naturally, Stalin did not like any such tendencies in countries that (like Yugoslavia) he viewed as client states. The Soviets therefore launched an extensive espionage network within the Yugoslav Communist Party from 1945, some of which was uncovered.

Tensions increased in late 1948, when Tito, Kardelj, and other top leaders decided to establish an independent economy, without Moscow's approval. To the Soviets, this was an act of extreme insubordination for any communist country to attempt, and the ensuing diplomatic escalation led to an impasse, resulting in mutual accusations. The Yugoslav-Soviet drama boiled over in 1949 when Stalin put his other Balkan proxies on a war footing, with Red Army backing from Hungary, on all borders (Romania and Bulgaria on the east, and Albania to the southwest). On June 28, Yugoslavia was expelled from the Cominform for allegedly "nationalistic" activities in the economic policy matter, Although a Soviet-backed invasion from multiple fronts did not happen in the end, the threat did have serious consequences as a state of emergency was declared in certain areas amid a large-scale crackdown on tens of thousands of real or perceived "Stalinists" in Yugoslavia. Elsewhere in Europe's communist east, Stalin returned the favor by having alleged "pro-Titoists" purged from the ranks of national communist parties.

While the 1948 break with Stalin had considerable negative repercussions for Yugoslavia, it also had some positive ones. Tito confirmed his independent-minded spirit within the socialist sphere, while gaining for the country a new opportunity from the West. By detaching itself from the USSR, Yugoslavia was suddenly eligible to win American aid through programs overseen by the Marshall Plan (the comprehensive U.S. relief plan for rebuilding postwar Europe). While this arrangement brought Tito some much-needed assistance in rebuilding Yugoslavia, he kept his political options open and did not rely on the West thereafter. Thus, while he improved relations with the West, Tito also improved relations with the Soviets again after 1953 when Stalin died. With the dictator no more, Yugoslavia began to receive Soviet aid too. By ending the "Trieste Question" the following year in London, Tito was also able to demonstrate to Western European a conciliatory approach.

STATE SECURITY, REPRISALS, AND THE HUNT FOR WAR CRIMINALS (1946-1966)

While these kinds of overt threats demonstrated quite clearly that vigilance was necessary for the stability of postwar Yugoslavia, they also suited the personal interests and power-centralization goals of Tito and his top lieutenants, who included the Serbian Partisan veteran and longtime communist Aleksandar Ranković (1909–1983). Since Serbia constituted the largest, most populous, and most powerful state of Yugoslavia, it was clear that a communist Yugoslav country could not survive without some concessions to Serb interests. Aleksandar Ranković came to be associated with this accommodation as one of those within the leadership who envisioned a strong, centrally administered state, as opposed to the views of others (often, non-Serb) who favored more power-sharing and devolution of administration at the federal and regional levels.

Tito was able to maintain the delicate balance of power and interests for two decades. In 1946, one year after the war, he had wartime Chetnik rival Draža Mihailović and several of his generals arrested and executed for alleged treason. This demonstrated to the Serb nationalists (and, to the Croat, Slovene, and other populations) that Tito was ready and able to take on any potential challengers from Yugoslavia's largest republic. But at the same time, he also extended Belgrade's historic role as headquarters of most security institutions. From the remaining units of the Partisans, he formed the Yugoslav People's Army (*Jugoslavenska narodna armija*, hereafter, JNA). Building on the wartime ranks of 800,000 Partisan soldiers, the JNA eventually became the fourth-largest European army, following the recovery of Croatia and its naval capacities, as well as the central transport corridor creating a strong infantry basis and air corridor stretching from the Hungarian to Greek borders. The primacy of Belgrade as JNA headquarters was given some balance by giving Croatia the headship of the Yugo-slav Navy in Split.

Another security appointment that helped Tito placate Serbian mistrust of his rule was the decision to make Aleksandar Ranković interior minister, and to task the former Partisan commander with organizing and running Yugoslavia's state security agencies, which were (as before) largely influenced by Serb interests. Ranković created the ruthlessly efficient State Security Administration (*Uprava državne bezbednosti*, or UDBA), with its headquarters in Belgrade and stations in different capitals on the federal levels of Yugoslav states. The UDBA was basically an extension of the military intelligence group the Par-tisans had created in May 1944—the Department of People's Security (*Organ Zaštite Naroda—Armije*, OZNA). Thus, from the beginning, UDBA not only gathered information but also engaged in sabotage, kidnappings, and assassinations. Such activities would be synony-mous with the UDBA for decades to follow, with numerous "dark operations" carried out both at home and around the world against real and perceived enemies of Tito and the Yugoslav state.

Aside from residual resistance elements such as the Chetniks and Stalin's aggression, the major initial task for Yugoslav intelligence was to bring Nazi collaborators—most often, the Croatian Ustaše—to jus-tice. This was a considerable task, first, because many of the former Ustaše leaders had gone into hiding after the war. Argentina (under President Juan Domingo Perón) and Spain (under Franco's military dictatorship) were two favorite destinations, though Austria, Italy, the United States, and other countries also hosted high-ranking Croat war criminals, most of who were never brought to justice. Over time, these fugitives would create nationalist networks that agitated for the downfall of Yugoslavia and restoration of an independent Croatian state.

Yet, before chasing down any escaped Ustaše elements, the Yugo-slav authorities had to first worry about the situation closer to home; whether it was suspected signs of insurrections or simple politi-cal dissent, Tito's regime tended to respond robustly. From early on in postwar Yugoslavia, it was apparent that dissent would be dealt with in Soviet style. In place of gulags, there existed labor camps and prisons—the most infamous being that of the Croatian island Goli Otok (literally, "Barren Island"), an uninhabited Adriatic island which hosted roughly 16,000 political prisoners between 1949 and 1956. While many of those detained there were accused of pro-Stalinism (during that early scare to the system), others were simply nationalist or other dissidents. Over time, hundreds died of malnutrition and disease.

The authorities did, of course, also deal with more legitimate security threats. One of the first major UDBA successes was the 1948 disruption of an Ustaše plan to start an insurgent campaign against JNA military forces. Ante Pavelić, who had escaped to Italy under Vatican protection, and fellow exiled Ustaše leaders in Austria and Germany believed that the new East-West rivalry would create the conditions for the Ustaše to overthrow Tito. However, the Yugoslav intelligence service anticipated their plot, which was to liaise with so-called crusaders (*križari*), scattered bands of Ustaše soldiers who had not surrendered at war's end. Although UDBA was run on a national level by Ranković in Belgrade, its stations in the republics' capitals fell under control of the relevant interior ministry; the counteroperation, dubbed "Operation Gvardijan" thus required, in this case, leadership from Croatia section Interior Minister Ivan Krajačić and his UDBA agents both inside and outside of Yugoslavia.

Gvardijan was a complex campaign of infiltration, deception, and paramilitary action that rolled up almost 100 Ustaše fighters, including wanted war criminals like Ljubomir Miloš, a former commander of the NDH's Jasenovac concentration camp. Miloš and other Ustaše leaders like Ante Vrban and Luka Grgić had been sent to liaise with remaining bands by an Austria-based Ustaše outfit under Božidar Kavran (a mission known to them as "Operation April 10"). However, UDBA achieved a total victory in its infiltration of the organization's communications and was able to act decisively in remote territory. Coming at the height of fears for state security due to the break with Stalin, Operation Gvardijan was an early example of how Tito's secret services would operate in the decades to come.

Although generally unknown outside of Croatia today, Ivan Krajačić (1906–1986) was one of the most important Croats of the communist era. He had originally come to know Tito in the 1920s as both were Croatian railway engineers dedicated to communism. Like Tito, Krajačić had several brushes with the law under royalist Yugoslavia, but later took on a more international role by volunteering in the Spanish Civil War on the communist side. Thus, he was able to significantly increase his own (and Tito's) profile in Europe and build an extensive network of contacts from across Europe and the Soviet Union. This would come in useful both during WWII (in which Krajačić was seriously wounded fighting for the Partisans) and afterwards, when his UDBA networks fed the Yugoslav leadership with secret intelligence and other services. After stepping down as interior minister in 1953, Krajačić continued to hold a series of senior positions and retain influence, as with many other Yugoslav apparatchiks, from the shadows.

Capturing war criminals outside of the country was a much bigger challenge, however. Although Spain had remained neutral in WWII, its military dictatorship was well aligned with both Nazi Germany and the Catholic Church. For his part, Argentina's president Perón was a former general and public admirer of German, Spanish, and Italian fascism, and a charismatic leader at home. His legacy is complex. While Argentina under Perón provided safe passage through diplomatic and Vatican channels to thousands of Nazis—including Holocaust perpetrators like Josef Mengele, Adolf Eichmann, and Franz Stangl—the president also put many Jewish Argentines into positions of power and sought good relations with Israel after it was founded in 1947. Perón enjoyed cultivating a wide range of peoples fleeing the war and found a role for many—even appointing Ante Pavelić as his security advisor for a time. In the 1950s, Argentina became home to an often fractious Yugoslav diaspora, which was considered both a threat and an opportunity to intelligence planners back in Belgrade. Pavelić quickly resumed his political ambitions, declaring himself head of a sort of Croatian diaspora government in 1951.

The UDBA's different responses to different threats illustrate the complexity of the Cold War. Unsurprisingly, the organization sought to kill the politically active Pavelić, though the first assassination attempts failed. Finally, on April 10, 1957, Pavelić was shot by a Montenegrin Chetnik in Argentina, Blagoje Jovović. Although he survived and was soon on the run again, this time to Spain, the Ustaše leader would die there two years later as a result of injuries sustained. At the same time, for those antiregime figures not perceived as threats to Tito, there were other solutions aside from assassination. One example was the Croatian Catholic priest Krunoslav Draganović, who had been the chief organizer of the "ratlines" escape route used by Pavelić and other Ustaše fighters during his time at the Vatican's San Girolamo monastery. As a suspected CIA informant and anti-Communist, Draganović was a person of great interest to the UDBA; indeed, he returned rather mysteriously to Yugoslavia in 1967 and (after over a month in the spy agency's custody) made a public statement praising Tito's brand of freedom and democracy—unsurprisingly, infuriating the Croatian diaspora. Draganović was allowed to live out his days in peace; whether or not the price of this relative freedom was cooperation with the secret service will probably remain a mystery for the ages.

These events marked the end of a relatively quiet period of dark operations for the Yugoslav secret service. Ironically, many of the roughly 200 assassinations for which UDBA was credited occurred in the two decades after 1966—that is, just after structural reforms and resignations had been announced in an attempt by Tito to increase public trust and placate internal unrest among the various ethnic populations. The best-known event in this process was UDBA chief Aleksandar Ranković's dismissal, following a dubious scandal in which he was accused of wiretapping Tito's office. The process of adjudicating the matter (one quite possibly orchestrated by internal rivals) took place at a closed party plenum on Tito's private island of Brioni, on the Istrian coast in July 1966. The removal of the third-most powerful man in Yugoslavia, after Tito and Kardelj, was partly due to the result of bickering between two sides of the party, with the one supporting a less centralized, Belgrade-oriented federation winning out. As Ranković was associated strongly with the centralist camp and with Serb nationalism, his dismissal was seen as a sort of victory for non-Serbs. But it also meant that UDBA would continue and indeed expand upon its activities—especially as subsequent reforms would give more decision-making power to spy chiefs at the level of individual Yugoslav republics.

CROATIA AND SLOVENIA UNDER THE ECONOMY OF "SELF-MANAGEMENT" (1948–1968)

The Tito-Stalin break of 1948 had many causes and effects, but was most visibly related to the Yugoslav economy's management system. The Soviet Union had expected that, as with other communist countries in Eastern Europe, Yugoslavia would follow Moscow's central planning in this sphere. However, Tito had other ambitions, choosing a form of communism that steered slightly toward forms of economy previously known to his own country—that is, various measures of feudalism, free-market economy, and royalist centralization. As in negotiations over the Slovenian border, Tito assigned much of the policy formulation task to Edvard Kardelj, working together with Milovan Đilas (1911–1995), a Serbian communist (and later, dissident), and Vladimir Bakarić (1912–1983), a Partisan veteran who would serve as chairman of the Croatian League of Communists until 1969, making him another of Yugoslavia's most powerful figures.

The new economic policy they established for Yugoslavia was to be known as the "workers' self-management" system. In this version of socialism (also referenced as "Titoism" in its economic form), the workers themselves would collectively own their share of state-owned enterprises. In theory, at least, the system would make the laborers both liable for the operation and management of companies and capable of profiting from their success. In June 1950, parliament approved the bill (finalized by Milovan Đilas and Tito) concerning labor self-management (*samoupravljanje*). By 1953, this communist experiment in economic production had become the basis of the whole Yugoslav labor system. Workers' self-management in the workplace was meant to fuse elements of both communism and capitalism in a cooperative and democratic format that also included profit-sharing and workplace democracy. The system did not actually function as hoped, but Yugoslav officials were able to cover for its failings through bureaucratic sleight-of-hand, new foreign loans, and government propaganda campaigns.

The economic system imposed by Tito and his Slovene comrade Kardelj was complemented by massive infrastructure projects meant to bolster a sense of Yugoslav national unity and postwar reconciliation. These were undertaken by youth labor brigades, working voluntarily and invoking the honor of the new "heroes" of their local towns and cities from the Partisan side of the conflict. In this manner, several of Yugoslavia's major highway and railway projects were built, which in particular helped better connect Bosnia's mountainous territory with Croatia and Serbia. Such labor projects brought together young people from the different constituent Yugoslav republics; the government media portrayed this participation as a prestigious and patriotic duty.

Beyond volunteerism, the development of Yugoslavia as a provider of world-class economic products and solutions involved the retention and education of capable staff for large state-owned companies that could fulfill both domestic and international infrastructure projects. One of the major companies was Energoprojekt, a Belgrade-based company that specialized in large-scale engineering projects after its founding in 1951. Through Tito's expansive diplomatic alliances, Yugoslavia was able to contract (especially to Middle East, North African, and Eastern European countries) for the implementation of major infrastructure projects abroad. This provided opportunities for not only Yugoslav laborers but also enhanced the country's reputation as a source of well-educated engineers and scientists.

While modest by Western standards, Yugoslav wages in the 1950s and 1960s were somewhat above those of communist countries within the Soviet orbit, and Tito made strides to develop what was a largely undeveloped and agriculture-based society. Slovenia and Croatia, as the two previously most industrialized republics, benefited most from this trend. Tito's desire to make Yugoslavia a military power to be reckoned with came as a boon to the shipyards of the Croatian coast.

Croatia's own specific area of expertise for national development inevitably relied on innovation and modernization of its historic industry as a country focused toward maritime trade. Coastal towns that had been historic centers of this craft, like Trogir near Vis island, expanded and modernized their production with assistance from the federal government and educational sector. Thus from 1948 experts from the Institute of Oceanography in Split helped designers at Brodotrogir, the major local shipbuilding interest, to modernize their designs and productions, and fully transition from wooden to steel-hulled ships. Brodotrogir soon became a notable producer of vessels for the Yugoslav Navy, which led to new export markets in future when diplomacy allowed it as with, for example, the navy of India. Larger still was Brodosplit, the main shipbuilding company in Croatia's largest coastal city. It was founded in 1922 and expanded after WWII. Under Tito, Brodosplit employed thousands of workers and produced not only naval vessels for domestic and international customers but also ferries, cargo ships, and luxury yachts. Both of these shipyards would survive the transition from communism after the 1990s and remain important to modern Croatia's industrial base today.

Industrialization in Slovenia, historically already a leading center, achieved even more sophisticated levels through communist times. Indeed, the strength and diversity of Slovenian industrial productions and exports (ranging from chemicals and pharmaceuticals to electronics and automotive goods) made Slovenia the economic motor of Yugoslavia. Despite comprising less than one-tenth of the overall Yugoslav population, Slovenia was responsible for roughly 20 percent of national gross domestic product (GDP) and one-third of all exports at the height of the Yugoslav communist experiment. This imbalance would, in the 1980s, become a major reason for Slovene nationalists to begin pressing for independence.

Achieving this economic rank was not, however, historically necessitated, even if Slovenia was a historically industrialized nation. Other factors assisted in its growth, such as Tito's fear of a Soviet invasion of Serbia—and, possibly, the communist leadership's desire to "balance" the traditionally dominant place of Serbia. For example, the automotive producer TAM Maribor, from the eponymous Slovenian city, was just one of seventy major companies relocated from Serbia to Slovenia by 1955. Slovene politicians of influence like Kardelj, despite their rhetoric about equality, essentially reified the pre-existing developmental disparity levels between regions. The value-added economy of Croatia, and especially Slovenia, meant that the lower-value economies in the south of the country remain for the most part agricultural, as providers of raw materials. No wonder, then, that Slovenia became ever more industrialized and sophisticated, while backwaters like Kosovo continued to stagnate. Special federal economic development funds for such regions were unable to bridge the gap. Throughout the 1970s, meanwhile, the Yugoslav authorities continued with U.S. firm Westinghouse to build their first nuclear power plant in Slovenia (as of 2020, it remains the only nuclear facility in any former Yugoslav republic).

During the 1960s, Yugoslav authorities also looked to the allure of Croatia's Adriatic coast and the charm of the Slovene Alps for another means of making a profit. Tourism emerged as an important growth industry for these two republics, further separating them from the rest of Yugoslavia. Tito's smart diplomacy in the Non-Aligned Movement allowed him to present the country as a welcoming destination to people from the world over. While the Soviet Union and its Eastern European satellites were relatively restrictive to outsiders, Yugoslavia was somewhat more open. For economic and ideological reasons, Tito sought to keep the country an indispensable link between East and West, hosting frequent educational and cultural events and programs.

Urban areas in Croatia and Slovenia also grew as communist Yugoslavia developed. Emigration from villages continued likewise, as people without means or party connections were forced to seek work opportunities elsewhere. In fact, while Tito had in the early postwar years tended to suppress migration, he increasingly allowed it after the early 1950s because Yugoslavs working abroad tended to send money home to support their families—thereby helping to shore up the experimental state's communist system. Yugoslavs, in fact, were one of the main beneficiaries of West Germany's "guest worker" (*Gastarbeiter*) program, created to restart the German economy and rebuild infrastructure after the war. A large Turkish diaspora arose in Germany as a result of this program, which also included over 400,000 Yugoslavs throughout the 1960s when Tito lifted restrictions on emigration. Due to overlapping political events across Europe from the late 1960s, the Croat diaspora in Germany—already large, and subsequently increased considerably by the guest worker program—would soon start a quiet but bloody war with UDBA agents targeting suspected neo-Ustaše Croat nationalists speaking out against Tito's government from Germany. This marked a turning point in the Yugoslav experiment, as was reflected by contemporaneous events.

DISSENT, THE "CROATIAN SPRING," AND THE NEW CONSTITUTION (1967–1974)

These events were both domestic and international in nature, and resulted in a further battle for power decentralization by the time Tito and his advisors had crafted a new constitution for Yugoslavia in 1974. This document gave individual Yugoslav republics unprecedented control over their internal management and finances, while also giving a specific autonomous status to Serbia's Kosovo and Vojvodina provinces. While these changes did not satisfy all protest elements, they did show pragmatism on the part of Tito, who sought to balance concessions with purges (by 1972, over 200,000 members of Croatia's League of Communists alone had been expelled from the party). The Yugoslav leadership saw, however reluctantly, that some reforms were warranted, while also remaining well aware that it could not control the larger world events that had galvanized protest movements in the previous few years, indirectly affecting Yugoslav thought in myriad ways.

By 1968, worldwide protest movements in the United States and Western Europe generally opposed the Vietnam War and right-wing governments, while calling for civil rights and left-wing causes. In early June, students in Yugoslavia participated in several days of protests and strikes in Belgrade, as well as in Sarajevo, Zagreb, and Ljubljana. These protesters had some overlap with the "Prague Spring" protests of that spring (which would prompt a Soviet invasion in August) in support of liberalizations; but as with the contemporaneous student protests in Paris, the Yugoslavs were also agitating against economic policies and perceived social injustices. While these demonstrations were all broadly leftist in nature, they also caught the attention of various nationalist elements (including the neo-Ustaše and Serb nationalists in the diaspora) as the potential for any instability in Yugoslavia regardless of cause could hypothetically expedite divergent political visions for the country.

While Tito acted mildly toward the student protesters, conceding that they expressed legitimate grievances, the Yugoslav government was unnerved by the 1968 demonstrations as they were the first significant sign of public disenchantment with Tito since the war. Indeed, one unplanned weakness arising from Tito's policy of openness was that it exposed young Yugoslav scholars to foreign political doctrines at variance with his own. From the mid-1960s, Croat, Slovene, Serb, and other Yugoslav students began returning from studies in Europe and North America with degrees incorporating topics like sociology and political philosophy. The universities in Yugoslavia (primarily, those of Belgrade, Zagreb, and Ljubljana) became hotbeds of dissent against the "orthodox" communism of the Yugoslav federal government.

Intellectual debate and protests over Yugoslavia's political and economic path took on nationalistic dimensions as well, further complicating the issues while also in a sense clarifying what issues mattered most to specific populations. The most significant event in this regard for future events was the 1971 "Croatian Spring" (*Hrvatsko proljeće*), also referred to as the "Mass Movement" (*masovni pokret* or MASPOK). The Croatian Spring harnessed national frustrations with limited political freedoms and economic mismanagement in Tito's Yugoslavia, with some of its youth activist leaders later becoming important figures in modern times (for example, the first president of the post-Yugoslav independent Croatia, Franjo Tuđman, first gained prominence as an activist in the cadres of the Croatian Spring movement from the late 1960s).

The original development of this movement, compared with other left-wing protest movements in Europe at the time, was somewhat coincidental. Croatian activists were first emboldened to speak out in 1967 by two events that had occurred the year before, events which they considered auspicious for their cause. The first, of course, was the dismissal of Interior Minister Aleksandar Ranković during the Brioni Plenum of July 1966, by which they expected Serb influence within Yugoslavia would be lessened. The second event was the 1966 restoration of diplomatic ties between Yugoslavia and the Vatican. This came after the three-year Second Vatican Council, and was a significant boost to Croatian nationalist aspirations, as the Catholic Church had historically been central to educational and cultural life of the Croat (and Slovene) peoples. However, due to the church's collaboration with the Ustaše and political support for nationalism, Tito had repressed public religious events. With restoration of relations in 1966, however, many of these prohibitions were loosened. Further, while it did not try to interfere with politics, the Catholic Church in Croatia did provide moral support for the reformist movement on a personal level.

After months of careful coordination, Croatian anti-Tito activities began in early 1967. To better protect themselves from any possibly harsh response from the authorities, the movement sought to gather a critical mass of intellectual support around an issue with symbolic national resonance, which was not yet directly confrontational to the authorities. To show this, activists gathered 130 influential Croatian poets and linguists (the large majority of them, Communists) to back a March 1967 declaration concerning the status and name of the

Croatian language—ironically but not incidentally, the same issue that state-builders of earlier centuries like Ljudevit Gaj had highlighted in arguing for greater, not lesser, unification with Serbia.

Croat activists were able to use the linguistic issue as a spearhead for attracting wider public support, especially from student groups and young members of Croatia's League of Communists, for their larger goals. These included not only demands for greater civil rights but also political, economic, and even military requests. The Croat protesters opposed, for example, the established practice of having young JNA conscripts perform their military service in other Yugoslav republics, a system that Tito had originally envisioned by Tito as beneficial for postwar "brotherhood and unity," in that it brought together young men from formerly adversarial parts of the country. The Croatian activists also called for economic decentralization reform, which the public could easily get behind when presented with statistics revealing the extent to which profit made by Croatian tourism and industry were being redistributed to shore up less affluent parts of Yugoslavia. (The same general observation, of course, was also made by Slovene critics of the Tito-Kardelj system during this period.)

By 1970, Croatia's League of Communists was under the leadership of a more independent-minded second-generation; most notable for the reform movement were Ante Miko Tripalo (1926–1995), a respected communist with wartime experience, and Savka Dabčević-Kučar (1923–2009), an accomplished politician and bureaucrat; indeed, in having served as the Yugoslav equivalent to a prime minister (in Croatia, from 1967 to 1969), Dabčević-Kučar was the first woman to be appointed head of government in any European country after the war. She was able to build on the momentum created by the 1967 Croatian language declaration (and subsequent grassroots activism), gaining attention for the national cause in a January 1970 speech before the Central Committee of the League of Communists of Croatia. This was far more dangerous, however, in that it concerned more practical economic issues: Dabčević-Kučar noted that while Croatia's per-capita GDP significantly exceeded the national average, it took relatively little from the Belgrade-managed federal solidarity fund, which primarily benefited the ethnic-Albanian majority Serbian province of Kosovo. Other sensitive issues pointed out by Croat critics included the central management of Yugoslavia's investment fund.

The two Croat communist leaders then joined forces with overtly nonpolitical activist groups in 1971 (the Croatian Spring demonstrations), calling on Belgrade to decentralize the economy and allow more democratic input on the level of individual Yugoslav federations. With the endorsement of Croatia's legitimate communist party leaders and a wide range of citizens, their cause seemed promising, though it also caused significant alienation with Croatia's ethnic Serbs, the Republic of Serbia, and the JNA, which saw itself as the ultimate guarantor of state stability.

Several months of generally nonviolent protests ensued in Zagreb and other cities, peppered by symbolic events like banned publications of the Croatian language. By December 1971, when Tito negotiated an end to the internal impasse, Dabčević-Kučar, Tripalo, and other prominent Croatian communist leaders resigned from public life, and some of the key concessions were granted—fatefully, including the right of individual Yugoslav republics to have greater control over their own investment decisions. In the long term, this would have negative and uneven results due to poor decision-making on local levels, which would aggravate trade deficits and economic losses.

During and after the Croatian Spring, roughly 2,000 activists were arrested and prosecuted, while over 25,000 people were expelled from Croatia's League of Communists. Among other things, this decisively severed the Belgrade leadership's ties with the last generations of Croats to have had some personal experience with WWII and the fight against fascism—something that in the longer term would create space for the return of more far-right ideologues in the neo-Ustaše diaspora (men who were themselves then arming and training for potential paramilitary or terrorist activities to try and topple the country).

Today, Croats remember the events of 1971 as something of a mixed success; the Croatian Spring achieved some of its objectives, though its own apparent downfall (with the government's robust efforts to restore order) led in turn to something called the "Croatian silence" (*Hrvatska šutnja*), the long period until 1989 during which Croatian politicians generally avoided seeking further major system changes. This revisionist view tends to downplay the important role that Croats continued to play at the highest levels in Tito's Yugoslavia. For example, Milka Planinc (1924–2010), the woman who replaced Dabčević-Kučar within the Croatian League of Communists after 1971, would go on little over a decade later to become the first female prime minister of the Yugoslav Federation. In the big picture, the events of 1967–1971 in Croatia are probably most important in that they hastened the decentralization of the country, as would be codified with the new federal constitution of 1974. With this document, the individual republics and autonomous regions were given greater control over their administrative and economic decision-making. While formally still in charge, aging dictator Tito was, through the constitutional changes, increasingly supplanted by a bureaucratic system—setting the course for what would be a tense and increasingly dysfunctional decade following Tito's death in 1980.

THE DEATH OF TITO AND UNCERTAIN TIMES (1980–1986)

Tito died just three days before his eightieth birthday on May 4, 1980 due to complications from a leg amputation endured months earlier. The government's awareness of his impending death allowed it to secretly organize what would be the world's largest state funeral in history. All in all, some 128 countries and numerous international organizations were officially represented at the May 8 funeral in Belgrade, which included the presence of four kings, thirty-one presidents, and twenty-two prime ministers. Indeed, this international representation attested to how influential Tito had really been in navigating the challenging waters of Cold War politics and finding a unique diplomatic place for Yugoslavia between East and West.

Although Tito himself was somewhat of a figurehead by 1980, the heartfelt reactions to his death among ordinary Yugoslavs revealed the affinity and respect that people had for him—whether or not they were fond of his communist system of rule. Yugoslavia would continue to live off of its "cult of Tito" for the following decades, emphasizing the themes of unity and brotherhood that the communist leader had preached, and commemorating him with specific annual rites (one vivid example of such memorial acts, a moment of silence for Tito's memory, was the blasting of sirens throughout major towns and cities in Yugoslavia each May 4th at 3:05 p.m., the time of Tito's passing). In part, the country needed to do this because there was no clear successor. Edvard Kardelj, the second main architect of communist Yugoslavia, had died just over a year before Tito in February 1979. There was no single leader with Tito's charisma and appeal to Yugoslavs of different nationalities, ethnicities, and religions.

Tito himself had been well aware of this fact. For the interest of preserving Yugoslavia's future as a unitary and functional state, he had left plans for a power-sharing system that would rely on rotating presidencies among the Yugoslav republics—a further innovation from the sort of decentralization that was codified in the 1974 constitution. However, time would show that this system was a better idea in theory than in practice as it would prove inefficient and prone to manipulation by nationalist interests.

In April 1982, the Croatian politician (and Partisan aide during WWII) Milka Planinc was elected to lead the Yugoslav government, primarily based on this legacy. However, while the annually rotating Yugoslav presidency gave individual republics and provinces direct participation at all levels of power, it hampered effective decision-making and policy continuity, ironically damaging the federation's leadership capacities and widening existing inequality rates of development on local levels. As Tito had already purged the Croatian (and, much of the Serbian) League of Communists during the Croatian Spring, there remained few "second-generation" communist politicians who, like Planinc, had personally experienced Tito's ideals of "brotherhood and unity" in wartime. The very sense of what it meant to be a Yugoslav would become increasingly questioned in a Europe that was rapidly heading toward reintegration and trending toward German expansionism (following the fall of the Berlin Wall in 1989 and creation of the European Union three years later).

The one sector of the Yugoslav state that did follow Tito's mission with the greatest vigilance—the military—continued to uphold its perceived role as ultimate protector of the nation. However, its upper echelons also became increasingly dominated by Serbs and Montenegrins, leading to new reinterpretations of what the national interest was specifically. Through the early 1980s, the JNA kept a watchful (and even, paranoid) eye over the largely powerless central government in Belgrade and tried to keep apprised of the fluid events that comprised the final years of the Cold War. Yugoslavia's nonaligned orientation had kept the country constantly prepared for conflict with both major powers at the same time. This vigilance was as much a part of Titoism as were the oft-stated values of brotherhood and unity; indeed, well into the 1980s, drills were held in Yugoslav schools in symbolic preparation for either a Western or Soviet invasion.

As time passes and more official information from the late Yugoslav period becomes available to researchers, it has become increasingly clear that the military and intelligence services of Yugoslavia were becoming increasingly challenged and confused by the changing international situation in the years following Tito's death. Further, while it would continue its policy of assassination and perceived threats to national security in the Yugoslav diaspora throughout the 1980s, the UDBA was also becoming involved with business and political corruption at local levels within the federation. This would lead to one of the most important (though relatively little-known) relationship dynamics in the fall of Yugoslavia and the resulting "transition period" from communism to capitalism: that of competing (and, sometimes, cooperating) networks comprising intelligence officials who would cohere around nascent political actors and economic oligarchs. The myths of UDBA linkages to prominent events in late Yugoslav history (and indeed, to murky political and business events in the years thereafter) remain part of the popular culture throughout the former federation to this day.

In the absence of Tito as a uniting figure, old ethnic grievances soon resurfaced. In 1981, Kosovo Albanian demands for a status upgrade (from autonomous province to constituent republic) aggravated relations with Serbia, and particularly, the minority Serbian population in the territory that had once comprised Serbia's medieval heartland. For decades, Yugoslavia had been pouring money into Kosovo, but aside from some showy building projects, had nothing to show for it. The central government never succeeded in raising standards in Kosovo, fueling anger locally and in other republics for opposite reasons. What was a necessary expenditure for Serbia was seen as a waste by many other Yugoslavs, and relations worsened between Kosovo's Serbs and Albanians over the decade. In all of the republics, new generations of political leaders were taking control of the League of Communists parties on local levels. However, most had local and ethnic-nationalist sympathies, in contrast to the avowedly antinationalist views of Tito and his generation. The best known of these new leaders was Slobodan Milošević (1941–2006), who from 1987 became identified with the cause of Serb nationalism in Kosovo, Montenegro, and Vojvodina. In fact, other Yugoslav leaders resented how Milošević sought to influence the communist reform movements within these places to develop alliances that would help Serbia outvote the other republics in matters of internal affairs, within the new system Tito had left behind. This would be a recurring story right until the end of the communist experiment (Milošević's relationship with Croatia and Slovenia during the 1990s Yugoslav civil wars is discussed in the following chapter).

In Slovenia, the most important future leader to emerge after the death of Tito was Milan Kučan. Born in 1941 in the rural Prekmurje region of Slovenia, Kučan was a lawyer who had been involved in communist political organizations since the 1960s. By 1982, Kučan was representing Slovenia's League of Communists at Yugoslavia's Central Committee in Belgrade, four years after becoming head of the Slovene League. Like other reformers opposed to the Serbian leadership, Kučan sought further decentralization and justified this with new arguments based on human rights and European democratic ideals. Similarly in Croatia at the time, political trends were moving, as at previous times in history, away from unification and toward independence.

Franjo Tuđman (1922–1999), a WWII Partisan veteran, historian, and first president of today's independent Croatia, was one of the three most important politicians associated with the Balkan conflicts of the 1990s. Elected in 1990 and re-elected five years later, he oversaw Croatia's efforts to fight the War of National Independence (1991–1995) while also building new diplomatic alliances with Western powers. (Embassy of the Republic of Croatia)

Prominent former Partisans who broached the idea of greater autonomy ran into trouble with the authorities, as was the case with Franjo Tuđman (1922–1999), following his 1981 visit to Sweden. Once the youngest general in the Yugoslav army, Tuđman had been upsetting the authorities for his nationalist views since the 1960s, and would become Croatia's first president following the break-up of Yugoslavia.

One of the key issues for the future would be the status of Bosnia and Herzegovina, in general, and, in particular, for Croats, of the region's historic Croat population, especially from western Herzegovina. Likewise, the Serb Orthodox and Bosniak Muslim populations of Bosnia (both there and in the diasporas) had strong and conflicting opinions. The contentious nature of Bosnia-Herzegovina, indeed, had been anticipated by national sports planners as an opportunity to project unity on a world stage, which was achieved with the successful hosting of the 1984 Winter Olympics in Sarajevo. At the height of Tito's strength in the mid-1960s, local communist leaders like the Bosnian Croat Branko Mikulić (1928–1994) could pride themselves on solidifying an ethnically inclusive economic and political system. However, the old approaches were no longer relevant when it came time, in a different context two decades later, for Mikulić to assume leadership of Yugoslavia from the outgoing Planinc government on May 15, 1986. Mikulić's government was most associated with the final years of economic crisis which brought about Yugoslavia's demise, scarcely a decade after that of its founder.

ECONOMIC COLLAPSE AND THE UNRAVELING OF THE YUGOSLAV SYSTEM (1985–1990)

Apart from ethnic disputes, political protests, and an inefficient bureaucracy, Yugoslavia might have survived but for the severe and systemic economic shocks endured during the country's final decade. One year after Tito's death, Yugoslavia was almost $20 billion in debt to foreign creditors—a cumulative situation due, in part, to bad decision-making and mismanagement throughout Yugoslavia following the 1971 decentralization program sought by the Croatian Spring protesters. Unemployment also began to rise sharply as the role of diaspora cash remittances grew ever-more important to keep up the image of consumer affluence presented by designer shops and cafés of urban centers like Belgrade and Ljubljana.

The national economic crisis was caused by a wide range of factors, including foreign concerns over internal political stability and losses from investment abroad due to wars and an energy crisis. Energoprojekt, for example, lost much of its established business in the Middle East and North Africa when the oil-producing rulers of those countries were forced to seek out cheaper Asian alternatives for big engineering projects, which had typically also employed thousands of Yugoslav laborers, as well as project managers and engineers. Industry export losses also began to affect companies in Croatia and Slovenia.

While all this was occurring, the Yugoslav dinar continued to lose its value against the dollar and German Deutschemark (a key currency of remittance from the Yugoslav diaspora in Europe). All of the government's attempts to rectify the situation only worsened it as the country was built on an experimental economic foundation, and had allowed itself to be opened to Western capitalism prematurely. Yugoslavia was forced to spend considerable revenue from exports just to pay down a fraction of its debt, rather than grow the economy—in any case a complicated one, based on the fuzzy concepts of "market socialism" that had once seemed visionary in Edvard Kardelj's theories of workers self-management. Yugoslavia fatefully expanded its exposure to the Western-dominated banking system by taking out increasing loans from the International Monetary Fund (IMF) under difficult reform conditions by which the IMF and other foreign creditors essentially sought the destruction of that system.

In May 1987, following a rash of workers' strikes, the Mikulić government threatened to call in the military against a citizenry unhappy with its unpopular reforms. Six months later, Mikulić launched a policy of hyperinflation, slashing the value of the Yugoslav dinar by one-quarter. Unsurprisingly, this wreaked havoc in the economy, and especially the banking system, while allowing opportunities for some to get rich overnight simply by repeatedly reconverting dinars to foreign currencies and back again for internal payments, a practice abetted by certain flaws in a financial system that had never anticipated such a threat. The stage was set for numerous bankruptcies of state-owned companies, leading to significant further losses in the productive economy. Finally, the Mikulić government achieved a Standby Agreement with the IMF in 1988. Public dissatisfaction with these measures was high. The republic-level governments of Croatia and Slovenia unsuccessfully sought to gain a no-confidence vote against Mikulić in May, but the sentiment was kept alive by the thousands of protesters demanding Mikulić's resignation during the summer. By year's end, the objective was achieved—Mikulić became the first and only communist Yugoslav leader to resign. He was replaced by Ante Marković, another Croat, in March 1989.

As Yugoslavia's federal leader and a well-educated economist by background, Marković was strongly supported by the West as a potential savior for the country. In 1989, he visited U.S. president George H. W. Bush to arrange for financial assistance. The agreed package obliged Yugoslavia to continue further economic reforms, including currency devaluation while blocking wage raises, slashing public spending, and similar "austerity measures." Most remarkable was the agreement to do away with the legacy of Tito and Kardelj specifically by ending the socially owned, workers self-managed system of companies. While there were some promising signs, briefly, from attempts to implement the program, it was a case of too little too late. Internal fractiousness also prevented the reforms from being accepted. For example, the governments of Serbia and Vojvodina refused to carry out the inflationary measures. Instead, they called for customs taxes on goods imported from Croatia and Slovenia; Serbia also requested an additional $1.5 billion from Yugoslavia's national bank to pay for their increased salaries and pensions, as well as to subsidize loss-making companies, which angered Croats and Slovenes and fueled opposition political rhetoric in the latter republics. In a largely decentralized and experimental system, the federal government clearly lacked the capacity to keep reforms on track.

Equally significant for the future (and for Marković's personal legacy) were his agreement at the U.S. talks to liberalize the conditions for foreign investors and his 1990 program for privatization of previously worker self-managed companies. Thus would begin the infamous era of "transition" in Yugoslavia, during which a new oligarch class emerged due to behind-the-scenes collaboration between small groups of insiders in Yugoslavia's political, intelligence, military, and business elite. In fact, the new federal laws on privatization of 1990 encouraged company management boards to privatize by selling discounted company shares to employees. While technically a "fair" means of redistribution, the rate of inflation and in many cases real devaluation of companies meant that the shares were virtually worthless, allowing would-be tycoons associated with state structures to scoop up entire businesses on the cheap. This was not restricted to Serbia, Croatia, and Slovenia, or to areas of Yugoslavia that eventually suffered from war, but was more widespread.

As the Yugoslav economy reached the point of no return, political conditions were ripening as well for popular unrest to be transformed into political agitation. This was particularly the case in Slovenia and Croatia, which also commanded interest from their historic near-abroad, Central/Western Europe. Throughout the 1980s, several key European states (including historic partners Italy, Austria, and Germany) had been working increasingly together to standardize their economic and political cooperation toward something that would soon become known as the European Union. At the same time, protest movements were occurring elsewhere in Eastern Europe against the aging Soviet Empire. While the state security apparatus was still something to be feared, by the late 1980s, Yugoslav citizens had become more restive and increasingly emboldened to criticize a government that was clearly incapable of solving the country's many problems.

They did this through strikes, protests, and through the formation of new semipolitical organizations that more or less gravitated toward the historic ethnic or territorial orientations of different regions and communities. By the late 1980s, it was clear that the mainstream no longer feared challenging Tito's traditional one-party system when it came to ideal future outcomes for the country. These tended to range from a multiparty, but centralized federation (something many Serbs wanted) to a loose federation or even semi-independent grouping of states (a preference of many Slovenes and Croats). However, Bosnia, with its three major populations, added a further degree of complexity to the issue.

In Croatia, the desire for independence was fueled both by exasperation with the incompetence of government and economic losses, and by diaspora-led nationalism that depicted the Serbs, as in WWII, as impeding the national will. On June 17, 1989, the increasingly popular Franjo Tuđman founded the Croatian Democratic Union (HDZ), a nationalist Croatian movement strongly oriented toward the Roman Catholic Church and the historical figures associated with Croatia's secular and ecclesiastical past. The HDZ was greeted with great suspicion by the authorities in Belgrade, and by Serbs in Croatia, as many of their most ardent supporters were far-right Croatian diaspora figures who were Ustaše apologists.

To understand how touchy of a subject Croatian nationalism was during the mid-1980s, one must also consider two additional personalities of the time whose role—or potential role—in the Balkans was seen as suspicious by rivals of the Croats. The first was the then fairly new Polish pope, John Paul II, whose own election to the papacy was broadly understood as a manifestation of political mobilization of the Christian West against Soviet communism. Second was the revelation, by Austrian journalists in 1986, that the country's new president (and two-time former secretary-general of the UN), Kurt Waldheim (1918–2007), had actually been a Nazi intelligence officer stationed in Yugoslavia during the war. A detailed, but debated report from the U.S. government reiterated this and claimed that the Yugoslav and Soviet authorities had known about Waldheim's wartime activities but somehow blackmailed the UN leader into following their wishes by not revealing so. The entire affair caused a stir in Yugoslavia, where renewed curiosity about the Nazi past could have tangible impacts on interethnic, and even international relations.

At the same time in Slovenia, a number of grassroots organizations bridging the gap between cultural and political life had become influential. In the 1970s and 1980s, Yugoslavia had developed a thriving rock music and artistic scene, with considerable collaboration from performers from across the federation. Most popular acts in late Yugoslavia did not attempt to involve themselves in political issues; those that did, like Slovenia's somewhat avante garde group Laibach, had a more limited audience, but still garnered influence because their sometimes controversial political imagery put them into the public spotlight.

Named after the German-language moniker for the city of Ljubljana, Laibach was formed in 1980 and became the musical arm of the Slowenische Kunst ("New Slovenian Art" in German), a politically minded art collective. Referred to by its acronym of NSK from its founding in 1984, the collective is still active today, drawing on themes of totalitarianism and political repression for its main areas of expression. Drawing on a certain ambiguity of symbolism from the Nazi past and Yugoslav communism, NSK sought to indirectly spark dialogue about the peculiarities of Slovenia's political experience in the broader shared culture of Habsburg Austria and the wars that followed it. The performances of Laibach and NSK sometimes brought censure from the official communist authorities as did publications of historians, psychologists, and political philosophers associated with what became known as the *Nova revija* (New Review) intellectual circle.

From the mid-1980s, Milan Kučan and his reformist faction took charge of the Slovenian League of Communists. As Slovenia was the most advanced and Westernized republic historically, they sought economic and political change to bring Slovenia closer to its neighbors, particularly Austria and Germany. They tapped into the popular sentiment, particularly in the wealthy republics of Slovenia and Croatia, that their republic's economic potential was being unfairly restricted by the ineffective federal reforms. This led to protests in 1987 and 1988, ending with the so-called Slovene Spring movement for self-rule. This was expressed in a 1987 manifesto (which was quickly censored), written by several leading intellectuals and published in the *Nova revija* journal. Pushing a "Slovenian National Program" that would include anything from greater democratization to national independence, these intellectuals angered the Communist regime, which, however, did not take significant measures against them.

More significant steps toward political independence occurred as Yugoslavia's economy continued to fail, sparking inflation and bankruptcies that prompted workers to take to the picket lines. A 1988 strike at the Litostroj heavy machinery plant in Ljubljana resulted in the declaration of Yugoslavia's first independent trade union. Furthermore, a political organization was soon inaugurated from the protest movement (the Social Democratic Union of Slovenia), which was followed that May by a self-declared "Peasant Union of Slovenia." Soon after, the prodemocracy movement gained another rallying point when four Slovenian journalists were arrested and accused of leaking state secrets by the JNA. Their ensuing trials caused protests around Slovenia. Further aggravating things was the fact that Slovenia's ruling communists were fundamentally opposed to the goals and activities of the Serbian League of Communists, their ostensible partners in governance.

However, under the direction of Slobodan Milošević, the Serbian communists pressed a nationalist agenda that drove Slovenia's governing communists toward a shared vision with the protesters. Thus, on September 27, 1989, Slovenia's parliament unilaterally declared numerous amendments to the 1974 Yugoslav constitution; most significantly, they voted to end the one-party system and to allow Slovenia the right to leave Yugoslavia entirely. Hundreds of pro-Yugoslavia Milošević supporters attempted to rally in Ljubljana on December 1, with instructions to overthrow the local government, but were thwarted by select nationalist police forces. Soon after, on January 23, 1990, the League of Communists of Slovenia walked out of the main event at the 14th Congress of the League of Communists of Yugoslavia, in protest against what they considered Serbian domination of the federal system. In a coordinated move, the League of Communists of Croatia also walked out on the event, leaving the once all-powerful national political structure essentially impotent. For all intents and purposes, even if not formally so, the Yugoslav state that Tito had created was formally dead.

9

The Yugoslav Wars of Secession and Their Legacy (1990–2007)

ELECTIONS AND ESTRANGEMENTS: THE HDZ'S ELECTION AND ETHNIC DIVISION IN CROATIA (1990–1991)

The dawn of a new decade in Yugoslavia brought sudden change and a continual recalibration of interests that increased the tendencies of local ethnic groups to seek new forms of political organization in an increasingly uncertain environment. After both Slovene and Croat League of Communist delegations walked out on the League of Communists of Yugoslavia's January 1990 party congress, in reaction to Milošević's veto of their demands for a looser federal system, new reactionary political forces began to gather support across all Yugoslav republics. At the same time, diaspora Yugoslavs of all ethnicities became increasingly proactive in defending what they considered to be captive homelands potentially poised for historic moments of liberation.

In April and May elections, Franjo Tuđman, leader of the nationalist Croatian Democratic Union, or *Hrvatska demokratska zajednica* (HDZ), comfortably defeated his main rival Ivica Račan of the Party of Democratic Change (SDP), a reformed communist grouping. The margin of victory surprised many, but reaffirmed the extent to which anti-Yugoslav and anti-communist rhetoric had been embraced by the majority of Croats just ten years after the demise of the national founder. Tuđman, who had campaigned on Croatia's independence, had a strong mandate from the election, with a relatively strong hand owing to his decisive victory, though for federal authorities in Belgrade and Croatia's own indigenous Serb populations, the HDZ's goals were concerning. Even before the election had taken place, the national climate was polarized along ethnic lines, with clashes and provocations witnessed especially in contested areas of Slavonia and Dalmatia.

Some of the animosities that were emerging in Croatia could be traced back to Tito's most controversial legacy document, the 1974 Yugoslav constitution. The special autonomy statuses given to ethnic Albanian-majority Kosovo and ethnically mixed Vojvodina—two provinces of Serbia—had not been extended equally to protect similarly ethnically mixed regions of Croatia and Bosnia-Herzegovina, where Serbs comprised considerable historic minorities. Therefore, the reaction of Serbian political forces in Croatia following the years of anti-Belgrade protests from Croat communists and non-communists alike was predictable.

Thus, in preparation for the elections, in February 1990, Croatian Serbs (who had vivid memories of atrocities carried out against their ancestors in WWII by the Ustaše regime) began to mobilize for their own political demands. Jovan Rašković (1929–1992), a psychiatrist whose family had been killed during Ustaše's government, launched a political bloc—the Serb Democratic Party (SDS)—in the ethnic Serbian stronghold of Knin in Dalmatia. The party's early position supported the rights of Serbs to be autonomous in certain areas, and to even redraw municipal lines within Croatia to reflect the ethnic balance, which in turn alarmed Croatian nationalists. Rašković also suggested the need to create a similar Serb-minority party in Bosnia-Herzegovina to Radovan Karadžić, who would go on to become the most important Bosnian Serb political leader of the wars of the 1990s. Although SDS did not win enough seats in the spring 1990 elections to be a major factor, Tuđman was keen to discuss the future of Croat-Serb relations with Rašković, who had become the de-facto minority representative in the country by summer of 1990. However, when HDZ portrayed Rašković in an unflattering light, it only antagonized the Serbian community further against the new Croatian government. Rašković was soon replaced by politicians closer to centralists in Belgrade, where he himself would die of a heart attack two years later.

Tensions with the Serbs (both inside and outside of Croatia) increased with the HDZ government's first decisions once in power. Thus on May 30, 1990, the new Sabor met for this first time under President Tuđman, who declared plans for a new Croatian constitution, with numerous reforms envisioned in the context of a future decentralized confederation of sovereign countries within a vestigial Yugoslav state—a virtual declaration of war as far as Belgrade was concerned. Soon after, on July 25, the parliament passed further constitutional amendments, including the removal of the prefix "socialist" from Croatia's name. The HDZ government also sought to redress what nationalists had considered a historic wrong by purging large numbers of ethnic Serbs from state jobs, including in particularly sensitive areas like the police. From the Croat nationalist point of view, the communist Yugoslav governments had long given Serbs preferential treatment and employment quotas significantly higher than their actual 12 percent total of the national population. This official state policy unsurprisingly further alienated local Serbian populations. The situation was further aggravated by Tuđman's tendency to make high-profile gaffes that sparked media uproar in Serbia, benefiting Milošević's own attempts to characterize the new Croatian government as an existential threat to the safety of local Serbs. Media on both sides did their part in sensationalizing the political rhetoric.

In response to the perceived threat to their future, Croatian Serbs announced a parliamentary boycott, while taking steps to physically demarcate their territory. On July 25, citizens of Srb (a town north of Knin) declared their own Serbian Assembly as the political representative of Croatian Serbs, thus repudiating the HDZ government's national legitimacy. Under the new leadership of Milan Babić, a Knin dentist, the Assembly in Srb argued that if Croatia could break away from Yugoslavia, then local Serbs could do the same from Croatia. To add muscle to their secessionist bid, the entity soon created paramilitary units, led by Milan Martić, Knin's police chief. Given the high level of interethnic tension and segregation within the Croatian society for Serbs, and their concern that Croatian authorities would seek to recreate Ante Pavelić's Nazi puppet state, confrontation was almost unavoidable.

At the same time, for Croats, the combination of geography and seasonality made the fast-paced events particularly alarming. Minority enclaves affected were not simply on the borders with Bosnia or Serbia;

Knin was the largest town in the Krajina region of Dalmatia, and the authorities saw these new protests as unhelpful to the traditional summer tourism industry on the nearby coast. Moreover, that summer, Croatia was playing host to the 1990 European Athletics Championships in the Dalmatian coastal city of Split. Thus when rebellious Serbs began blocking roads across the country (from August 17, with the so-called Log Revolution), the country found itself basically cut in two. Underscoring the gravity of the situation, Croatian special police helicopters dispatched to clear the roads were intercepted and turned back by Yugoslav Air Force fighter planes. This major humiliation for the fledgling government angered Croatian nationalists, while encouraging local Serbs to believe that Belgrade would back their secessionist aspirations.

The estrangement between Croats and Serbs worsened by the end of the year as armed incidents between national police and paramilitaries escalated. Finally, the passing of Croatia's so-called Christmas Constitution on December 21, 1990 left the Serbs dissatisfied with their status because it categorized them as a minority group among others, as opposed to a constituent nation. For most Croats, it was a difference of semantics only, but the heated atmosphere and the general negative course of events accelerated the trend toward secessionism. Babić declared the parallel creation of a new political structure, the Serbian Autonomous Oblast of Krajina (or SAO Krajina) on the same day as the Zagreb parliament ratified its new constitution. The decision of the Krajina Serbs to declare autonomy, while not unexpected, raised the stakes and put Croatia further on a course toward civil war.

Soon after, on February 21, 1991, the Croatian parliament began the process of disassociation from federal Yugoslavia, declaring its national constitution and laws as superior to those of Yugoslavia. The following day, the municipal council of ethnically mixed Pakrac, a town in eastern Croatia, voted to join the SAO Krajina, forcing the Constitutional Court of Croatia to intervene six days later. The council's decision to handover the control of Pakrac police station to Krajina caused a Croatian government police intervention, marking the first significant armed event in the growing conflict on March 2, in which Croatian special police stormed the town and engaged in a day-long firefight with Serb officers. Following negotiations between the Croatian government and the JNA—which had sent tanks in preparation for a military operation—the Serbs relinquished control of the police station. The JNA only left Pokrac following promises from the HDZ government to remove Croatian special police units, which at the point was the closest thing that the preindependent country had to an army.

However, interethnic tensions soon worsened further on March 31, which happened to be Catholic Easter. Croatian special police launched a highly dangerous mission near the usually idyllic Plitvice Lakes National Park, where they were ambushed by Serb paramilitaries; the ensuing day-long gun battle resulted in fatalities on both sides. Eventually, the police got the upper hand and withdrew with numerous Serb prisoners, among them Goran Hadžić, who would later become president of the self-declared Republic of Serbian Krajina (RSK). The JNA responded in late April by imposing a blockade on the Croat-populated village of Kijevo, which in turn caused a massive backlash from the Croatian public. On May 6, a protest in the city of Split against the JNA, ostensibly organized by the Croatian Trade Union Association of the major local employer, the Brodosplit Shipyard, drew 100,000 people to demonstrate in front of the military's local headquarters, leaving a nineteen-year-old Macedonian JNA conscript dead. The televised images of protesters climbing atop a tank and trying to pull out soldiers shocked viewers elsewhere in Yugoslavia and became a defining one for the beginning of the war. The possibility of armed conflict still seemed unreal to regular people across Yugoslavia, and the hostilities in Croatia rapidly accelerated Macedonia's own plans to leave the federation, though it was in a very weak position for other reasons.

The negative repercussions of such incidents, then and thereafter, were worsened by confused and inaccurate reporting that inflamed public sentiment across the Yugoslav republics, providing ideal conditions for politicians to score points on combative rhetoric. It was the Croatian president himself, after all, who had called on the public to "end" the Kijevo blockade by taking to the streets. After the federal government refused his demand to declare a state of emergency in Croatia on May 15, Serbia's Slobodan Milošević denounced the federal presidency's authority categorically. This came two weeks after the Croatian parliament's vote for a full independence referendum— following the earlier example of Slovenia, which had voted to become independent from Yugoslavia in December 1990.

Thus, on May 19, 1991, in a vote characterized by high turnout, over 93 percent of Croats voted to secede from Yugoslavia. The Serbs in Krajina, of course, boycotted the referendum. In fact, they had already held their own plebiscite the week before on May 12. The Serbs voted to remain in Yugoslavia; neither they nor the Croatian government recognized the validity of the other's referendum. While Zagreb opposed the moves of the RSK, they had at the time no military capacity to enforce their claims, leaving Croatia in a precarious and divided state. On June 25, the Croatian parliament declared its full independence from Yugoslavia in careful coordination with their neighbor to the north, Slovenia.

THE TEN-DAY WAR AND SLOVENIAN INDEPENDENCE (1991)

While never a guaranteed outcome, war in Slovenia became much more likely following these turbulent events in Croatia, especially after the December 23, 1990 referendum, in which almost 90 percent of Slovenes voted for independence from Yugoslavia. In response, the JNA announced that Tito's old doctrine of defensive units and supplies at the republic level would be abolished, with the protection of local areas being centralized fully under the JNA. The Slovenian authorities had prepared for this eventuality, however, through legal means like a constitutional amendment of September 28, 1990 that obliged Slovene Territorial Defense or TO (*Teritorialna obramba*) units and equipment to remain within the republic. This bureaucratic safeguard would buy time for Slovenian defense planners seeking to confound the JNA in advance of the expected war.

What is most intriguing (and, in a sense, most Slovenian) about the resistance movement is the efficiency, secrecy, and ingenuity with which it was prepared and carried out. Throughout its long history of duchies and semiautonomous imperial Habsburg regions, Slovenia had maintained a variety of impromptu militias and (during the world wars) a Home Guard tradition maintained during Tito's Yugoslavia. One iteration of that was the TO, a sort of reserve structure created by Tito in 1968 in response to the Soviet invasion of Czechoslovakia. However, while it was given arms and a certain structure, Slovenia's TO was never required to perform any duties as the Soviet threat never materialized. In 1990, however, the Slovenian government quietly brought the TO back to life as an alternative command structure in anticipation of the Yugoslav Army's administrative centralization.

Known in full as the Maneuver Structures of National Protection (*Manevrska struktura narodne zaščite*, or MSNZ), this TO had few members and outdated weaponry by 1990. However, it did have one thing—a certifiable structure—which the proindependence government needed to outwit the JNA. Therefore, even before the JNA could attempt to take over Slovenia's TO stored military inventory, the Slovenian government secretly launched the MSNZ chain of command. By October 1990, they had thus secretly commissioned over 20,000 Slovenian TO soldiers and policemen. The federal government in Belgrade remained somewhat unaware of this operation. By the time war was actually announced the following June, MSNZ personnel had thus become a coordinated fighting force. Today, the story of how Slovenia was able to deceive the well-informed and experience Yugoslav military and intelligence apparatus remains one of the great unresolved mysteries of the war.

Slovenia's military strategy was also drawn up well in advance of the actual fighting. Its architect was the defense minister, Janez Janša. Born in 1958 (and himself the son of a former Home Guard member), Janša became famous in 1988 as one of several journalists arrested and charged by the JNA for allegedly revealing state secrets. The ensuing trial helped launch the Slovenian Spring movement. By that point, Janša (who also later served several terms as prime minister) was already well known in the nascent civil society movement as a reformer of the republic's League of Communists.

The war strategy prepared by Minister Janša and his colleagues was made with the awareness that superior JNA forces could not be defeated in pitched battle or for long periods of time. Instead, the Slovenian units would have to rely on a combination of guerrilla warfare, sabotage, ambush, and deception, adapted to the unique conditions offered by their largely rural and mountainous homeland. To have any chance of success, the rebels would have to isolate and trap the JNA's heavy mechanized weaponry and tank columns when passing through narrow passages. Crucial to this strategy was securing modern replacements for the TO's aging antitank and antiaircraft missile inventory, and the Slovenian defense ministry indeed obtained these discreetly from West German arms producers.

Slovenia finally declared independence on June 25, 1991, in coordination with Croatia, immediately sparking the Ten-Day War (*desetdnevna vojna*), also sometimes referred to as the Slovenian Independence War (*slovenska osamosvojitvena vojna*). While Slovenia relied on highly motivated volunteers, most did not have real military experience. On the other side, the JNA by that time was dominated by Serbs and Montenegrins in the officer corps and conscripts in the ranks. The confused allegiances of the military structures at this time was compounded by the ideological divide between those who wanted a strong and centralized Yugoslavia—an already vanished dream, by then—and those who sought different forms of decentralization or independence. As the goal of independence was achieved, the Ten-Day War remains a great point of pride for Slovenes today—one which has left relatively few scars, making it relatively uncontroversial compared to other Yugoslav secessionist conflicts. Indeed, the war caused less than fifty JNA casualties, while the Slovene side lost only eighteen, with 182 wounded. Damage to military hardware was more extensive, but property damage was similarly limited, and only twelve foreigners died in the fighting (war reporters and several Bulgarian truckers accidentally killed in JNA airstrikes).

Such limited casualties and such a short period of hostilities make the Ten-Day War barely register as a conflict, which was just as Slovene military planners seeking a quick and painless exit from Yugoslavia had hoped. The Slovene side had several advantages going into the war, for which it had been preparing for months in advance. This included both onsite logistical efforts and basic observations of the greater global context in which the struggle was being waged. For example, China's harsh reaction to the 1989 Tiananmen Square protests was still fresh on the minds of international observers at the time of the war, and Slovene propaganda strategy was successfully able to target Western audiences by depicting their own liberation war as a heroic struggle against similarly insurmountable odds.

For this reason, much of the actual "war" in Slovenia was not fought on the battlefield. Although it would have been relatively easy for the JNA to capture and pacify Slovenia quickly in a conventional war, this would have still left the question of what to do next. As such, considerable confusion and disagreement existed within the JNA command structures and at the level of the Yugoslav federal leadership. Any long and bloody war—right on the country's borders with the West—could have had negative repercussions. Thus, though the previous years of unrest had given the JNA ample time to prepare for all secession scenarios, it was stymied by internal dissent and competing strategic goals from the military and political leaderships, particularly at the republic level in Serbia. The JNA thus finally chose a lackluster and ineffective war strategy, which played to the strengths of the rebels, that is, their unique knowledge of local terrain.

After catching Belgrade off-guard with the earlier-than-anticipated independence declaration on June 25, Slovenia sought to secure its land borders and international airport, as did the JNA, which began dispatching troops from bases in neighboring Croatia and from ones within Slovenia. This show of force caused public protests but was slow to turn violent as neither side wanted to fire the first shot. This gave the Slovenian authorities ample time to spread their narrative of a small and democratic country fighting alone against a communist giant. Their cause attracted sympathy and was generally covered favorably in the Western media.

Meanwhile, the JNA continued to underestimate the threat posed by Slovenia's phantom military. After it disregarded warnings from Slovenian authorities to stop flying helicopter missions from its base in Zagreb into Slovenia, the Yugoslav military was shocked to see the rebels actually shoot down two of their aircraft—and with new German-made missiles, no less. Ironically, one of the first JNA pilots killed in this manner was actually an ethnic Slovene. Although the JNA succeeded in capturing many border points, its forces were soon surrounded by TO forces, and numerous JNA barracks and arms depots throughout Slovenia were seized, while desertion became a problem only five days into the war. A JNA airstrike on Slovenia's international airport left two Austrian and German journalists dead, adding to the anti-Belgrade sentiment internationally. Diplomatic efforts soon ratcheted up, with Western European countries growing increasingly concerned about the risk of spillover violence or refugee waves affecting their own countries.

The first major turning point in the war occurred on July 1, when nonmilitary developments made clear that Slobodan Milošević's Serbian government did not particularly care if Slovenia left Yugoslavia. The republic lacked a historic Serb-minority population, whereas Croatia and Bosnia were completely different cases. The Serbian government was much more concerned about protecting their interests in the latter republics. The Serbian representative to the Yugoslav presidency, Borisav Jović, infuriated the JNA by blocking Defense Minister General Veljko Kadijević's belated proposal to authorize an all-out attack on Slovenia on July 1. Indeed, JNA Chief of Staff General Blagoje Adžić had argued for this from the beginning and was predictably furious with both bureaucrats; it had been Kadijević, after all, who rejected the total invasion strategy in advance of the war. By withholding Serbia's support for further action against Slovenia, Jović essentially undermined the authority of the JNA, which had since Tito's time regarded itself as the federation's ultimate guarantor. In the mind of the generals, the army and its matériel were being sacrificed for no clear reason in Slovenia, where the only side with any personal stake in the matter was the rebel one.

On the evening of July 2, 1991, the Slovenian presidency offered a ceasefire, but this was rejected by Belgrade. However, the massive JNA convoy that set off from the capital the following morning to seize Slovenia never reached its destination as further diplomacy prevailed with international assistance. Over the next three days, the Ten-Day

War slowly subsided and the Slovenian government was granted control of all border points and facilities. War officially ended with the signing of the Brioni Accord in Croatia on Tito's favorite getaway, the Brijuni islands. Slovenia and Croatia agreed to a three-month delay in their independence declarations, which was for all intents and purposes irrelevant. Slovenia's TO units, the unexpected heroes of one of Europe's shortest wars, were internationally recognized as the official security organs of the new Slovenian state. Further, the agreement stipulated that Slovenia could keep much of the JNA's heavy weaponry and stock, which would thereafter be utilized in the new army or sold to Croatia or other warring parties in Yugoslavia. The defeated JNA was obliged to pull out what remained of its units and equipment, which it did by late October. By that point, Macedonia had also declared independence (on September 8), ensuring that the war for what was left of Yugoslavia would primarily involve Serbia.

THE CROATIAN WAR OF INDEPENDENCE: OUTBREAK AND CEASEFIRE (1991)

For four years starting from the summer of 1991, parts of Croatia were gripped by an on-again, off-again conflict of varying intensities between government forces and rebel Serb paramilitaries, the latter often backed by the JNA, which sought to defend Serb-populated regions from the Croatian army and police. Cumulatively, this conflict is now known to Croats as the Croatian War of Independence. While large portions of the country were unaffected by fighting, this and the near-simultaneous Bosnian War (which also heavily involved Croats) kept the country preoccupied with war and constant refugee waves through the first half of the 1990s. Croatia had to start from scratch in forming an army, and this brought it very quickly into tacit alliances with old allies (like Germany, the Vatican, and Italy) and new ones (pivotally, the United States), while making extensive use of its wealthy and geographically dispersed diaspora for support. This effort was heavily ramped up during the period immediately following the war in Slovenia, when all sides prepared for the larger war that was expected to follow the three-month suspension of independence negotiated in early July.

The Krajina Serbs, meanwhile, tried to establish new facts on the ground in the interim, with the support of Belgrade in late July. Police stations in the Banovina villages of Glina and Kozibrod in central Croatia were targeted in the so-called Operation Stinger (*Operacija Žaoka*), which resulted in the evacuation of Croat civilians by police with coordination of the JNA. Glina had become a flashpoint for its highly symbolic value; in 1941, the Ustaše had massacred over 1,000 local Serbs there. The Krajina Serb operation in Glina in 1991 was timed to occur around what was then the fiftieth anniversary of the original WWII Ustaše massacre. The historic cycle of violence was thus perpetuated as clashes continued throughout this strategic area of Croatia into the fall of 1991. Adding to the general confusion was the fact that while the Krajina Serb entity had a nominal structure and JNA support, on the ground level it relied on a handful of loosely organized local militant bads—something that, decades later, would still leave war crimes prosecutors uncertain as to the responsibility for specific attacks.

The war in Croatia, in its early phases at least, was complicated by the imbalance of forces as Croatia did not have an army and relied on police as well as civilian protests and blockades to thwart JNA movements from their established bases. The JNA had been built up over Tito's time into the fourth-largest fighting force in Europe, but these conventional strengths were of no use when it came to subduing internal dissent. Having witnessed how Slovenes had systematically taken over former TOs and held JNA barracks hostage, the military strategy in Croatia was adapted to achieve goals that would impair Croat ability to seize matériel or attack barracks in highly populated areas. Nevertheless, the long-standing institutional presence of military units in such areas complicated JNA efforts to protect them, particularly on the coast.

Thus, after Croatians laid siege to an important JNA barracks near the coastal city of Šibenik, fighting broke out when army units were ordered to break the siege in mid-September. After a week of fighting, however, troops of the Croatian National Guard (*Zbor Narodne Garde*, or ZNG) had captured naval facilities, dozens of vessels, and some other posts, forcing the JNA to negotiate a retreat by which it kept much of its supplies but failed to keep the city under Yugoslav control. In general, the early war on this front was thus frequently a blocking campaign, in which the JNA and Serb paramilitaries sought to control transport infrastructure to create conditions for Croatian negotiations. In this way, the army could secure a safe retreat without loss of heavy weaponry, and with guarantees for the safety of JNA personnel, without having to fight its way out at the same time.

This characterized events like the Battle of Zadar, which occurred over several weeks in September to October 1991. Belgrade—which also provided naval support—ordered commanders to take this port city, though that was never actually achieved. Instead, the battle became another protracted siege, in which thirty-four civilians were killed. The JNA and Krajina Serb forces on the outskirts of the city won the strategic Maslenica Bridge, thereby severing access to the all-important highway running along the Adriatic Sea and isolating Dalmatia from Zagreb and the rest of Croatia. This blockade created conditions by which the government was forced to negotiate. After an agreed ceasefire period, the JNA was allowed to peacefully evacuate its local garrison, removing almost 4,000 personnel and family members, and over 2,000 truckloads of weaponry and other equipment. Contrary to the agreement to remove all of its supplies from Croatian territory, the JNA allowed the Krajina Serbs to keep some of the Zadar artillery, bolstering its capabilities against the HDZ government. Nevertheless, though it did not seem a tremendous victory at the time, the fact that Croatia was successfully able to impel the JNA to leave its existing bases without a major fight was advantageous.

In other contested parts of the country, like Eastern Slavonia and Syrmia on the border of Serbia proper, the Battle of Borovo Selo in May (again, supported by the JNA) laid the framework for local Serbs to demand autonomy. But on August 1, a massacre of over fifty Croats in the eastern village of Dalj was followed by the evacuation of hundreds more by boats and barges along the Drava River to Osijek, which generated considerable Western sympathy for Croatia, particularly from Germany. This was particularly noteworthy considering that Germany's controversial past in the Balkans made it historically reticent to get involved with controversial matters. Germany finally announced its intention to recognize Croatian independence on December 19, 1991, following the example of recently independent ex-Soviet Ukraine and Latvia, as well as NATO member Iceland, putting the issue squarely into an emerging East versus West showdown.

A turning point that guaranteed Western support for the Croatian cause during the remainder of the war soon materialized in the eighty-seven-day Battle of Vukovar in eastern Croatia, which became the largest single bombardment of a European city since WWII. Starting on August 26 and tasting well into November, it pitted 36,000 JNA troops and a small number of Serb volunteers against only about 1,800 Croatian defenders. By November, the city had been all but destroyed by continued artillery barrage and was under JNA control. The army also continued to resettle an increasing number of Serb refugees from other parts of Croatia in eastern Slavonia as various massacres continued through the latter half of 1991.

Although the ruined area would not fully return to government control until international peacekeepers returned it in 1998, the JNA's victory at Vukovar was pointless. Indeed, Vukovar became an early and emotive rallying cry for Croatian nationalists seeking to blame Serbs for unprovoked war crimes. The siege also bogged down the JNA's heavy weaponry at a time when it could have been used elsewhere. However, it should be remembered that Belgrade's reactionary military policy at the time was at least partially due to the indignation of top commanders who had been denied a major assault on Slovenia—an offensive that, rightly or wrongly, they had assumed would deter the Croats from daring to engage in full-scale rebellion. On December 19, 1991, the SAO Krajina officially renamed itself as the RSK; though it remained unrecognized as a political entity, it gained support from other Serb groupings in Croatia, such as the SAO in eastern Croatia, which joined the RSK on February 26, 1992. Thereafter, Goran Hadžić, leader of the eastern Croatian Serbs since September 1991, became RSK president.

On the Croatian side, the new HDZ government faced constant crises and, while supported by a patriotic public, was under fire for its inability to defeat the Serb secessionists. Fortunately for the fledgling nation, it did have some officials with the capacities and connections to take advantage of the increasing bad public image that the JNA and RSK attacks were creating for the Serbian side, while also capable of finding pragmatic solutions to the Croat military. One of the most important figures for the war effort in the HDZ government, thus, was Minister of Defense Gojko Šušak (1945–1998). A native of Široki Brijeg in western Herzegovina, Šušak emigrated to Canada in 1969. In the following two decades, he worked in construction and restaurants while moonlighting as a diaspora nationalist—something that won him influential friends, such as the future president, Franjo Tuđman. He was one of several diaspora Croats to return to join the new government from 1990 to 1991 liaising with Croat donors abroad for economic aid as the minister of emigration, and from the same year moving to the defense ministry. By September 1991, Šušak became minster, meaning that the war effort was largely in his hands.

The challenge he inherited was formidable. While Croats—both at home and abroad—were not lacking patriotism, they were operating at a massive disadvantage during the early stages of the war. The JNA controlled the army and, crucially, the balance of air power, meaning that the separatist-friendly government in Belgrade could consistently reinforce Serbian Krajina territory with military and nonmilitary supplies, allowing the rebels to hold large pockets of national territory. While Croatia commanded a long coastline, the Yugoslav Navy still maintained access to the sea from neighboring Montenegro just to the south and (as the naval siege of Zadar had shown) the ability to obstruct Croatian ports.

As of July 1991, the ZNG, forerunner to the Croatian Army (*Hrvatska Vojska*, or HV), consisted of just three brigades, augmented by various local and national police units. Unlike the situation in ethnically homogenous Slovenia, Croats had not enjoyed the element of surprise or an advance opportunity to raid their own Yugoslav-era territorial defense units for matériel. As territorial losses mounted and the defense ministry used up over half of its supplies defending Vukovar, Minister Šušak sought ways to rearm the country, reorganize its leadership, and restructure it. Thus, by early December, he had created sixty ZNG brigades.

The challenge of defending the new nation was also in murky legal waters as from September 25 the UN announced an arms embargo against the Croatian government, which began to produce its own munitions, guns, and tanks to the extent that it could. As in all such conflicts, the embargo also increased the presence of internal organized crime and arms smuggling—not only to Croatia but to the other warring factions elsewhere in Yugoslavia as well. Under heavy international diplomatic pressure, representatives of the belligerent parties (Yugoslav defense minister General Veljko Kadijević, Serbian president Slobodan Milošević, and Croatian president Franjo Tuđman) signed a ceasefire, known as the Geneva Accord in Switzerland on November 23, 1991. However, while the international body began planning for an ambitious peacekeeping force, United Nations Protection Force (UNPROFOR) of soldiers from around the world, the ceasefire did not hold and the local arms race intensified.

It would not be until after January 2, 1992, when Minister Šušak and JNA General Andrija Rašeta signed a temporary ceasefire agreement in the Bosnian city of Sarajevo, that the pace of the conflict slowed somewhat. However, that time also saw the spillover of conflict into Bosnia itself, ensuring that Croatia's road to peace would be much longer and more complex than had been the case for Slovenia.

CROATIA AND THE WAR IN BOSNIA (1992–1995)

The complex multiethnic nature of the Yugoslav Republic of Bosnia and Herzegovina, owing to its historic division between Serbs, Croats, and the Bosniak Muslims, made for a much different environment than either Slovenia or Croatia. The eventual final result—of a unitary country with territorial autonomy between the three populations—was never in doubt, but was prolonged by mutual mistrust and political brinksmanship that punctuated four years of war. The cessation of hostilities with the 1995 Dayton Agreement, signed in Dayton, Ohio under the sponsorship of the UN and Clinton administration, resulted in a tripartite federation with rotating presidencies and much reduplication of bureaucracy. For over two decades following its peace, the question of whether Bosnia and Herzegovina would be able to survive in the long term under such an arrangement remained an item of interest for foreign policy experts, media, and local residents alike.

Over the years, the high casualty rate and damages suffered in Bosnia have made attributing guilt a preoccupation of Western media and the political class. With over 100,000 dead and 2.2 million civilians displaced, the Bosnian War was Europe's deadliest since WWII and has attracted a certain notoriety that permeated from media into Western popular culture. Although there is more than enough blame to go around between the three sides (and various foreign actors), decades of controversial media reports and scholarship have tended to oversimplify the conflict by depicting it as a war of Serbian aggression; leaders like Milošević, Karadžić, and Bosnian Serb General Ratko Mladić (all later tried for war crimes at international tribunals) have been widely portrayed as having attempted the ethnic cleansing of Bosniak Muslims, in particular, as well as Croats. Of course, the realities of the war were much more complex. As in the Slovenian, Croatian, and late Kosovo war of 1999, the full picture included both remarkable games of geopolitics and seemingly incongruous acts on the ground level, such as cooperation between ostensibly rival factions. Aside from ethnic differences and historic grievances, the Bosnian (and other Yugoslav) wars were characterized by the simple desire for financial gain, as was seen in the massive smuggling of sanctioned weapons, fuel, and other goods that enriched politicians, bureaucrats, and businessmen from all over the world during the crisis.

War began in Bosnia in April 1992 following two years of escalating tensions between the three communities, influenced by the breakdown in Yugoslav governance capacities and the independence movements in Slovenia and Croatia. Bosnia's most significant leader and president of the multiethnic republic presidency was Alija Izetbegović (1925–2003), a lawyer, former anti-Tito dissident, and Islamist whose views over the role of religion had alienated him from Croats, Serbs, and communists alike. Nevertheless, Izetbegović was a shrewd politician and managed to win support from the West (as well as numerous Muslim countries) for the Bosniak cause, while entertaining rival settlement offers and often going back on agreements in the hopes of gaining a better deal—something that both guaranteed a civil war and then perpetuated it once fighting broke out.

Thus, Izetbegović supported but then rejected a June 1991 peace plan that would have kept Bosnia whole (and in fact enlarged it, expanding to include 60 percent of the territorially contiguous Serbian province of Sandžak, which itself had a Bosniak population) and in Yugoslavia. That deal was negotiated by Adil Zulfikarpašić of Izetbegović's Party of Democratic Action (SDA) and Radovan Karadžić, president of the Bosnian Serbs' party (Serb Democratic Party, SDS). Most importantly, Serbian president Slobodan Milošević supported the deal. Nevertheless, Izetbegović backed out of the agreement, demanding (with the Croats of Bosnia) nothing less than independence. In January 1992, there seemed to be a breakthrough when European negotiators came up with the Lisbon Agreement, by which Bosnia would become a Swiss-style cantonal state. Yet, once again, Izetbegović renounced his agreement (reached with Karadžić on behalf of Bosnia's Serbs and Mate Boban on behalf of its Croat population). Instead, Izetbegović pushed forth on February 29, 1992 with an independence referendum that the Serbs (who constituted 32 percent of the population) boycotted; only with the combined support of Bosniaks (at 44 percent), and Croats (at 17 percent) was the referendum to secede from Yugoslavia successful.

Unsurprisingly, this led to an outbreak of civil war by April 1992. Izetbegović had achieved one strategic objective as the international community generally recognized Bosnia's declaration of independence. However, he presided over a very weak government and had almost no army with which to defend his new state. Soon, the JNA and the Bosnian Serb entity it supported, Republika Srpska (RS), controlled 70 percent of Bosnian territory. With its capital in Banka Luka, the RS had support from the regular Yugoslav army and its own Army of Republika Srpska (*Vojska Republike Srpske*, or VRS). In fact, the VRS was established in May 1992 when the JNA discharged 80,000 soldiers of Bosnian Serb background, allowing the self-proclaimed state within Bosnia to defend itself with heavy weaponry inherited from JNA stockpiles. The historic TOs and other arsenals throughout Bosnia were similarly raided or resold by Bosniaks and Croats in areas under their control.

Croatia itself played a key role in directing the war in Bosnia, both imitating the Serbs' own breakaway actions and providing a pivotal arms pipeline from Croatian ports to arm both Bosnian Croat fighters and, during periods of alliance, troops in the Bosniak-majority Army of the Republic of Bosnia and Herzegovina (ARBiH), loyal to the SDA government in Sarajevo. Croatian government officials took particular concern of the ethnic Croat population in Herzegovina, which had been declared on November 18, 1991, as the Croatian Community of Herzeg-Bosnia, a self-declared autonomous zone similar to the RS and the SAO Krajina within Croatia.

A military body called the Croatian Defense Council (*Hrvatsko vijeće obrane*, or HVO) was also created on April 8, 1992, to defend Bosnian Croat interests. Operating thus in his land of birth, Defense Minister Šušak was able to use his local knowledge and diaspora contacts to establish strong connections between Zagreb and the Bosnian Croat separatists. This was problematic at times as in 1992 when a separate Croat nationalist militia, the *Hrvatske obrambene snage* (HOS), briefly arose in Bosnia due to far-right diaspora participation. Disagreements over possible negotiations with the Serbs, or cooperation with the Bosniaks, led to several internal Croat assassinations and ultimately the disbanding of the HOS in late 1992.

In the early months of 1992, the HVO generally fought alongside the ARBiH against the Bosnian Serbs. However, an internal Croat-Bosniak war soon broke out, especially in the area around Mostar, the ethnically mixed town nominated by the Croats as the capital of their own rival ethnic entity. This war-within-a-war occurred due to mutual mistrust over suspicions that the opposing sides were secretly negotiating a separate peace with the Serbs. Croat mistrust in Herzegovina was also high due to the atrocities committed against them by several thousand mujahideen from Muslim countries, who had been funded by Saudi Arabia and set up in bases with Iranian military trainers. In an irony typical of the nasty and complex Bosnian conflict, these fighters and some of the weapons they would use against Bosnian Croats (and Serbs) were actually being moved into Bosnia via logistics centers in Croatia, administered by the Croatian government itself.

Indeed, much remains unclear about Croatia's actual intentions during the war, which is unsurprising, considering that Croatia itself was still gripped by civil war with the Serbs during the entire Bosnian conflict. Much of the uncertainty about Croatian intentions derives from differing interpretations, then and now, of the motivating factors behind decisions taken by key leaders. For example, President Tuđman's own prewar public statements hinted at a preference for ethnic self-determination, while diplomatic efforts to divide Bosnia on ethnic terms with Serbia were pushed early on in the conflict. At the same time, though, Croatia supported Bosnian independence and clearly relished the role of being the ARBiH's major arms supplier as this was (especially during the wartime UN arms sanction period) very profitable.

In the end, larger diplomatic forces pushed Croatia to resume the local military alliance with the Bosniak Army. Izetbegović proved very successful at lobbying for his cause in Western capitals, at the UN level, and in the Muslim world, leaving Serbia almost without allies. By 1993, the HVO was reorganized by the Croatian defense ministry to resemble the HV. Indeed, during the overall conflict, HV units were often engaged directly against VRS forces in eastern Herzegovina. Some HVO units were incorporated into the Sarajevo government's army. This paved the way for a united force against the VRS as NATO began preparations for airstrikes against Bosnian Serb targets in 1994. By mid-1995, the combined Bosniak and Croat armies, supported by NATO air power, tipped the balance of the war. The ensuing peace negotiations at Dayton ended up creating a tripartite state remarkably similar to the kind that had been foreseen by numerous observers local and foreign alike since well before the war.

With the safety of Bosnia's Croats guaranteed by the treaty and the continuing large presence of international observers overseeing Bosnia's day-to-day political and administrative life, a smaller version of the HVO was incorporated into the Army of the Federation of Bosnia and Herzegovina (VFBiH) in December 1995.

SLOVENIA'S PROGRESS UNDER JANEZ DRNOVŠEK (1992–2007)

After the brief drama of Slovenia's Ten-Day War had subsided, the country was rapidly stabilized and ushered back into the fold of Western European nations; especially keen to help its economic postwar redevelopment were old allies like Germany, Austria, and Italy. While Slovenia played a minor role diplomatically during the remainder of the Yugoslav Wars, and also took in refugees from Bosnia and Croatia, it did not suffer any further instability after its quick and triumphant liberation in July 1992. Further, its ethnic homogeneity meant that, unlike other ex-Yugoslav republics, ethnic nationalism was of a limited nature. Indeed, with their preferences for pragmatic and even bland political options, Slovenes showed themselves to be the most "Yugoslav of the Yugoslavs," a sort of cross between efficiency-minded Germans and socialist intellectuals in the style cultivated by leaders like Tito and Kardelj.

The postwar reverse from temporary nationalism to a seasoned socialism was soon apparent. The government that had delivered the independence referendum and the war effort (known as the DEMOS coalition) was replaced in 1992 by another, more traditionally liberal coalition with strong relations to the Yugoslav old-guard, led by Janez Drnovšek (1950–2008). Nominated as a compromise candidate following a crisis in the DEMOS coalition, Drnovšek had briefly served as president of Yugoslavia in its final troubled years of 1989–1990. Previously, he had specialized in the banking sector and worked as a Yugoslav economics advisor abroad. In 1992, Slovenes hoped that his experience would help propel national growth following the damage and uncertainty that had been caused by the unceremonious break-up with Belgrade.

Drnovšek's government included left-wing remnants of the DEMOS coalition, including the Liberal Democratic Party (*Liberalno demokratska stranka*, or LDS), which itself was the legal successor of the Association of Socialist Youth of Slovenia (*Zveza socialistične mladine Slovenije*, or ZSMS)—the former youth wing of the Communist League of Slovenia. Drnovšek was elected LDS president and spent much of his political career with the party, serving as prime minister from 1992 through 2002, and subsequently as Slovenian president for one term.

For postindependence Slovenia, the presence of relatively young leaders like Drnovšek, who had active experience of late-Yugoslav economics, was highly advantageous because a similar ideological class was taking power at the European level in the early 1990s. In fact, there were many similarities between Yugoslavia had attempted to achieve, and what the aspiring EU theoretically wanted to achieve, in terms of centrally planned political and economic policies. In 1992, someone like Janez Drnovšek was not perceived as a throwback to an earlier time, or a progenitor of a failed political experiment, in the halls of power in Brussels or Strasbourg, where European technocrats met. Rather, he was a fellow traveler on a similar mission—to unite Europe under generally left- or center-left political values.

Another Slovenian politician with experience in late-Yugoslav economics, who played a key role in the new country's economic growth, was Mitja Gaspari. Born in 1951 in Ljubljana, Gaspari became an expert in monetary policy, obtaining degrees in economics from universities in his home city and in Belgrade, where by 1988 he had become vice-governor of the National Bank of Yugoslavia. As such, Gaspari gained valuable insight into real-life crisis economics and the international crisis negotiations from that period, in which the Ante Marković government was trying to save Yugoslavia's economy with the help of international institutions like the IMF and World Bank. Indeed, in September 1991, Gaspari became a World Bank senior advisor. The following year, he was able to make a rather seamless transition back to national politics, joining the Drnovšek government as economy minister from 1992 through 2000. The two men deserve much of the credit for developing a stable and increasingly prosperous economy, transforming the old Yugoslav model and applying it successfully to the rules applicable in Europe.

In general, a key part of their policy was to take a gradualist approach regarding the transition from a state-managed economy to a capitalist market economy. Knowing the risks posed by changing the system too quickly in places where institutions were not yet fully developed (as was the case in Russia, Ukraine, and other Eastern Bloc countries in the early 1990s), Slovenia took a more cautious approach. For his part, Gaspari was particularly effective in taking an organized and firm orientation to public finances, budgets, pension reforms, and bank restructuring. Issues like monetary sovereignty and rectification of external Yugoslav-era debt were dealt with responsibly, according to a plan, with macroeconomic stability and sustainable growth being generally agreed policies of the bipartisan government, reflecting overall agreement in Slovenian society about the national interest in the years after Yugoslavia.

Another issue that most Slovenes agreed on was the benefit of joining the EU, at that point a newly established grouping of states that had emerged from the European Economic Community (EEC) that developed in the decades following WWII. After German reunification in 1991, a prevailing mood of optimism presented the future as a simple and natural process of finalizing the so-called European Project for an "ever-closer union" among countries on the continent, both politically and economically. The continuation of war in Croatia and Bosnia, of course, was vivid proof that such a moment had not yet quite arrived, but for Slovenes, the ongoing wars next-door were also proof that membership in the European club would be a safeguard from any future return to instability. The same argument was put forward regarding potential membership in NATO, and official governmental efforts to join both soon began. The country's EU membership application was officially submitted on June 10, 1996, leading eight years of further discussions and reforms before it eventually joined the bloc.

As a pragmatic country keen to benefit from its achievements, Slovenia began its relationship with the EU as an extension of its inherited relationship with the EU from Yugoslavia. Thus, with the Cooperation Agreement of September 1, 1993, Slovenia simply took on the rights and obligations laid out in a 1980 agreement between the EEC and Yugoslavia. Following further reforms, Slovenia replaced this with the so-called Europe Agreement (the country's de-facto membership application) signed on June 10, 1996 with EU representatives. This broad agreement covered harmonization of trade laws, reorienting Slovenia's economy toward establishing a free-trade area with the EU, and stipulated certain technical and financial assistance from the EU to Slovenia. A year later, parliament ratified an amended version of the Europe Agreement, which allowed a four-year transition period to take effect; it also allowed for greater foreign ownership of Slovenian real estate, which generated mild controversy at the time. As with the pace of economic reform, however, these negotiations with the EU were done on the basis of gradual implementation, with the agreement coming into effect only on February 1, 1999.

By 1998, the EU had become Slovenia's main trade partner, with 65 percent of its exports made to EU member states and 69 percent of its imports coming from the EU. Of this, Germany, Italy, and France comprised Slovenia's main trade partners. All in all, Slovenia had achieved a remarkable success, considering that the effects of war and economic devastation would continue to haunt much of its neighbors in other former Yugoslav republics for years to come.

While the European Commission (the bureaucratic leadership body overseeing the EU) and European Parliament occasionally voiced criticism of Slovenia for slow or incomplete reforms to its domestic market, judiciary, and so on, there were never any major issues or questions about human rights issues that affected other EU applicant states. Slovenia was considered fairly universally as a model candidate, and the frequent public affirmations from Brussels that things were moving on the right track helped the center-left government remain in power throughout the 1990s. In a June 1999 speech, the prime minister voiced his optimism that Slovenia would be admitted to the EU by 2002 and to the single currency. Otherwise known as the Euro, this new currency was set for implementation on January 1, 2001, in select European countries. Although his estimate would be off by two years, Drnovšek showed his economic acumen with this comment as Slovenia in 2007 would become the first of the new members of the EU to replace its national currency (the Tolar) with the Euro. (As of 2020, several EU countries had still not fulfilled all the conditions for assuming the Euro, or did not want it.)

On March 23, 2003, a largely symbolic referendum was held asking Slovene citizens whether they would like to join the EU and NATO. Voters approved of the former by almost 90 percent, though only 66 percent supported the latter. According to Drnovšek, the president of Slovenia at the time, support had been dampened somewhat by popular opposition to the U.S.-led intervention then beginning in

Iraq. However, the public opinion also indicated a sense of perspective among a small country of 2 million who, if not entirely pacifistic, were much more attuned to economic well-being and daily-life issues than international geopolitics. After five decades at the center of Tito's Non-Aligned Movement, bordered by former countries with lingering problems, many Slovenes found it most sensible to look forward to the benefits of EU membership and try to stick out as little as possible otherwise.

This was generally the case though there were moments of exception. For example, on June 16, 2001, Drnovšek hosted the first-ever meeting between U.S. president George H. W. Bush and Russian counterpart Vladimir Putin in Brdo Castle near Kranj in Upper Carniola. Drnovšek had a personal taste for involvement in such high-level foreign affairs, something that had only been heightened following his 1999 diagnosis with kidney cancer. This personal setback undoubtedly affected Drnovšek's outlook, and after successfully winning the Slovenian presidency in 2002, he became more attuned to various humanitarian and environmental causes. However, the government (which had swung back to the conservatives for the first time since 1992) and general citizenry did not share the new president's vision of a proactive Slovenia engaged in solving crises like Darfur in Africa or even Kosovo, a former neighboring Yugoslav territory. Ironically, by the time of Drnovšek's death, in 2008, it was the absolute success of his policies that allowed Slovenes to enjoy a life free of major crises the humanitarian-minded president had wanted them to care about.

CROATIA AT WAR: THE FINAL YEARS (1992–1995)

On January 15, 1992, twenty-four nations (among them, twelve EU members) officially recognized Croatia's independence. This diplomatic achievement coupled with the agreement of the temporary ceasefire earlier that month sparked hopes among Croats that the war would be over sooner rather than later. In November 1991, Croatia, Serbia, and the JNA signed the Vance Plan (named for UN negotiator and former U.S. secretary of state Cyrus Vance), creating the Geneva Accord. However, while the plan envisaged a ceasefire, enforced by UN peacekeepers on the ground, the actual deployment of this group, UNPROFOR was delayed and not fully achieved until May 1992.

Following the Croatia-JNA negotiated ceasefire of January 1992 and subsequent expansion of the war to Bosnia, fighting temporarily subsided in Croatia. An unsanctioned operation in April against JNA and

Krajina Serb forces near the towns of Belišće and Valpovo resulted in quick gains for the HV, but the central government soon interceded and leading officers were reassigned because of their overzealous action. In the eyes of otherwise friendly Western allies, the episode raised concerns that the government did not have full control over the army, and the fact that it needed to provide reassurances also played a role in the government's decision.

Thus, only small skirmishes continued to occur during this time, and Croat officials were generally optimistic about their standing with the West. The fact that they hosted international peacekeepers across disputed territory was beneficial to an extent that the government could control access to information and conceal their intentions from UNPROFOR or deflect responsibility onto it before the public, whenever suitable. The peace plan was meant to demilitarize the SAO Krajina, allow for return of refugees, and restore the peace. However, as Croatia increased its own covert role in Bosnia's war and local antagonisms increased, the UN plan soon fell apart. Although UNPROFOR officers were present in Croatia and in contact with senior military and political officials, they were essentially powerless to stop the fighting and confused or deceived by official explanations. For example, following an HV assault on June 21–23, known as the Battle of the Miljevci Plateau, UNPROFOR asked the Croatian side to withdraw to prior positions, to which they were told that the elaborately planned operation had in fact not been organized.

During this period, the HV achieved some clear victories, though, such as Operation Tiger in July 1992. This two-week operation was launched in southern Dalmatia and western Herzegovina, and succeeded in driving back VRS forces near the key border port city of Dubrovnik. Two months earlier, the HV had already succeeded in defeating VRS forces in a battle in the Neretva River valley. The concentration of Croatian and Bosnian Serb forces in this key southern Dalmatian corridor had been allowed by events of the previous fall. In October 1991, the JNA had overrun most of the territory between the coastal Pelješac and Prevlaka peninsulas but not Dubrovnik. The city came under a Yugoslav Navy blockade and suffered extensive shelling in its historic old town. Although human casualties due to shelling during the Siege of Dubrovnik were not tremendous, there was extensive building damage and the Croatian government achieved a public relations victory by depicting the JNA as barbaric for bombing the UNESCO heritage site.

The HV action in July 1992 resulted in the capture of a strategic transport corridor and, following further skirmishes, led to a negotiated

JNA withdrawal from nearby Konavle, thwarting the VRS force's effort to connect to the Adriatic coast. Further HV offensives chipped away at the VRS territories in Herzegovina, threatening the important town of Trebinje, while the JNA's withdrawal took southern Dalmatia mostly off of the map of battle, with UNPROFOR demilitarizing and then administering the Prevlaka Peninsula until 1996. Croatian military operations in the summer and fall of 1992 eliminated the strategic threat that the JNA had originally posed, that is, establishing a secure area under Yugoslav control between the Montenegrin border and Knin. That would have essentially prevented Croatia from functioning as a state, and, due to the geographic and logistical factors at work locally, represented numerous military scenarios witnessed in Dalmatia since medieval and ancient times.

Entering into 1993, the Tuđman government sought to expand on these gains in southern Dalmatia by launching new operations in the province's north. The so-called Operation Maslenica of January 1993 aimed to recover land in northern Dalmatia and Lika held by RSK forces, as well as to prevent Serbs from threatening coastal cities like Zadar again. The operation, which caught the Serbs by surprise, was also politically motivated; the HDZ and Tuđman personally faced local elections in early February, and more right-wing parties had long been criticizing the government for failing to defeat the rebels. However, while Serb casualties were higher than Croat in the ensuing battles, the HV lacked the heavy artillery needed to capitalize on its initial gains. Politically, the operation was criticized by the UN Security Council. In February, an obscure attempt was made at improving relations between the RSK and Croatia when a secretly negotiated treaty, the Austrian-supported Daruvar Agreement, was signed contrary to the knowledge of top RSK leaders. The results of this debacle were forced UN staff changes and international reconsideration of general conflict resolution methods.

With the Bosnian Croat army engaged in skirmishes with the Bosniak Muslim and Serb armies throughout 1993, fighting in Croatia itself eased until September. The very controversial Battle of the Medak Pocket (*Operacija Medački džep*), centered around the village of Medak, saw the HV attack RSK forces near Gospić in the Lika region. While the Croat HV gained some ground, the conflict acquired additional notoriety because of claims that the army also targeted UN peacekeepers and Serb civilians. An official report from Canadian UNPROFOR peacekeepers, who engaged in heavy firefights with the HV, reported that the Croats had systematically destroyed eleven villages in the Medak Pocket during their UN-negotiated withdrawal.

General Janko Bobetko, the HV commander of that operation, would later be indicted for war crimes before an international tribunal set up in the Netherlands, though he died before his case went to trial. Nevertheless, several other HV military personnel involved in the killing of Serbs and destruction of property at the Medak Pocket would later be tried by national and international courts, representing a significant hindrance to the pace of Croatia's postwar entrance into the EU.

In 1993, however, that was still a distant dream. One key result of the Battle of the Medak Pocket was that it damaged Croatia's image internationally, both in the media and among the UN, with the head of the latter stating in 1994 that the incident had damaged trust in UNPROFOR among Croatian Serbs, and thus been a disincentive to UN calls for the RSK to disarm and implement other goodwill measures. Fortunately, for Croatia's government, however, these events coincided with a sea change in American foreign policy. Whereas the former Republican administration of George H.W. Bush had taken a relatively neutral stance, preferring to let the UN and European leaders try to sort out the conflict, the new Democratic administration of Bill Clinton took an activist stance, won over largely by the wily Izetbegović to the side of Bosnia's Muslims. Indeed, by the fall of 1993, American college campuses were littered with posters announcing events ultimately funded by public relations companies for the Bosnian government's cause against the Serbs. The same dynamic was witnessed in Washington, D.C. For Croatia, joining together—however unwillingly—with the SDA and its unclear goals for Herzegovina was increasingly seen by leaders as a package deal that would lead to long-term victory.

The Clinton administration would increasingly single out Slobodan Milošević and Serbia for criticism in the Yugoslav wars. As Croatia tried to stick with the ceasefire and pursue a diplomatic course, American diplomacy began to unilaterally outpace the efforts of the UN and Europeans, while, of course, still working with them officially. One key result was the Washington Agreement signed between Bosnia's SDA government and the Bosnian Croats' self-declared Republic of Herzeg-Bosnia on March 18, 1994. According to the agreement, the cumulative territory then controlled by the Croat and Bosnian government militaries would be divided into ten autonomous, Swiss-style cantons, thus establishing the Federation of Bosnia and Herzegovina. The general purpose was to create a unified Bosniak-Croat front against the Serbs—both in Bosnia and in Croatia.

At the same time, Defense Minister Šušak had become the major Croatian leader for the United States throughout 1994. He was especially close with U.S. Secretary of Defense William Perry, who helped provide military training solutions by directing Šušak to private U.S. military companies since Croatia was still under an arms embargo. While Šušak continued to scour the arms bazaars of the world (with a heavy focus on the former Soviet Union) for his military refurbishment plans, the U.S. technical assistance was also vital to train Croatian officers. On November 29, 1994, Šušak led a Croatian delegation to Washington that signed a cooperation agreement with Pentagon generals.

By that time, the Croatian defense ministry was in the concluding phase of an expansion and reorganization plan for the entire military. The government had provided over $1 billion for arms and training for a combined force of 96,000 men, including air force, navy, and national guard components. This was clearly a force created—as Šušak told his American supporters in a February 1995 visit to Washington—with the conquest of Serb-occupied areas and total victory in mind. While the Clinton administration was uncertain that Croatia was still strong enough to actually achieve this, they allowed the military solution to prevail over a diplomatic one. The last possibility for a peaceful resolution (the so-called Z-4 Plan of January 1995 created by an international expert group) was not even read by the RSK leadership as the Serbian leadership did not like the terms. The Croats, too, were unimpressed.

This policy change occurred in parallel with the beginning of NATO airstrikes against the Bosnian Serbs in 1995, something that further sapped at the Krajina Serbs' ability to gain reinforcements. The Croatian government carried out its own operations against the Serbs in the Knin area, as well as further north and east into Slavonia, in two 1995 actions—Operation Flash and the more notorious Operation Storm. In these combined offenses, a much better-equipped and commanded army swept rapidly across Serb-held territory; Operation Flash, waged in May, captured 215 square miles of RSK-held territory forces around Okučani in Slavonia, forcing the majority of the region's 14,000 Serbs to flee.

Later, during Operation Storm in August, the HV established a front stretching almost 400 miles, making it the largest land battle in Europe since WWII. With backing from the Croatian special police coming from the Velebit Mountain and the Bosnian government army coming from the Bihać Pocket, the HV was able to breakthrough the RSK's main positions. Over the two weeks of battle and mopping-up operations, almost 200,000 ethnic Serbs were forced to flee, and numerous war crimes were committed against those who did not escape in time.

The various refugee columns sought to go to Serbia or RS, but suffered numerous hardships along the way from both military and civilian forces, even those of fellow Serbs. Although Serbian and Croatian officials disagreed (and continue to disagree) categorically over the extent of damages, casualties, and crimes, in general Operation Storm would be remembered as a great final act of liberation by the Croats, as well as a grave act of ethnic cleansing by the Serbs.

POLITICAL CHANGE AND REORIENTING CROATIA (1995–2007)

After Operation Storm, the war in Croatia was essentially over. On November 12 in the eastern village of Erdut, the Basic Agreement was signed between Croatia and Serbs who had been holding the Eastern Slavonia and Syrmia regions, allowing a peaceful end to the war. This occurred just under two weeks after the Dayton Agreement was signed in the United States, ending the Bosnian War. Although there were UN-protected zones in different regions of Croatia until as late as 1998, the country had achieved its major strategic goal of unifying the country under borders broadly similar to those of the Yugoslav Croatian republic.

A major issue after the war was refugees, not only the ethnic Serbs of Croatia who had departed, in most cases, for good, but also the Croats. Since the beginning of the war, over 200,000 Croats had been internally displaced by fighting, and fierce battles such as the Medak Pocket battle left entire areas uninhabitable. The government had also hosted hundreds of thousands of Bosniaks made homeless by the fighting in neighboring Bosnia-Herzegovina. Wartime laws over occupation of property and a continually fluid situation would affect the ability of war refugees to reclaim their property, or to get legal recourse.

After the war, the duties of the government shifted from the immediate, humanitarian-related concerns to broader economic recovery. Croatia's economy had been reduced by a quarter since 1990, incurring almost $37 billion in property and other physical damage. Unquantifiable damage had been done to the country's cultural heritage and infrastructure as well.

In 1995, the first postwar elections were held, which were won by Franjo Tuđman and his HDZ party. They had already proven capable of arming and organizing a military that could liberate the country; however, now their challenge would be completely different. Despite Croatia's military success, the country had lost valuable time (compared to countries like Slovenia) in modernizing and reforming its society to incorporate the kind of reforms demanded by the EU. Considering that the international tribunal set up in Holland for investigating war crimes was also keenly interested in investigating Croatia's top brass, the challenges to progress were truly complex and long-lasting.

The government's steps to rebuilding the economy in 1995 included the creation of a Ministry of Privatization. Given Croatia's appeal as a tourist destination, with its thousands of islands and Mediterranean climate, government officials were aware from the beginning that property sales and tourism development would be a big part of the postwar recovery. Therefore, this new administrative portfolio was considered an important addition to the overall efforts (then still in their infancy) toward turning Croatia into a free-market capitalist economy. While government planners had lost valuable time compared to countries like Slovenia because of the war, they also had the chance to learn from the latter's experience of economic and administrative reforms during that time.

In 1997 presidential elections, Franjo Tuđman was elected to a second five-year term, his still ruling HDZ party benefiting from greater consumer confidence and economic growth, as well as nationalistic achievements, like the final reintegration of the Eastern Slavonia/Syrmia and UN-overseen Dalmatian territories in 1998. The peak achievement was reached on October 3 of that year when a longtime influential friend of Croatia, Pope John Paul II, beatified the controversial Cardinal Alojzije Stepinac, who had led Croatia's Catholic community during the Nazi-era Ustaše regime. For Serbs who had suffered from the more recent war, this was just adding insult to injury. Even for non-Serbs, the pontiff's actions could be seen as a whitewashing of history as Stepinac had been aware of Ustaše crimes against civilians and the Vatican-led "ratlines" that helped thousands of Nazis from Croatia, Germany, and elsewhere escape to South America after WWII.

President Tuđman died in 1999. The HDZ government finally ran its course in 2000, losing parliamentary elections that year due to a poor economy. A center-left coalition led by Prime Minister Ivica Račan was created, while concomitant presidential elections brought veteran moderate Stjepan Mesić to power. At this time, efforts were being heightened to fulfill national goals for EU and NATO membership. The Račan government used these goals, in part, to justify amending the constitution to change Croatia's political system toward the type more often encountered in Europe: no longer the semipresidential system used by HDZ during the war years, it would instead become a parliamentary system, in which most powers were handed over to the parliament and the prime minister's cabinet.

Mesić did retain, however, the president's traditional role as commander-in-chief; this would prove vital in late September 2000 when he took the bold decision of forcibly retiring seven senior military officers who had signed the so-called "Twelve-Generals Letter" that complained about alleged disrespect of Croatian war veterans and the legacy of the war itself. While largely forgotten today, the president's move probably expedited Croatian progress toward EU and NATO accession by several years, as some of

Born in 1934, Stjepan "Stipe" Mesić is among modern Croatia's most eminent leaders. Only the second to have been elected president twice (in 2000 and 2005), Mesić first came to prominence due to his activist views in the 1967 "Croatian Spring" protests. As president, he was most notable for his pragmatic, reform-minded steps meant to weaken the influence of ethnic nationalism linked with the war. (NATO)

the letter's signatories (like General Ante Gotovina, a commander in Operation Storm) would be tried for war crimes at the Hague Tribunal in later years. Mesić's swift response to the letter caused considerable controversy in Croatian society and media, but did serve a purpose for the future by helping to separate the old-guard, more nationalistic militant elements from the country that sought to reform into a model EU member along the lines of Slovenia.

The president's instincts proved correct in July 2001 when the International Criminal Tribunal for the former Yugoslavia (ICTY), located in the Netherlands, issued sealed indictments to the Croatian government regarding General Gotovina, former special police commander

Mladen Markač, and Ivan Čermak, a former deputy defense minister. The tribunal sought their arrest and extradition for war crimes allegedly committed during Operation Storm in August 1995 against the Krajina Serb civilian population. A fierce debate was instantly sparked in Croatian society over the legality and rightness of the request. For his part, Gotovina immediately went into hiding, successfully evading war crimes prosecutors and various intelligence agencies searching for him for over four years.

Aside from this drama, the Račan government enjoyed brief popularity through big infrastructure rebuilding projects, economic growth, and tourism revival. It also took tangible steps toward connecting Croatia internationally. The country became a World Trade Organization member in November 2000. Eleven months later, the government signed a Stabilization and Association Agreement with the EU, formally applying for EU membership in February/March 2003.

Later that year, new parliamentary elections brought the nationalist HDZ party back to power, under the leadership of Ivo Sanader, an entrepreneur and former deputy foreign minister. His premiership was instantly drawn in by the controversy over whether Croatia should allow the extradition of its generals to the ICTY over cases of war crimes in the former Yugoslavia. This highly emotive issue cut to the core of different understandings of the war, patriotism, and what seemed to be the price of admission for Western bodies anxious to see signs of "reforms" in relevant areas, such as the judiciary, military, and human rights.

Nevertheless, in 2004, the European Commission finally gave its recommendation that Croatian accession negotiations should begin, emphasizing in its findings the country's progress in building sound economic and democratic institutions. Official EU applicant status came on June 18, 2004, but negotiations were delayed until December 2005, after the dramatic capture of General Ante Gotovina from his hiding place, the Spanish island of Tenerife. EU member states like Great Britain and the Netherlands had made Gotovina's capture or surrender a precondition for Croatian EU accession, something that was predictably unpopular among Croatian nationalists. Gotovina was arrested by Spanish police and flown to the Netherlands, where he pled not guilty before the court, thus beginning a long and controversial chapter in international justice. (Originally found guilty of participation in a "joint criminal enterprise" to drive out the Krajina Serbs, Gotovina was freed on appeal in 2012.)

Croatia had larger problems impeding its EU accession than the location of a few former generals, however. The EU membership negotiating process slowed over both perceived reform problems and, specifically, by Slovenia's decision as an EU member to block Croatia's EU accession from December 2008 until September 2009 over a territorial dispute regarding ownership of the Bay of Piran. It was an ironic reminder that the two former Yugoslav republics most eager to depart the Balkans for the West could still engage, if even peacefully, in the kind of disputes befitting the historical mindset of the region.

10

Rejoining the West
(2007–2020)

CROATIA: MESSY JUSTICE AND EU MEMBERSHIP (2008–2013)

By July 1, 2009, when he abruptly announced his decision to resign as prime minister and abandon politics, Ivo Sanader had been in office since 2003—a longer run than any prior head of government in the young country's history. The veteran HDZ leader's sudden announcement surprised many Croats as he had been tipped as a possible presidential candidate for the 2010 elections. Until Slovenia decided to play hardball by obstructing Croatia's EU membership talks because of an unresolved border dispute, Sanader had been expected to lead Croatia in negotiations with Brussels. Instead, the nationalist who had managed to make painful compromises and work with the opposition for reforms was suddenly out of power. Indeed, this cumulative experience created a cloud of confusion over national happenings. When he finally fled Croatia for Austria in December 2010—only to be extradited to face corruption charges in July 2011—it was hard to tell who was more pleased. The old guard he had sidelined within his own

HDZ and the archrival Social Democratic Party (SDP), which he had toppled from power following a three-year administration in 2003, both saw benefits from Sanader's downfall. Despite their individual dominance, HDZ and SDP have since independence always needed other, smaller parties to form government coalitions—something that has led to frequently volatile and short-lived governments.

Even well before these unexpected developments derailed his premiership, Ivo Sanader's time in office had coincided with turbulent domestic events (such as massive protests over General Ante Gotovina's war crimes indictment and later arrest), as well as international ones (such as the war in Iraq and the global financial crisis of 2008). This inevitably meant that Sanader participated in numerous key events. In February 2005, he became the last statesman to visit Pope John Paul II at the Vatican, a few weeks before the Polish pope died on April 2. It was in a way fitting: Sanader had grown up in a large and poor family and, following a venerable Croatian tradition, gained his higher education in Rome and later Austria under the tutelage of the Catholic Church. He went on to play an important role in the 1990s Tuđman governments, mostly at deputy level, a connection that would be brought up again in corruption trials decades later as Croatian prosecutors looked to burnish their reform credentials in a so-called war on corruption that, all too often, targeted Sanader and his close associates.

As of 2019, Sanader had been convicted and freed several times, with retrials, orders, and sentences quashed by the Constitutional Court over procedural and other issues. For a certain segment of rival politics and society, the on-again, off-again nature of Sanader's trials was either confusing or perhaps deliberately opaque; a sign that Croatia, despite a declared "war on corruption," was unable or unwilling to tackle alleged corruption among senior politicians. On the other hand, Sanader had at one point been considered a voice of moderation, early in his mandate indispensable to "cleaning out" the war-era nationalist wing of the HDZ that supported initiatives such as the 12 Generals' Letter and the Ante Gotovina cause. Further, in 2003, the ethnic minority Independent Democratic Serb Party supported Sanader's government. In a sign of goodwill, the Catholic premier even went to celebrate Orthodox Christmas with the Serb minority. When Gotovina was finally captured by Spanish police on the island of Tenerife in 2005 and extradited to the International Criminal Tribunal for the former Yugoslavia (ICTY), significant pressure was alleviated from the Croatian government, which could be seen as no longer potentially complicit in hiding suspects of war crimes. The trajectory of EU negotiations was swift, and, for a time, it appeared that the "reformed" HDZ government under Sanader might lead Croatia into the union.

An additional hazard that got in the way, however, was the global financial crisis of 2008. This ultimately turned out to be the major cause for the downfall of the national leader. Croatia's economy sputtered and foreign investment declined in Sanader's second term, which in any case took place after a closer-than-expected 2007 election, a result requiring a three-party coalition to be created for HDZ to rule instead of SDP. After Sanader's resignation, Deputy Prime Minister Jadranka Kosor replaced him, becoming Croatia's first female leader. The reason for the sudden resignation of the long-serving HDZ leader came from the global banking crisis itself and the failings of the Austrian Hypo Alpe-Adria-Bank, which had branches in Croatia and several other Balkan countries. In 2011, Croatia's anticorruption agency accused Sanader of having taken a bribe in 1995 so that the Austrian bank could enter the local market, at a time when other foreign banks had not yet invested. Sanader vehemently denied the charge and pointed to findings from Austria's own investigation of why the bank had been allowed to give out so many loans in the first place. (The bank would eventually have to be completely restructured.)

It remains unclear whether the Croatian politician had in fact been guilty of anything or whether he had just fallen afoul of political rivals and a new thirst for anticorruption actions taken to please critical EU negotiators. Making things tougher for Sanader, the Hypo Alpe-Adria-Bank case was soon merged with another one, this time in the energy sector that claimed he had illegally profited from the sale of the Croatian oil company INA to Hungary's oil firm MOL. In the latter case, Sanader was convicted in 2014 of allegedly taking a bribe of ten million euros for selling the state energy company. Political archrival (and national president from the SDP party from 2010 to 2015) Ivo Josipović declared Sanader guilty of treason for this affair. However, in 2015, the Constitutional Court canceled the verdict while dividing the two cases, declaring that the trials would start from scratch. Sanader's trial in the INA-MOL case resumed in 2018.

The state's case against the former prime minister quickly became a long odyssey and was highly influenced by its context. For the government, it was a useful distraction from Kosor's unpopular budget-tightening "austerity measures" during the economic crisis, while it was also presented as evidence that Croatia was proactive in its fight against political corruption at a time when it was, hopefully, in the last stages of negotiating EU membership, which it finally won in 2013. It is possible that some relationship existed between these events as a sort of political and judicial theater playing out before the eyes of the Croatian public and EU political observers. Thus, on November 20, 2012, Sanader was sentenced to ten years in jail, becoming the most senior politician sentenced on corruption charges. At the time, it seemed a huge victory for the anticorruption cause, while Sanader claimed his trial was politically motivated. However, a year after acquiring EU membership, the Supreme Court reduced Sanader's sentence, while in 2015 the Constitutional Court threw out the whole verdict based on procedural errors. A predictable uproar ensued as critics and defenders of both sides argued over the continuing drama. However, other cases were brought up too, and in October 2018, Zagreb County Court convicted Sanader of accepting bribes of about 485,000 euros from the Austrian bank in late 1994 and 1995 when he was the young deputy foreign minister. Sanader was hardly the most important HDZ official of the time, and if any officials had really managed to profit illegally from the war, they were either long deceased by 2019, or simply managed to conceal their wealth more discreetly.

In the end, Sanader's saga with the uneven judicial system was paralleled by the war crimes spectacle of Ante Gotovina and a handful of other Croat generals sought by the ICTY over Operation Storm and other 1990s military operations. The entire episode, from Gotovina's indictment and subsequent escape in 2001 to his 2005 capture, conviction, and ultimately his acquittal on appeal in 2012, was marked by emotive media coverage and the intervention of politicians and the church. (For example, faithful Catholic Croats were known to hold large masses praying for the acquittal of generals fighting in the "Homeland War," as the Croatian War of Independence is also known.)

Gotovina and fellow war veteran General Mladen Markač were convicted by the ICTY in 2011. As was the case with Sanader in the realm of politics, this showed many previous critics of the country's war record that it too would be held responsible before the international community for war crimes as was demanded of all parties in the Yugoslav and other conflicts. Thus, when the ICTY acquitted Gotovina and Markač on November 16, 2012, in a 3–2 vote, many were shocked. The acquittal reinforced the longtime Serbian view that the ICTY was a hypocritical and politically directed chamber designed specifically to punish Serb defendants and not other protagonists in the conflict. For their part, many Croats were jubilant to see perceived war heroes freed. The court ruled that the original charge of a joint criminal enterprise meant to eliminate the Serbian population during 1995 operations could not be corroborated. For the many critics of this ruling, of course, any military commander embarking on a full-on assault such as Operation Storm would surely have been aware that it would cause a massive civilian exodus.

Nevertheless, the final appeals ruling gave the generals the benefit of the doubt, and in so doing paved the way for Croatia's EU accession, which took place on July 1, 2013. While it will never be known for sure, it is highly likely that the international tribunal—long a source of controversy and concern over a politicized orientation—was subject to lobbying not so much for the benefit of Croatia or its generals but for the image of the union itself. After all, it would not be considered in keeping with the liberal and semipacifistic "European values" long promulgated by Brussels for it to be seen as a group in which member states were guilty of war crimes. On the other hand, the more mundane and universal crimes of political corruption remained something that could be encountered anywhere and dealt with. In retrospect, the complex and intertwined tales of Sanader, Gotovina, and the outcomes of HDZ's internal wars are bound to remain opaque, charged with emotion, and with consequences for future generations.

AN AMBIVALENT DISPUTE: THE CROATIA–SLOVENIA BORDER NEGOTIATIONS (2009–2019)

Although they had become generally amicable neighbors since becoming independent from Yugoslavia, Slovenia and Croatia inherited a few disagreements that, while small in number, were acute and in need of diplomatic resolution. These inherited differences primarily reflected historic disagreements over territorial borders—particularly, concerning the narrow strip of seacoast at the northeastern edge of the Adriatic, the Bay of Piran—and became politically sensitive because EU accession rules required all members to agree unanimously over any potential candidate's progress in complying with the application process. As an existing member, Slovenia enjoyed plenty of leverage over Croatia and could use it politically to force the latter to compromise on the disputed areas. It was the sort of scenario that had happened numerous times between existing and aspiring member states for years already by that time.

The Slovene perspective, it should be remembered, was informed by a historical perception of having already lost considerable national territory in the coastal area—after all, Tito's failure to keep Trieste in Yugoslavia meant that the large ethnically Slovene populated sections of Adriatic Italy would never be incorporated in a Slovenian state. Therefore, while the post-1991 Slovenia did have some access to the Adriatic, with the large port of Koper and a small one of Izola, the country's total access to the Adriatic was still tiny in comparison to both Italy and Croatia. The Gulf of Piran, in particular, remained controversial as it involved disputed access to international waters. Although a UN-sanctioned arbitration panel in 2017 finally decided in Slovenia's favor, Croatia did not accept the verdict, having left the talks in 2015 after claiming the tribunal was biased in Slovenia's favor. After 2017, isolated incidents continued in which police boats from both countries would get in the way of fishing vessels in the Gulf of Piran, making symbolic shows of force more reminiscent of Balkan dispute resolution of the past than a supposed new era of friendship under the collective EU future.

Back in 2001, Slovenian Prime Minister Drnovšek and Croatian counterpart Račan had signed an agreement; however, Croatia's parliament refused to ratify it, claiming that it implied a coastal concession to the Slovenes. Thereafter, Slovenia blocked Croatia's EU accession talks, throwing off the process that Croatia (under Prime Minister Sanader in early 2009) had expected to start. At that time, Sanader and his Slovenian counterpart Borut Pahor met with members of an EU-initiated negotiations team to try and make progress on the issue. Croatian president Stipe Mesić feigned bemusement in public comments, implying that Pahor (and Slovenia in general) were afraid they would lose if the border case were heard before the International Court of Justice; that was why, in his view, they sought to use their leverage as an EU member against Croatia instead to force a dispute resolution on favorable terms. The president's view seemed to be justified when Slovenia did not accept certain negotiating recommendations of the EU committee in spring and summer of 2009.

Later, in 2009, Sanader's successor Jadranka Kosor signed an agreement with Pahor, allowing Croatia's EU accession talks to continue while the border dispute continued to be discussed. The latter even intimated that a solution such as "shared sovereignty" of the disputed region could be found. At the same time, however, the nationalist Slovene People's Party (SLS) announced plans to collect signatures from the public to hold a referendum concerning precisely how the bilateral arbitration agreement over the border would work. The process for holding such a vote got underway as diplomacy continued. Thus, an arbitration agreement between Croatia and Slovenia was signed in Stockholm on November 4, 2009. The promised Slovenian referendum was finally held in June 2010 and narrowly passed, by a margin of fifty-one percent to forty-eight percent, allowing an international arbitration tribunal to try and resolve the dispute.

At long last, on May 25, 2011, the process got underway when representatives of both countries submitted their preliminary arbitration agreement to the UN. According to the agreed format, talks would only start after Croatia's signing of its EU accession, representing a win for Zagreb. The ad-hoc arbitral tribunal commission set to resolve the dispute would comprise experts in international law and would be charged with comparing different territorial claims not only involving the Bay of Piran but also various outposts, river borders, and settlement areas where claims to national sovereignty had shifted over the years. This was a complex issue not only because of the two world wars but because of the role that various noble families had long played under the Habsburgs, meaning that (as with other regional border zones) a plethora of cadastral and aristocratic property documents making overlapping claims could be compared.

Little happened on the border dispute until, as envisaged, Croatia joined the EU in July 2013. Then the expert tribunal slowly began to get to work, drawing relatively little interest among the public at first. However, on July 22, 2015, an investigation by a Croatian newspaper set off a major scandal, claiming to show evidence that the tribunal itself was corrupt and secretly lobbying on behalf of the Slovene side through arbitration commission judge Jernej Sekolec, an ethnic Slovene. Claiming that he had worked clandestinely with Slovenian officials, the Zagreb newspaper claimed Sekolec was pressuring other judges to rule against Croatia on different issues. Although all involved denied any wrongdoing, it was enough to force the Slovene's resignation and to inspire a united Croatian parliament to vote to stop the UN arbitration talks. On July 26, 2015, Croatian prime minister Zoran Milanović announced that the country would abandon the arbitration process completely, significantly damaging the credibility of the institution as well as regional border stability, coming during a summer marked by a historic migrant crisis in which over one million migrants passed through on the nearby "Balkan Route" from Turkey through Greece, Macedonia, and Serbia, heading toward Germany.

Although Croatia did not return to the talks, the UN arbitration commission merely continued where it had left off, clearing itself of any wrongdoing with an internal investigation and changing some of the judges and other personnel to please both sides. Finally, a verdict was released on June 29, 2017. Slovenia reacted favorably to the general decisions of the international body, but Croatia announced that they would not be acknowledged as the government had left the trial in 2015 and not returned. This event later caused Slovenia to take

Croatia to the European Court of Justice, lodging the complaint that Croatia had violated European law by not accepting the verdict, which included several border areas as well as the central Bay of Piran access issue.

Remarkably, the disagreement continued to acquire new dimensions, with the Slovenian government in April 2019 temporarily recalling its ambassador to Croatia for consultations after a Ljubljana television station reported that Croatia's Security and Intelligence Agency (*Sigurnosno-obavještajna agencija*, or SOA) had been responsible for wiretapping the Slovenian UN judge in 2015 before the first Croatian media reports came out that sparked the scandal over border negotiations. Politicians in Slovenia were quick to call for urgent National Security Council meetings while trying to turn the issue into one of human rights infringement. It was the kind of cloak-and-dagger spat that had characterized decades of political life within the Yugoslav League of Communists' republic-level governments, now broadcast onto the far bigger screen of the EU. It was more than a bit ironic that the EU—which had long prided itself on a vision for a "borderless" Europe in which national restrictions were removed—would end up in a situation where two of its newest members made such a fuss about their own boundaries. Yet in the case of Croatia and Slovenia some things, as they say, come with the territory.

SOCIAL AND POLITICAL TRENDS IN TODAY'S CROATIA AND SLOVENIA (2013–2020)

Although the occasional old disputes such as the unclear status of the border continued to exist, relations between Croatia and Slovenia remain generally solid. In recent years, both countries have been equally impacted by European and global trends of all types affecting their social and political orientations. These trends include political participation, impact of EU membership, orientation toward key global issues among others.

The participation of women in politics, already quite visible in Slovenia, picked up after the premiership of Jadranka Kosor in Croatia. Following her own 2015 election, Kolinda Grabar-Kitarović became the first Croatian female president, representing the conservative HDZ. Meanwhile, Alenka Bratušek, a career public servant, was appointed Slovenia's first female prime minister in 2013, representing the center-left Positive Slovenia (*Pozitivna Slovenija*) party created by businessman and former Ljubljana mayor Zoran Janković in 2011. After her resignation, the next center-left coalition government that arose in 2014 made gender equality one of its explicit goals. An emphasis on gender equality was seen in the selection of a near-equal number of male and female cabinet ministers under the leadership of the new prime minister Miro Cerar. This new cabinet was also Slovenia's best-educated with one-third of ministers holding a PhD degree. Interestingly, the 2014 Slovene decision on cabinet creation foreshadowed a similar decision of the new European Commission in 2019. After European Parliament elections in the latter year, the commission decided to appoint an equal number of male and female commissioners to run the body's bureaucratic structures in Brussels. As had been the case when it was first applying for EU membership, Slovenia was again ahead of its time on gender equality.

An interest in politicians from alternate points of view has been attested as well. In 2017, a forty-year-old former comedian, Marjan Šarec, almost beat the seasoned political veteran and incumbent Borut Pahor in run-off voting for the presidency. Previously twice mayor of the small Alpine town of Kamnik, Šarec brought a fresh perspective and appealed to voters primarily by entertaining them through his political satire. In the following year's parliamentary elections, Šarec entered parliament, running with a party named after himself, and became prime minister of a coalition government. He was an early member of Positive Slovenia, the party that gave the country its first female prime minister, before going on to form his own.

In terms of contemporary trends, Croats and Slovenes are also generally known for being attuned to the environment. This is partly due to the importance of tourism in local economies but also due to the broader global trends in regards to climate change. This has affected both political engagement and local activities. For example, thousands of climate activists participated in the global climate change protests that were held in late September of 2019. In Croatia, protests were held in Osijek, Rijeka, Split, and Zagreb, while activists also took to the streets in Slovenia. At the same time, in the Climate Change Summit in New York, Slovenian prime minister Šarec spoke at a World Economic Forum debate on sustainable development, discussing Europe's role on climate and green growth while calling on all countries to move toward the environment friendly policies supported by Slovenia.

While its traditional conservative-dominated political outlook remains strong, EU membership has colored the Croatian perspective as well since 2013. Typically in Europe, supporters of the EU project have espoused relatively liberal views, including initiatives toward "shared sovereignty" and common decision-making in economic policy (the internal European market) that have been criticized by

Euroskeptics as testifying to an overreach of authority from Brussels—the core of the problem in the Brexit debate, for example, by which the United Kingdom voted by referendum to leave the EU in 2016.

However, for new members and small countries especially, the change for an otherwise impossible contribution to leadership is an incentive for conservatives built into the EU project. For example, member states take part in decision-making by leading a European Commission (one for each country) and participating in decision-making committees at the European Parliament and related bodies. Further, every so often the position of the six-month European presidency becomes available; though largely ceremonial in nature, this function allows the host country to put its own emphasis on the EU's agenda during the period assigned. Croatia got to experience the role of EU president in January 2020, handing off to Germany in June of that year.

In announcing the government's plan for the EU presidency, Croatian leaders in October 2019 revealed that they would follow the motto of "a strong Europe in a challenging world," and called for a "stronger union," an attempt to please both liberal and conservative factions in the country and continent. "Guided by its Christian roots, traditions and culture, the Croatian people have always expressed affection and belonging to the European family," Prime Minister Andrej Plenković said at the time. "For us, the European Union is a project of peace and hope." Plenković went on to specify that Croatia's goals during the presidency would also include strengthening social rights, rebooting the enlargement process for Western Balkans aspirant members, and taking measures to reverse Europe's declining birthrate.

In addition to the large demographic problems faced by EU countries, most of them being Eastern European ones, is the question of brain drain. Faced with the challenges of aging populations and an increasing percentage of young people going abroad to study and work, Croatia and Slovenia have been among those countries challenged to find ways to keep young people—especially in rural areas—interested in staying at home. In recent years, countries like Germany and France and the Scandinavian countries have attracted much interest from young people seeking education and work opportunities, from across the Balkans. Since the factors behind the phenomenon of brain drain and emigration remain complex, governments have been unable to find a simple solution. In Croatia's case, the decision was made in 2019 to launch new outreach mechanisms to the general diaspora in the hopes of reviving interest and engagement with the homeland. Given the realities of demographic decline and brain drain, however, such initiatives will require considerable time and effort before major results can be obtained.

VICTORIES AND GROWING PAINS: TOURISM, SPORTS, AND MUSIC (2011–2020)

In recent years, Slovenia has been increasingly known as a tourism destination, with its combination of Adriatic coast, Alpine villages, caves, and well-kept cities, attracting a diversity of visitors. Indeed, in 2017, it was recognized as the world's "most sustainable" country by National Geographic for its environmental policies and high quality of life. The well-organized national plan for tourism development had followed, in typically methodical Slovenian style, from a baseline in 2016 to see continuous gradual expansion over the following five years.

Thus, Slovenia tourism increased year on year through 2019, with some goals from the 2017–2021 national tourism strategy having been realized early. The number of total arrivals and nights spent in the country by foreign tourists grew in 2018 by 7.1 percent while revenues from foreign tourism rose by three percent over the year before. By comparison to the year 2016, foreign tourism revenue had increased by twenty-four percent to 2.7 billion euros in 2018. However, the 2019 bankruptcy of the national air carrier Adria Airways severely impacted passenger numbers at Ljubljana Airport late in the year, leading to uncertainty over the long-term outlook for what might essentially remain a regional airport without a greater capacity for growth. The reality is that in a regional market marked by numerous competitors, and other larger factors such as environmental policies at play, several other Balkan cities will remain keen to compete with Ljubljana and Zagreb for air traffic in the years to come.

Developing Croatian tourism did not need too much effort, but even there a stroke of fortune helped in a most unexpected way with one single decision. Croatia's landscape and historic architecture were captured as the setting for numerous episodes of the HBO epic fantasy series *Game of Thrones*, which ran from 2011 to 2019; this spawned an entire tourism subindustry in tours based on filming locations. These locations include Dubrovnik, Split, and the island of Lokrum. Such business has had a profound effect; one 2017 study found that between 2012 and 2015 alone, an estimated 240,000 tourists spent 126 million euros visiting Dubrovnik alone, drawn entirely by the historic city's place in the fictional world of a television series.

Since then, the global popularity of the series sparked a whole new relationship with Croatia's main historic attractions for new generations of tourists, with travel-related media literally putting sites related to the filming "on the map" for anyone visiting or learning about the country online. The enduring effect of the decision to film *Game of Thrones* in Croatia consists of whole new associations with places like the Palace of Diocletian in Split or Dubrovnik's Old Town. During the same period, Croatia cashed in on its impressive natural beauty to become a filming site for major Hollywood series like *Star Wars*, which appears to continue for the foreseeable future.

However, the burgeoning popularity of Croatia, Slovenia, and the Adriatic Sea coast in general has not come without problems or controversy. Much like its former imperial master across the bay, Venice, Dubrovnik began to buckle under the weight of so much tourism, with quick-stop cruise tourism being singled out in both cases for presenting an oppressive burden on local services and the environment. In August 2019, the Italian government announced that large cruise ships would be banned in future from docking at the lagoon city's central port. Long-simmering opposition to the mass tourism industry among local Venetians and environmentalists alike was sparked by a cruise ship's docking accident earlier that summer, causing authorities to declare the ban and promise that large ships would be redirected to other ports.

The fight against cruise ships and the general idea of "overtourism" had begun a year earlier in Croatia when Dubrovnik mayor Mato Franković limited the number of such vessels docking in the harbor to no more than two per day. The city proved largely successful throughout 2019 in sticking by the limits, and the mayor expanded his program by closing down the majority of souvenir stands in the Old Town, while putting the idea of a five-year ban on new restaurants opening there up to a city vote in December 2019. The move was reminiscent of Venice's ban on new fast-food eateries and reflected a general perception among local residents that excessive tourist waves were detrimental to the city's well-being.

Similar opposition was rising just to the south in the Montenegrin port of Kotor, where a unique maritime environment marked by fjords was in danger, according to scientists, from pollution caused by the massive cruise ships. In general, the Adriatic being a long and narrow sea is prone to poorer circulation of water than other seas and oceans, and currents tend to distribute plastic waste north from Greece and Albania to Croatia, as the local Zmergo environmentalist group noted in 2018. They were among approximately 10,000 Croats who took part in an annual day called the "Blue Cleaning" in waters along the coast. These volunteers participate in cleaning up plastic waste from beaches and the sea after each tourist season while calling on the government and EU to do more in terms of passing laws against plastic waste.

In a period of world history dominated by public discourse over climate change and the environment in general, it is likely that these initiatives will continue to have political and social ramifications as Croatia tries to balance its tourism windfall with the impact that this economic producer has on both land and sea. As one prominent example, in April 2019, it was announced that environmental activists had won a European competition for their idea of making the island of Zlarin free of single-use plastics in 2020. The Dalmatian island, located near the city of Šibenik, would thus become the first plastic-free Croatian island. Although having only 300 permanent residents, the island's population reaches over 4,000 during the summer tourist season. Initiatives like these can be expected to increase in the years ahead.

In 2020, some twenty-five years after the end of the Yugoslav wars, Slovenia and Croatia remained the only two former Yugoslav republics to be EU members. While occasional national provocations persisted, most rivalries remained where they had always been—in the field of sports, an area in which teams and players from the whole former Yugoslavia continued to distinguish themselves in soccer, basketball, handball, tennis, water polo, and other sports. In the 2012 Summer Olympics, Croatia won the gold medal in water polo and took silver at the 2016 Games.

Most spectacularly, in 2018, Croatia reached the finals of soccer's World Cup held in Russia. Despite losing to France, the historic run is considered one of the country's biggest sporting successes. Their summer run was considered a genuine Cinderella story, and the Croatian national team developed a cult following from fans worldwide eager to see an underdog knock off one of the traditional big nations. The team's best-known star, Luka Modrić, won the coveted Ballon d'Or award, essentially recognizing him as the world's best professional soccer player of the year. The ascent of Modrić has sparked considerable interest at the highest levels in the future of Croatian soccer.

While not as accomplished in soccer, in 2017, Slovenia won basketball's European Cup in a hard-fought final against perennial powerhouse Serbia, winning in a game that was played in Serbia as well. The tournament showcased talented players like future NBA Rookie of the Year Luka Dončić. The Slovene athlete had started out playing for Spanish club Real Madrid at the age of sixteen, making a considerable impression for the premier European club. Dončić's arrival in the American League in 2018 was just the most recent of ex-Yugoslav players going back to the 1980s, such as the late Dražen Petrović and Toni Kukoč, both from Croatia, and Vlade Divac from Serbia. It can only be expected that these countries will continue to see their young athletes be represented at the highest levels of organized athletics, both in team and individual sports, including the more unusual ones. One example of the latter was Alenka Artnik, a Slovenian diver who set a world record in August 2019 when she performed a 111-meter free dive in the Caribbean Sea, with the help of a monofin.

Of all the successes enjoyed by contemporary Croatia and Slovenia in the cultural sphere, none is more unexpected—nor perhaps more fitting—than the story of Luka Šulić and Stjepan Hauser. The former, born in Maribor, Slovenia, in 1987, and the latter, born in Pula, Croatia, a year before, are better known today as members of the crossover classical-rock act 2CELLOS, the musical duo famous for its passionate classical renditions of rock and pop hits. Their unlikely story of being

2CELLOS, pictured here opening for Sir Elton John in Singapore in 2011, rocketed to fame with their innovative, impassioned classical renditions of pop and rock tracks. The Slovene-Croatian duo, comprising classically trained cellists Luka Šulić and Stjepan Hauser, has released several best-selling and critically acclaimed albums since 2011, and represent their countries' most notable current acts in popular music internationally. (Meisterphotos/Dreamstime.com)

"discovered" by YouTube viewers while working as classical musicians in England is both unusual and entirely fitting for the online era.

The two had met at a master's class in Pula as teenagers and kept in contact while pursuing different advanced studies and classical competitions and ensembles in the 2000s before hitting upon an idea to record a music video of a well-known pop song on only their two cellos. The chosen track (Michael Jackson's percussive, melodic "Smooth Criminal") was put up on YouTube in December 2010, when that platform was in its infancy. In just weeks, their video went viral; among the millions of viewers was Sir Elton John, who invited the duo to open for him on his world tour. Record label Sony Masterworks also put out the Croat-Slovenian classical duo's full first album of classically performed rock and pop songs. The challenge in creating the project was deciding which songs to record and to "find new ways to play the cello, like people had never seen before," recalled Šulić in a 2019 interview.

The cumulative result was four critically acclaimed albums backed by constant touring over the following seven years. The duo's instrumental arrangements of popular, classical music and film scores have enjoyed significant crossover appeal and put Croatia and Slovenia on the map in a most unexpected way. In 2019, 2CELLOS went on indefinite hiatus due to the exertion of almost a decade of constant touring and collaborations but expected new creative works to continue. In October, Hauser announced plans for his first "solo" tour (to be accompanied by a full orchestra) in spring 2020. The two continued to inspire both young people at home and around the world to develop a passion for music.

In the end, achievements like those made in music, sports, tourism, and culture by today's Croatia and Slovenia seem, perhaps, disproportionately large. Two small countries that have captured global attention and imagination in a thousand different ways, these Balkan neighbors on the periphery of Western Europe have managed to do something quite unique. Not only in that through painful transitions and transformations they have become better neighbors, but also in that through maximizing their natural offerings and human resources they have become more interesting to the outside world as well. In a region often associated with negative developments, Slovenia and Croatia have stood out as exceptions. Despite the inevitable growing pains faced by these or any countries, they will likely become more intriguing, and perhaps important, in European affairs in the years to come.

Notable People in the History of Croatia and Slovenia

Adam Bohorič (c. 1520–1598). Slovene Protestant reformer best known for the pioneering alphabet named after him.

Alojzije Stepinac (1898–1960). Croatian Archbishop of Zagreb during the World War II (WWII) Independent State of Croatia, later beatified controversially by Pope John Paul II.

Andreas von Auersperg (1556–1593). Habsburg field commander of troops from the Duchies of Carniola and Carinthia, who became known as the "Carniolan Achilles" in Europe following the 1593 Battle of Sisak against the Ottomans.

Andrej Plenković (1970–). Croatian politician, former European Union (EU) parliamentarian, and prime minister of Croatia.

Andrija Kačić Miošić (1704–1760). Franciscan monk from Makarska whose 1756 folk history of the Slavs proved very influential in the Croatian National Revival period.

Ante Gotovina (1955–). Croatian general during the 1990s independence war, whose role as a commander in Operation Storm led to his conviction (subsequently overturned on appeal) of war crimes.

Ante Marković (1924–2011). Croatian businessman and the last prime minister of communist Yugoslavia, who sought to implement emergency economic reforms to preserve the federation's unity in the late 1980s.

Ante Miko Tripalo (1926–1995). Croatian communist politician known for his activism during the early 1970s "Croatian Spring" protests against Tito's Yugoslav system.

Ante Pavelić (1889–1959). Croatian lawyer, politician, and head of the Ustaše fascist government that ruled the country as the Independent State of Croatia during WWII.

Ante Starčević (1823–1896). Lawyer, politician, and founder of the nationalist Croatian Party of Rights in 1861. He was involved in the Illyrian Movement and was the founding father of Croatian ethnic nationalism.

Ante Trumbić (1864–1938). Croatian member of the 1915 Yugoslav Committee, later noted for his work as a sculptor.

Anton Tomaž Linhart (1756–1795). Enlightenment-era author of the first Slovene-language theatrical work and the first history of Slovenes as a distinct ethnic group.

Balthazar Hacquet (c. 1739–1815). Habsburg Imperial war surgeon and professor of anatomy and chemistry who was active in the Slovenian Enlightenment and became the first to explore the Julian Alps.

Bernhard von Spanheim (1176–1256). Medieval Duke of Carinthia who expanded his autonomy to include the March of Carniola, spawning a familial dynasty.

Branimir (ruled 879–892). Croatian prince who brought the House of Domagojević to power in a coup against the Trpimirović clan, and famously allied Croatia with the Catholic Church against Byzantine Orthodox influence in an 879 letter to the pope.

Borut (8th century). Prince of Carantania and the founder of an early line of Alpine Slav nobles.

Borut Pahor (1963–). Slovene liberal politician who served as prime minister from 2008 to 2012 and as president of Slovenia thereafter.

Demetrius Zvonimir Svetoslavić (ruled 1076–1089). Croatian king and successor of Krešimir IV the Great who allied with the Catholic Church and the rising Norman power against Byzantium and formed a marriage alliance by marrying Hungarian Princess Helen.

Diocletian (244–311). Roman Emperor born in Croatia who brought stability to the empire by ending the Crisis of the Third Century and bequeathed the Dalmatian province with his palace, which still stands in the city of Split.

Edvard Kardelj (1910–1979). Slovene communist and close colleague of Josip Broz Tito who played an important role in the WWII Partisans resistance movement and, especially, in managing the communist Yugoslav Federation that followed.

France Prešeren (1800–1849). Slovene poet credited with definitively influencing the formation of a national culture through his verse in the National Revival period.

Franjo Tuđman (1922–1999). Croatian nationalist politician who oversaw the 1990s War of Independence as the first elected president of the modern Croatian state.

Frano Supilo (1870–1917). Croatian pro-Yugoslavist politician of the pre-World War 1 (WWI) period, particularly influential on the Dalmatian coast.

Gojko Šušak (1945–1998). Diaspora Croatian who became Croatia's first defense minister during the 1990s independence war, leading the country's armament efforts with the help of Western allies.

Gregory (10th century). Bishop of Nin, and associated with advancing the use of Slavonic as a liturgical language.

Hermann II (c. 1360–1435). A Count of Celje, he was rewarded with the Slavonian Croatian town of Varaždin for saving the life of Hungary's King Sigismund at the 1396 Battle of Nicopolis.

Hotimir (8th century). Prince of Carantania and nephew and successor to Borut who accepted Christianity for his people from the Frankish clergy.

Hrvoje Vukčić Hrvatinić (c. 1350–1416). Croat noble who contested Sigismund of Luxembourg's claim to Croatia from the late 14th century on behalf of an Angevin rival Ladislaus of Naples and in alliance with the Bosnian kingdom.

Ignjat Đurđević (1675–1737). Croatian Enlightenment poet who ran afoul of the Catholic clergy in his native Ragusa over his amorous poetic output.

Ivan Krajačić (1906–1986). Croatian interior minister in early communist Yugoslavia who played an important role in counterespionage and thwarting Ustaše reinvasion plans.

Ivan Lenković (c. 1520–1569). Uskok leader and Habsburg general known for his military works, such as the Nehaj Fortress in Senj, and his heroism in defending against the Ottomans.

Ivan Meštrović (1883–1962). Croatian politician active in the 1915 Yugoslav Committee.

Ivan Nelipić (14th century). Croatian noble at the time of King Charles I and founder of a noble line in 1330 that would have influence in Hungarian-ruled Croatia through the 15th century.

Ivica Račan (1944–2007). Croatian left-wing politician and prime minister from 2000 to 2003.

Ivo Josipović (1958–). Left-wing politician and jurist who served as Croatia's president from 2010 to 2015.

Ivo Sanader (1953–). Croatian prime minister from 2003 to 2009 who also served in the wartime *Hrvatska demokratska zajednica* government and later became associated with various banking and other scandals amid modern Croatian political feuds.

Janez Drnovšek (1950–2008). Slovene economist and first postwar prime minister and president of independent Slovenia.

Janez Janša (1958–). Conservative Slovene politician, former prime minister, and defense minister during the successful Ten-Day War against Yugoslavia that won Slovenia's independence in 1991.

Janko Drašković (1770–1856). Croatian intellectual and politician who championed national rights against Hungarian pretensions during the 1830s, patronizing the activities of the Illyrian Movement.

Jermej Kopitar (1780–1844). Slovenian scholar of the National Revival period and cooperator of Serbia's Vuk Karadžić on the latter's Yugoslav literary common language project.

Joakim Stulić (1730–1817). Enlightenment-era Croatian lexicographer who compiled the largest dictionary of the old Croatian dialects.

Josip Broz Tito (1892–1980). Slovene-Croatian communist activist, Partisan guerrilla leader, and architect of the communist Yugoslav Federation.

Josip Jelačić von Bužim (1801–1859). Croatian *Ban* from a storied military family who won prestige by helping the Habsburgs put down the Hungarian rebellion of 1848.

Josip Juraj Strossmayer (1815–1905). Catholic bishop, founder of the pan-Slavic People's Party and cofounder of the Yugoslav Academy of Sciences and Arts in 1867. He also refounded the University of Zagreb.

Jurij Dalmatin (c. 1547–1589). Slovene Lutheran minister who completed the first full translation of the Bible into Slovene in 1583, printed using the new Bohorič alphabet.

Kolinda Grabar-Kitarović (1968–). Croatian conservative politician, and from 2015, the first female president of Croatia.

Krešimir I (ruled 935–945). Croatian king and grandson of Tomislav I.

Krešimir IV (ruled 1059–1075). Croatian king known as Krešimir "the Great." He was acknowledged by the Byzantines as ruler of the Dalmatian city-states, including ports as far south as modern Albania.

Ljudevit Gaj (1809–1879). Croatian National Awakening intellectual in Zagreb associated with the Illyrian Movement, promoted the goal of a common Slavic language, and notably created a Croatian alphabet that bears his name.

Ljudevit Posavski (ruled c. 810–823). Pannonian Croatian duke who ruled from Sisak and led an uprising against the Franks in 818.

Marko Pohlin (1735–1801). Notable Slovene Enlightenment writer and grammarian.

Matija Čop (1797–1835). Important Slovene linguist of the National Awakening period.

Michael Krešimir II (ruled 949–969). Croatian usurper-king who ruled with his wife Helen for 20 years, lavishly endowing churches, especially in the Dalmatian coastal cities.

Milan Kučan (1941–). Slovene lawyer, politician, and first president of the modern independent Slovenian republic.

Milka Planinc (1924–2010). Croatian communist politician who became Europe's first female prime minister when she assumed this office for the Yugoslav Federation in the early 1980s.

Miroslav (ruled 945–949). Croatian king killed by his own *Ban* (provincial viceroy) Pribina, acting on behalf of a usurper, Michael Krešimir II.

Mitja Gaspari (1951–). Slovene financial expert who served as economy minister in the 1990s and helped the newly independent Slovenia reform its economic and financial systems to reach EU standards.

Muncimir (ruled 892–910). Croatian duke who restored the Trpimirović dynasty and tried to manage better relations between the Vatican and Constantinople, while confronted by a new threat from the Magyars (Hungarians) to the northeast.

Pavao Ritter Vitezović (1652–1713). Enlightenment-era historian, cartographer, and Habsburg diplomat from Senj, who wrote an influential history of the Slavs that supported Croatian nationalist pretensions in the National Awakening period.

Petar Kružić (16th century). Croatian Uskok pirate leader from Klis, famed for his victories over the Turks.

Petar Snačić (ruled 1093–1097). Croatian noble from Knin who launched a resistance to Hungarian attempts to take over the Croatian throne before the 1102 settlement.

Pribina (ruled 949–969). First historically attested Croatian *Ban* (provincial viceroy), Pribina killed King Miroslav during a civil war, and went on to serve under King Michael Krešimir II.

Primož Trubar (1508–1586). Protestant reformer who established the Lutheran Church in Carniola and published the first Slovene-language printed books.

Ruđer Josip Bošković (1711–1787). Ragusa-born Jesuit priest and mathematician, physicist, and astronomer, remembered for proving that the Moon has no atmosphere and computing planetary orbits.

Samo (ruled 623–658). Proto-Slovene king and founder of the first Slavic polity, maintaining an independent state against the Franks and Avars.

Savka Dabčević-Kučar (1923–2009). Croatian economist, communist official, and Croatian Spring figurehead in the early 1970s.

Sebastjan Krelj (1538–1567). Carniolan Protestant preacher best known for his contributions to Slovenian and Croatian linguistics.

Sigmund Zois Freiherr von Edelstein (1747–1819). Carniolan patron of the Slovenian Enlightenment and organizer of the "Zois Circle" of intellectuals in 18th-century Ljubljana.

Stanko Vraz (1810–1851). Styrian writer active during the Illyrian Movement in Croatia, known for his collection of rural folk tales from Croatia and Slovenia.

Stjepan Držislav (ruled 969–997). Late 10th-century Croatian king who improved relations with Byzantium over the issue of Dalmatian coastal cities.

Stjepan "Stipe" Mesić (1934–). Center-left Croatian politician, Yugoslav official, and two-time president of Croatia.

Stjepan Radić (1871–1928). The most influential Croatian politician of the interwar period who was tragically shot in parliament in 1928 sparking increased enmities between Serbs and Croats.

Tomislav (ruled 910–928). Croatia's best-known prince and then king from the Trpimirović dynasty, who defeated invading Bulgarian King Simeon in a key military campaign.

Trpimir (ruled 845–864). Duke of Croatia and founder of the Trpimirović dynasty who vied with Byzantium and the Bulgarians for local control in the late 9th century.

Trpimir II (ruled 928–935). Successor to Croatia's King Tomislav.

Ulrich II (1406–1456). The last Count of Celje who vied for royal influence. His death at the hands of the Hungarian Hunyadi clan saw the proto-Slovene territories be legally absorbed by Habsburg Austria.

Valuk (7th century). The first Duke of Carantania, in modern Austria and Slovenia.

Vatroslav Lisinski (1819–1854). Illyrian Movement activist in Croatia responsible for writing the first Croatian-language opera.

Višeslav (8th century). Duke of Dalmatia, an early Croatian lord known for baptizing his subjects into the new Christian religion.

Vladko Maček (1879–1964). Croatian politician who succeeded Stjepan Radić as head of Croatia's largest party, and proclaimed the so-called Zagreb Points, demanding a Yugoslav Federation in 1931.

Vojnomir (ruled 790–810). Prince of Pannonian Croatia and a military ally of Charlemagne against the Avars.

Bibliographic Essay

Scholarship on Croatia and Slovenia tends to be weighted toward the tumultuous events of the 20th century, with earlier centuries covered patchily and often in the context of other civilizations, whereas coverage of the 21st century is largely found in online resources. Thus, for basic facts about Croatia and Slovenia today, the reader will find the CIA World Factbook useful, with its dedicated pages to Croatia (https://www.cia.gov/library/publications/the-world-factbook/geos/hr.html) and Slovenia (https://www.cia.gov/library/publications/the-world-factbook/geos/si.html) providing all relevant information on facts ranging from geography to state symbols.

Other online resources for contemporary life and politics include the websites of the Croatian Ministry of Foreign Affairs (http://www.mvep.hr/en) and the Slovenian Ministry of Foreign Affairs (https://www.gov.si/en); the Croatian government (https://vlada.gov.hr/en) and the Slovenian government (https://www.gov.si/en/state-authorities/government); Croatian Bureau of Statistics (https://www.dzs.hr/default_e.htm), Slovenian State Statistics Office (https://www.stat.si/StatWeb/en); Croatian Tourism Board (http://croatia.hr/en-GB) and Slovenian Tourism Authority (https://www.slovenia.info/en). Both countries have numerous English-language media bodies, with the official state ones being HRT for Croatia (https://www.hrt.hr) and RTV Slovenija for Slovenia (https://www.rtvslo.si/rtv/english). The Balkan Insight website (https://balkaninsight.com) provides dedicated coverage of these and other Balkan nations from a generally liberal viewpoint.

For the ancient Illyrian period, see John Wilkes, *The Illyrians* (Oxford, 1995). For a detailed biography of life under the Roman Empire's great Dalmatian-born Emperor Diocletian, see Stephen Williams, *Diocletian and the Roman Recovery* (New York: Methuen, 1985). Detailed information on the imperial residence, now a key archeological site, can be found at http://www.diocletianspalace.org.

For the early medieval and Byzantine period in today's Croatia and Slovenia, see John V.A. Fine, *The Early Medieval Balkans: A Critical Survey from the Sixth to the Late Twelfth Century* (Ann Arbor, MI: University of Michigan Press, 1983). The most comprehensive general study of the Avar period in the Danube area, see Walter Pohl, *The Avars: A Steppe Empire in Central Europe, 567–822* (Ithaca, NY: Cornell University Press, 2018). Readers wishing to learn about the Slavic migrations in Croatia, Slovenia, and neighboring states can see Paul M. Barford, *The Early Slavs: Culture and Society in Early Medieval Eastern Europe* (Ithaca, NY: Cornell University Press, 2001), as well as Florin Curta, *Southeastern Europe in the Middle Ages, 500–1250* (Cambridge: Cambridge University Press, 2006). These studies also cover the medieval Croatian and proto-Slovenian kingdoms and duchies.

For the activities of other neighboring powers such as Hungary, Venice, the Turks, and the Mongols, see works such as Miklós Molnár, *A Concise History of Hungary* (Cambridge: Cambridge University Press, 2001); Joanne M. Ferraro, *Venice: History of the Floating City* (Cambridge: Cambridge University Press, 2012); Stephen Turnbull, *The Ottoman Empire, 1326–1699* (New York: Routledge, 2004); and Thomas T. Allsen, *Culture and Conquest in Mongol Eurasia* (Cambridge: Cambridge University Press, 2004). For the interaction of Vlachs and the Croatian kingdom, see Stanko Guldescu, *The Croatian-Slavonian Kingdom: 1526–1792* (Berlin: De Gruyter, 1970).

An excellent survey of renaissance Croatia's leading Dalmatian city-state is Robin Harris' *Dubrovnik: A History* (London: Saqi Books, 2006). Among the many books covering Austrian relations with early Croatia, see Robert A. Kann, *A History of the Habsburg Empire, 1526–1918* (Berkeley, CA: University of California Press, 1980). For insights into the complex centuries of war between Austria-Hungary and the Turks, waged frequently on Croatian soil, see Pal Fodor and Géza Dávid, eds., *Ottomans, Hungarians, and Habsburgs in Central Europe: The*

Military Confines in the Era of Ottoman Conquest (Leiden: Brill, 2000). To appreciate the internal religious and cultural competition in Austro-Hungarian Croatia and Slovenia that was caused by the Protestant Reformation and Catholic Counter-Reformation, see Howard Louthan and Graeme Murdock, eds., *A Companion to the Reformation in Central Europe* (Leiden: Brill, 2015).

At the point where Croatian and Slovenian state-building projects begin to converge in the 19th century, modern general histories provide the best view of both the preceding and following eras. For a few good examples, see Ivo Goldstein, *Croatia: A History* (Montreal: McGill-Queens University Press, 1999); Marcus Tanner, *Croatia: A History from the Middle Ages to the Present Day* (New Haven, CT: Yale University Press, 2018, fourth edition); Branka Magas, *Croatia through history* (London: Saqi Books, 2007); Marilyn Cvitanic, *Culture and Customs of Croatia* (Santa Barbara, CA: Praeger, 2010); and William Bartlett, *Croatia: Between Europe and the Balkans* (London: Routledge, 2002). For a general overview of Slovenian history, see Cathie Carmichael and James Gow, *Slovenia and the Slovenes* (Bloomington, IN: Indiana University Press, 2000), as well as Jill Benderly and Evan Kraft, *Independent Slovenia: Origins, Movements, Prospects* (London: Macmillan, 1996). For a more recent study, see Oto Luthar, *The Land Between: A History of Slovenia* (Bern: Peter Lang, 2008).

The best study of Croatia's leading political personality during the interwar years remains Mark Biondich's *Stjepan Radic, the Croat Peasant Party, and the Politics of Mass Mobilization, 1904–1928* (Toronto: University of Toronto Press, 2000). Among the many works on Josip Broz Tito available, see Neil Barnett, *Tito* (London: Haus Publishing, 2006); Richard West, *Tito and the Rise and Fall of Yugoslavia* (New York: Faber & Faber, 1995); and Ivo Banac, *With Stalin against Tito: Cominformist Splits in Yugoslav Communism* (Ithaca, NY: Cornell University Press, 1988).

An engaging account of life among Tito's Partisans was written by wartime British secret agent Fitzroy Maclean in his memoir *Eastern Approaches* (London: Jonathan Cape, 1949). Regarding the wartime Independent State of Croatia, see the new work by Pino Adriano and Giorgio Cingolani, *Nationalism and Terror: Ante Pavelić and Ustasha Terrorism from Fascism to the Cold War* (Budapest: CEU Press, 2018). For a study of how the Catholic Church aided Ustase fighters and other Nazi allies escape postwar Europe, see Uki Goñi, *The Real Odessa: Smuggling the Nazis to Perón's Argentina* (London: Granta Books, 2002).

Another study drawing insights from both royalist and communist incarnations of Yugoslavia is John R. Lampe's *Yugoslavia as History: Twice There Was a Country* (Cambridge: Cambridge University Press,

2000). For a study of Tito's Yugoslavia that isolates economic structural issues for its eventual failure, see Susan L. Woodward, *Socialist
Unemployment: The Political Economy of Yugoslavia, 1945–1990* (Princeton, NJ: Princeton University Press, 1995).

Among the many monographs concerning the 1990s Yugoslav wars,
see Marcus Tanner, *Croatia: A Nation Forged in War* (New Haven, CT:
Yale University Press, 2001); Sabrina P. Ramet, *The Three Yugoslavias:
State-Building and Legitimation, 1918–2005* (Bloomington, IN: Indiana
University Press, 2006); Marko Attila Hoare, *How Bosnia Armed* (Lon-
don: Saqi Books, 2004); Charles R. Shrader, *The Muslim-Croat Civil War
in Central Bosnia: A Military History, 1992–1994* (College Station, TX:
Texas A&M University Press, 2003); and John B. Allcock, Marko Mili-
vojevic, and John J. Horton, eds., *Conflict in the Former Yugoslavia: An
Encyclopedia* (Santa Barbara, CA: ABC-CLIO, 1999).

For insights concerning diplomacy and UN peacekeeping during
the conflicts, see Geert-Hinrich Ahrens, *Diplomacy on the Edge: Contain-
ment of Ethnic Conflict and the Minorities Working Group of the Conferences on Yugoslavia* (Washington, DC: Woodrow Wilson Center Press,
2007), and David N. Gibbs, *First Do No Harm: Humanitarian Intervention
and the Destruction of Yugoslavia* (Nashville, TN: Vanderbilt University
Press, 2009). For a study on Slovenia's economic transition carried out
by the World Bank, see Mojmir Mrak, ed., *Slovenia: From Yugoslavia to
the European Union* (Washington, 2004, available at http://documents
.worldbank.org/curated/en/197621468776951986/Slovenia-from
-Yugoslavia-to-the-European-Union).

Index

About the Author

CHRISTOPHER DELISO is an American expert on Southeast Europe who holds an MPhil in Byzantine Studies from Oxford University (1999). Based in the region since 2002, he has published articles in leading world media and has often presented his findings at events for U.S. government agencies and at international conferences. In addition to the current volume, he has written three other books for ABC-CLIO: *Culture and Customs of Serbia and Montenegro* (Greenwood); *Migration, Terrorism, and the Future of a Divided Europe: A Continent Transformed*; and *The Coming Balkan Caliphate: The Threat of Radical Islam to Europe and the West* (both from Praeger Security International).

Titles in the Greenwood Histories of the Modern Nations
Frank W. Thackeray and John E. Findling, Series Editors

The History of Argentina
Daniel K. Lewis

The History of Australia
Frank G. Clarke

The History of the Baltic States,
Second Edition
Kevin C. O'Connor

The History of Brazil
Robert M. Levine

The History of Bulgaria
Frederick B. Chary

The History of Cambodia
Justin Corfield

The History of Canada
Scott W. See

The History of Central America
Thomas Pearcy

The History of the Central Asian
Republics
Peter L. Roudik

The History of Chile, Second
Edition
John L. Rector

The History of China, Third
Edition
David Curtis Wright

The History of Congo
Didier Gondola

The History of Costa Rica
Monica A. Rankin

The History of Croatia and
Slovenia
Christopher Deliso

The History of Cuba, Second
Edition
Clifford L. Staten

The History of the Czech Republic
and Slovakia
William M. Mahoney

The History of Ecuador
George Lauderbaugh

The History of Egypt, Second
Edition
Glenn E. Perry

The History of El Salvador
Christopher M. White

The History of Ethiopia
Saheed Adejumobi

The History of Finland
Jason Lavery

The History of France, Second
Edition
W. Scott Haine

The History of Germany
Eleanor L. Turk

The History of Ghana
Roger S. Gocking

The History of Great Britain,
Second Edition
Anne B. Rodrick

The History of Greece
Elaine Thomopoulos

The History of Haiti
Steeve Coupeau

The History of Holland
Mark T. Hooker